PSYCHOANALYTIC REFLECTIONS ON THE HOLOCAUST: SELECTED ESSAYS

PSYCHOANALYTIC REFLECTIONS ON THE HOLOCAUST: SELECTED ESSAYS

Edited by
Steven A. Luel, Ed.D.,
and Paul Marcus, Ph.D.

HOLOCAUST AWARENESS INSTITUTE
CENTER FOR JUDAIC STUDIES
UNIVERSITY OF DENVER
and
KTAV PUBLISHING HOUSE, INC.
NEW YORK
1984

Library of Congress Cataloging in Publication Data

Main entry under title:

Psychoanalytic reflections on the holocaust.
Includes bibliographical references.
1. Holocaust, Jewish (1939-1945)—Psychological aspects—Addresses, essays, lectures. 2. Psychoanalysis—Social aspects—Addresses, essays, lectures. 3. Holocaust survivors—Psychology—Addresses, essays, lectures.
I. Luel, Steven A. II. Marcus, Paul.
D810.J4P8 1984 940.53′15′03924 84-4364
ISBN 0-88125-041-4

MANUFACTURED IN THE UNITED STATES OF AMERICA

Contents

Foreword

The Holocaust Awareness Institute at the Center for Judaic Studies, University of Denver, was established in 1982 to work within the Jewish community and with people of all faiths to explore the meaning of this horrible tragedy in the hope that we could play some role in preventing calamities of this nature from ever occurring again to any ethnic or social group. We have been encouraged by the response to our efforts to examine our individual and collective conscience and to find meaning in human existence through our multifaceted study of the Holocaust experience.

We are pleased to be able to help bring to the light of publication this fine collection of scholarly and thought-provoking essays which, in fact, accomplish precisely what the editors had intended, to "dispel any notions of a parochial Freudian approach cut off from the larger realms of history, ideology, and society when examining the Holocaust." The physical horror of this event has justifiably overshadowed its psychical dimensions. Nevertheless, just as the history, theology, and literature of the Holocaust have been created, scrutinized, and analyzed to reveal the kaleidoscopic somatic and spiritual impact of the Holocaust upon Western civilization, this offering from the psychoanalytic community will provide new and fresh perspectives on its psychological aspects—human motivation, aggression, hostility, perception of reality in an "unreal" world.

We believe that *Psychoanalytic Reflections on the Holocaust* will be viewed as a significant contribution in the field of Holocaust studies. May its lessons impinge upon the "conscious and unconscious of post-Holocaust generations."

Dr. Stanley M. Wagner
Director
Center for Judaic Studies
University of Denver

Preface

There is a plethora of books on the Holocaust. Historians, theologians, and the literati have grappled with this catastrophic event. There is, however, a serious gap in this literature. There are few, if any, scholarly psychoanalytic works on the Holocaust where analysts go beyond their consultation rooms in order to reflect on the human enterprise, psychoanalysis, and mankind's future in the post-Holocaust world. This volume attempts to assemble in one convenient place an array of thoughtful essays that provides the readership with an opportunity for a deeper understanding of the Holocaust as viewed by psychoanalysts and psychoanalytically oriented scholars.

This book is not a textbook. It is more of an anthology, in that it is a collection of essays revealing the diversity of opinion within the psychoanalytic community. This book is unified by each contributor's use of a broadly conceived psychodynamic perspective.

Since each essay is separately introduced, a brief remark will suffice here to give an indication of the diversity within the book. The contributors come from different backgrounds and disciplines, and this in itself indicates the powerful effect of the Holocaust on the history of ideas. The contributors include Jews and Gentiles, survivors and children of survivors, and persons not directly touched by the Holocaust. The authors' formal disciplines include literature and education as well as psychology and psychiatry.

Some of the essays are more technical than others (e.g., Hoppe; Krystal; Laub and Auerhahn) and require a greater familiarity with psychoanalytic terminology. However, where possible, the editors have tried to simplify the language, and a glossary of technical terms has been added. The introductory chapter provides a conceptual structure which should facilitate a greater understanding of the issues discussed in the papers.

In addition to the various essays, the book contains excerpts of a roundtable discussion in which four psychoanalysts responded to searching and perplexing questions concerning the Holocaust and its aftermath that were posed by the editors.

Finally, a brief personal note. This book is the result of a ten-year dialogue between the editors on a subject that has affected each of us both personally and professionally. This book, then, is our forum to wrestle with the demonic past. We invite the reader to join us and our contributors in this struggle and then look to the future, perhaps with hope.

Steven A. Luel and Paul Marcus

Forest Hills, New York
August 18, 1983

Acknowledgments

I am an only child born into a world in which I was loved and nourished by persons who had spent their young adulthood in the abyss of murderous terror that we call the Holocaust. My parents, one grandmother, aunts, uncles, and cousins were fortunate to have survived and to be able to successfully rebuild their shattered lives.

I know of no better way to acknowledge their role in my conception of this volume than to dedicate this book to my father and late mother. Their gentleness, generosity, and strength have been a guiding symbol of life-affirmation.

In addition, I would like to thank Lawrence Antinoph of the New York Freudian Society and Dr. Philip E. Kraus, chairman of the department of education at Touro College, for their encouragement and helpful insights.

Finally, I wish to thank Francesca, my soul mate for life and dear wife, for her valuable assistance in the preparation of this volume, her love, and her deep understanding of the Holocaust and its meaning in the life of one son of survivors.

S.A.L.

A book written on the Holocaust necessarily arouses strong feelings for both the reader and the editors—and this volume is no exception. Being an American Jew personally untouched by the Nazi experience, I have often asked myself why I was so moved by this event and why it remains so important to me. Without belaboring the point, I would like to briefly mention one aspect that has made the Holocaust so central to my personhood. I am speaking of the 1.5 million Jewish children murdered by the Nazis. This to me is a most horrifying and irreplaceable loss for the Jewish people and for mankind. This book, then, is my attempt to remember, honor, and in some way, help revive that tree whose roots were, in part, severed but from which Jewish history can still grow.

I wish to thank Dr. Philip Stone of the National Psychological Association for Psychoanalysis for his enduring moral support throughout this project. I am especially grateful to Irene Wineman of the Hampstead Child Therapy Clinic for her continual encouragement and helpful editorial suggestions.

International Universities Press for permission to reprint the article by Henry Krystal. Originally entitled "The Aging Survivor of the Holocaust" from the *Journal of Geriatric Psychiatry,* Vol. 14, No. 2, 1982.

William Alanson White Psychiatric Foundation for the Robert J. Lifton essay: "Medicalized Killing in Auschwitz" which originally appeared in *Psychiatry,* Vol. 45, November 1982.

Finally, both Dr. Luel and I would like to thank the Holocaust Awareness Institute of the Center for Judaic Studies at the University of Denver and its distinguished director, Dr. Stanley M. Wagner, for having participated in the sponsorship of this volume.

P.M.

Psychoanalysis and the Holocaust: An Introduction

STEVEN A. LUEL and PAUL MARCUS

A dark cloud hovers over the psychoanalytic enterprise—the Holocaust and its haunting legacy. The shift in historical conditions stemming from this event has given us a "chilling sense of conceptual unpreparedness."[1] Below, we will share our understanding of the impact of the Holocaust on the discipline developed by Sigmund Freud and his followers—psychoanalysis.

Freud still held out hope for the forces of reason and compassion as the first edition of *Civilization and Its Discontents* (1930) went to press. "Eternal Eros," he wrote, "will make an effort to assert himself in the struggle with his equally immortal adversary [Thanatos]."[2] But in his last years he anticipated the grave dangers stemming from mankind's aggressive and self-destructive tendencies. As Nazism gathered strength, he added the line "But, who can foresee with what success and with what results?" to the concluding paragraph of the 1931 edition of the above-mentioned essay.[3]

Freud did not live to see the results of the struggles of his "immortal adversaries." Nevertheless, looking back on the events of the past forty years, we can appreciate the prophetic quality of Freud's thoughts regarding human nature and cultural development: "The existence of this inclination to aggression, which we can detect in ourselves and justly assume to be present in others, is the factor which disturbs our relations with our neighbour. . . . In consequence of this primary mutual hostility of human beings, civilized society is perpetually threatened with disintegration."[4]

The validity of Freud's theoretical formulations concerning the existence of an innate destructive drive, the external manifestation of the death instinct, has been a subject of considerable scholarly debate. Max Horkheimer and Theodore Adorno (1947) offered a societal interpretation of Freud's words when they wrote that "horror and civilization are inseparable."[5] Because of the Holocaust, "history has to mean a progress toward Hell."[6]

Ironically, Freud—with his controversial insights into the nature and causes of human aggression and his hypothesis of an innate drive toward self-destruction—became the first psychoanalyst to shed light on the seemingly unfathomable actuality of the Holocaust. For he was arguing, in effect, that an understanding of the Holocaust, and of this most brutal of centuries, called for a confrontation with something inherent in the human organism. A review of historical and sociopolitical determinants was simply inadequate. As Waelder (1960) pointed out:

> . . . while it is possible and indeed indicated to explain many manifestations of aggressiveness—as reactions to frustration or danger, or as by-products of self-preservation or self-expansion, or as sexual manifestations, an attempt to explain all destructive behavior along these lines becomes strained. There seems to be an irreducible remainder of destructive phenomena which suggest the existence of destructive forces in man—at least in many men.[7]

Waelder referred to this "irreducible remainder" as essential destructiveness, an expression of a destructive instinctual drive.

In the years leading up to World War II, psychoanalysis gradually shifted its base from the European continent to the United States and, to a lesser extent, England and South America. Small pockets of psychoanalysts continued to practice within Europe, but the thriving and creative quality of the early 1900s and the interbellum period was essentially lost in the flames that consumed Freud's writings.

The problems facing the refugee analysts and all serious thinkers of the time concerned coming to terms with the unthinkable events that had transpired in their native Europe. To a greater or lesser extent, these refugee analysts and intellectuals had been traumatized by the Holocaust.[8] Some apparently concurred with the early Wittgenstein, who felt that "what we cannot speak about we must pass over in silence."[9] Others may have suffered a paralysis of initiative and nihilism like that of the profoundly pessimistic Adorno: "Auschwitz demonstrated irrefutably that culture has failed." "All post-Auschwitz culture, including its urgent critique, is garbage."[10] Some, like the critic Walter Benjamin and the poet Paul Celan, committed suicide (Benjamin before the Holocaust [1940], and Celan after [1970]).

Others, and this includes all the contributors to this volume, have attempted to approach the Holocaust in the way outlined recently by Bettelheim (1979): ". . . there is a group of survivors who concluded from their experience that only a better integration would permit them to live as well as they could with the after effects of their concentration camp experience."[11] While Bettelheim is referring to the actual survivors of the Holocaust, his concept of reintegration applies to all who have attempted to restructure their personalities and their world view rather than repress and deny the psychological ramifications of the Holocaust. Such a task can be an arduous one, laden with much ambiguity, but when studying the Holocaust we take the position that "only those questions which cannot be answered with laboratory precision have any real significance."[12]

We see the Holocaust as "nothing less than a moral equivalent of the Copernican revolution."[13] As Kren and Rappoport (1980) argue, "Western European culture is not an orderly, ethical center for our social universe, and the historical development of its moral instrumentalities—law and religion—was a failure ending in Auschwitz."[14] It is precisely this serious challenge to preexisting frames of orientation that calls the theory and practice of psychoanalysis into the picture. We are not referring to psychoanalysis primarily as a therapeutic tool, but rather as a systematized body of knowledge about human behavior and psychological functioning. The Holocaust raises the most troubling questions about man, and the conceptual veracity and possibilities of psychoanalysis can only be strengthened by self-scrutiny in light of the dominant psychic reality of the Holocaust.

There exists an extensive literature of a clinical nature dealing with the treatment of Holocaust survivors and their offspring,* but with the notable exception of Bettelheim[15] and papers by Wangh,[16] Mitscherlich and Mitscherlich,[17] and Eissler,[18] psychoanalytic reflections on the Holocaust per se and on its broader ramifications remain unavailable. Reich (1982) cogently assessed this problem in a discussion of a conference held at Yale University which focused on the development of a psychoanalytic theory of Holocaust trauma: "The tragic irony of the conference's limited

---

*For a comprehensive review of this literature, see *Psychological and Medical Effects of Concentration Camps: Research Bibliography,* prepared by L. Eitinger (Ray D. Wolfe Center for the Study of Psychological Stress, University of Haifa, Israel).

focus was never articulated. . . . the psychological damage that was inflicted upon those survivors, incomprehensible, brutal, and massive as it was, was still less compelling a problem of human experience than the physical exterminations themselves."[19] The inextensive psychoanalytic study of the Holocaust, as opposed to the study of the treatment of Holocaust survivors, was in Reich's view the outgrowth of a need on the part of the conference participants to concentrate on the more tolerable aspects of the Holocaust. We look for "some good in what happened, some decency, some selflessness, some light in that epoch of deepest darkness."[20] For the most part we only succeed in spinning self-protective fantasies—"conjured memories," as Reich courageously puts it.

We attempt to meet Reich's challenge by deemphasizing the technical study of individual clinical cases. Rather, our focus has been to have our contributors discuss specific aspects of the Holocaust that have a bearing on more general psychological, moral, and social problems, using clinical vignettes as illustrations when necessary. And if this book achieves anything, it will dispel any notions of a parochial Freudian approach cut off from the larger realms of history, ideology, and society when examining the Holocaust.

We approach the interrelationship between psychoanalysis and the Holocaust in a twofold fashion. First, we maintain that psychoanalytic insights help us to explore the deepest sources of human motivation. Moreover, psychoanalysis is the theoretical system which comes closest to conveying the turbulence of human behavior. It remains an unparalleled "science of the irrational." Other accounts of personality organization and functioning have much to offer, but they are relatively passionless when compared to the Freudian one. This view becomes more compelling when we recall that *passion* is a word that originally had much to do with human affliction and suffering. Secondly, as we argued above, the Holocaust has created a profound crisis in our efforts to construct a meaningful reality within which values which are part and parcel of a shared ethos of compassion can evolve. The psychoanalytic community ought to address Erich Kahler's searing assertion that "the most frightening aspect of our present world is not the horrors in themselves, the atrocities, the technological exterminations, but the fact at the very root of it all; the fading away of any human criterion."[21]

To strengthen our efforts to rediscover "the human center" and achieve new emotional and cognitive balance in a universe that seems to be ethically indifferent, the psychoanalyst is required to incorporate the essential meaning of Adorno's statement: "No poetry after Auschwitz." We agree with Tar that what Adorno meant by his famous dictum was that "no study of sociology could be possible without reflecting on Auschwitz and without concerning oneself with preventing new Auschwitzes."[22] What applies to sociology applies equally to psychoanalysis, if it is to remain a radical and imaginative vision of the human enterprise.

As Ostow (1982) observed regarding other Jewish-related issues, the Holocaust cannot remain a "private realm subject to an unspoken gentlemen's agreement of silence at psychoanalytic institutes."[23] For example, the application of a psychoanalytically oriented conceptual lens to the Nazi Holocaust has a direct bearing on our efforts to seek the prevention of a pan-Holocaust—nuclear global destruction. It is only recently that members of the psychoanalytic community have begun to use psychological knowledge derived from their understanding and study of the Holocaust in attempts to foster greater clarity of mind in dealing with our present crises.[24]

Psychodynamically based investigations of the impact of the Holocaust on our understanding of child-rearing, moral and ethical development, aggression and hostility, Jewish and Christian identity, group psychology, the psychogenesis of paranoia, and the conditions that make large-scale genocide possible are additional examples of issues that will benefit from serious psychoanalytic exploration.

All this emphasis on the need to confront the Holocaust and its unprecedented terror and destruction may sound unduly pessimistic or even macabre to some. On the contrary, we think that a proper psychoanalytically based study of the Holocaust as it took place—without self-protective distortion—will contribute to an inner ordering of one's experience and to the achievement of "ego integrity."[25] Because of the nature of the psychoanalytic process, with its focus on libidinal and aggressive drives, psychoanalysts are in a unique position to guide the way in our attempt to master our enormous destructive potential, that is, the exacerbated and unrelieved urge for violence. The present collection of essays represents our efforts both to address a serious gap in the literature and scholarship on the Holocaust and to foster constructive intellectual disquietude.

The study of the Holocaust aided by psychodynamic concepts inevitably leads to tragic comprehension that can stimulate preexisting inclinations toward denial and disavowal. But as Eissler observes: "truth, bitter as it is, may enlarge man's self—as it has so often in the past—and man, having shed one more denial, may enjoy the state of enlarged inner freedom despite the recognition of how merciless that reality is of which he is a part."[26]

When psychoanalysis and the Holocaust meet, as they do in the pages that follow, we can readily conjure up an image of a "fatally poisoned Eros trailing catastrophe."[27] But the restoration of the powers of Eros is not impossible.

As Reich, in the article cited earlier, notes: "the most powerful defense against the recurrence of a Holocaust is the memory of the one that took place."[28] To this we can only add that like Orestes in the great *Oresteia* trilogy of Aeschylus, we cannot deny or escape the dark side of life, the Furies. Greek tragic wisdom, as Barrett (1962) explains[29]—proposed the only solution: give the Furies their just and due respect and they will be propitiously renamed the Eumenides, or Gentle Ones.

The Holocaust poses a serious challenge to psychoanalysis. Will it serve as "an effective counter-vision in perpetuity,"[30] a preventive psychology, a means of ameliorating the pathology of contemporary society, or will its aims remain more circumscribed in nature—limited to treating individual disturbance and fostering adaptation to a decaying environment?

For psychoanalysis to remain a critical and profound theory, its practitioners and students will need to "work-through" the Holocaust and its numerous ramifications. Listen to Athena addressing the Furies (read Holocaust), for she defines our task: "Rather accept my honourable word that ye shall have a cave wherein to dwell among this righteous people, and enthroned in honor at your altars, shall receive the adoration of my citizens."[31]

The alternative to such a confrontation with the brutalization which took place is continued denial and rationalization of current social crises and persecution coupled with diminished access to the wellspring of our humanity and empathy. And so we have no choice but to deal, as Hoppe proposes, with "the dynamics of such a perverted pattern of modern man who gassed his soul in the ovens of Auschwitz."[32]

REFERENCES

1. Erik Erikson, *Insight and Responsibility* (New York: Norton, 1964), p. 208.
2. Freud, *Civilization and Its Discontents* (New York: Norton, 1961), p. 92.
3. Ibid., p. 92.
4. Ibid., p. 59.
5. Max Horkheimer and Theodore Adorno, *Dialektik der Aufklarung* (Amsterdam: Querido Verlag, 1947), p. 256.

6. Michael Landmann, in Zoltan Tar, *The Frankfurt School* (New York: Wiley, 1977), p. xvi.
7. Robert Waelder, *Basic Theory of Psychoanalysis* (New York: International Universities Press, 1960), p. 146.
8. The late Heinz Kohut, for example, viewed the trauma of his flight from Austria as important in the development of his theories concerning narcissism: "It was the end of a world, it was the end of an era. And I had the feeling that it was also the end of my life, in terms of the continuity of my cultural existence." "I've led two different, perhaps unbridgeable lives." It was that monumental disruption, Kohut believed, that made him "alert to the problems of the fragmented self and how it tries to cure itself." *New York Times Magazine,* November 9, 1980, p. 124.
9. Ludwig Wittgenstein, *Tractatus Logico-Philosophicus* (London: Routledge & Kegan Paul, 1961), p. 74.
10. Theodore Adorno, "After Auschwitz," in *Negative Dialectics* (New York: Seabury, 1973), pp. 366, 367.
11. Bruno Bettelheim, *Surviving* (New York: Knopf, 1979), p. 34.
12. E. F. Schumacher, *A Guide for the Perplexed* (New York: Harper & Row, 1977), p. 5.
13. George Kren and Leon Rappoport, *The Holocaust and the Crisis of Human Behavior* (New York: Holmes & Meier, 1980), p. 132.
14. Ibid., p. 137.
15. Bettelheim, *Surviving*.
16. Martin Wangh, "National Socialism and the Genocide of the Jews," *International Journal of Psychoanalysis* 45 (1964): 386–395.
17. Alexander Mitscherlich and Margarete Mitscherlich, *The Inability to Mourn* (New York: Grove Press, 1975).
18. Kurt Eissler, "The Fall of Man," *Psychoanalytic Study of the Child* 30 (1975): 584–646.
19. Walter Reich, "The Enemies of Memory," *New Republic,* April 21, 1982, p. 23.
20. Ibid., p. 22.
21. Erich Kahler, *The Tower and the Abyss* (New York: Viking, 1967), p. 151.
22. Tar, *Frankfurt School,* p. 158.
23. Mortimer Ostow, *Judaism and Psychoanalysis* (New York: KTAV, 1982), p. 150.
24. See Martin Wangh's essay in this book, below pp. 196-205.
25. The goal of integration in light of one's confrontation with the Holocaust is the subject of a paper (included in the present volume) by Henry Krystal, "Integration and Self-Healing in Post-Traumatic States." See below, pp. 113-133.
26. Kurt Eissler, *The Psychiatrist and the Dying Patient* (New York: International Universities Press, 1969), p. 312.
27. Erikson, *Insight and Responsibility,* p. 209.
28. Reich, "Enemies of Memory," p. 23.

29. William Barrett, *Irrational Man* (New York: Doubleday Anchor Books, 1962), pp. 276–280.
30. Erik Erikson, *Toys and Reasons: Stages in the Ritualization of Experience* (New York: Norton, 1976), p. 170.
31. Aeschylus, *The Eumenides,* in *The Oresteia,* trans. P. Roche (New York: New American Library, 1962), p. 192.
32. Klaus Hoppe, personal communication.

I

IDEOLOGICAL and CULTURAL PERSPECTIVES

INTRODUCTION

For the last five years Professor Lifton has been studying the Nazi doctors who officiated at Auschwitz and Nazi doctors in general. In this paper, he offers thought-provoking interpretations of the diverse motivations that permitted such physicians to preserve the illusion that they were performing a healing function while actually serving as vital cogs in a brutal killing machine.

Lifton suggests that there existed in Auschwitz and elsewhere a biomedical ideology in which political leaders ruled in the name of what was held to be a higher bioethical principle—mass murder as a healing and cleansing process. Bureaucratized killing became a therapeutic imperative, and the Nazi goal was nothing less than total domination over life and death, and over the evolutionary process itself.

Lifton discusses some of the psychological mechanisms surrounding the biomedical vision that made possible the "transformation from healer to killer." Of particular interest is "psychic numbing," diffusion of responsibility, and derealization (the feeling that the world seems unreal). This leads to a reduced capacity to feel, so that one avoids experiencing oneself as related to the brutality and killing. In addition, Lifton mentions the defense of "doubling," in which various elements of the psyche are compartmentalized. This permits the creation of two autonomous selves: on the one hand, the Auschwitz doctor could be brutal and kill, and on the other, he could remain gentle and kind in his family relationships while avoiding a sense of himself as a murderer.

Lifton's paper reveals how dedicated physicians can face their own mortality, terrifying forlornness, and lack of a unifying Weltanschauung in such a way that a dehumanizing and death-dealing ideology becomes appealing and eventually exerts a tyrannical hold over the individual. The essay concludes with the reader urged to see in collective violence not only extensive sadism but also the desperate striving for a greater sense of life and vitality.

Medicalized Killing in Auschwitz

ROBERT JAY LIFTON

I

Much of the study revolves around interviews I conducted in Germany and Austria with twenty-eight former Nazi doctors and one pharmacist. Five of the doctors had at some time worked in concentration camps. Six others had been involved with the so-called euthanasia program, which was mainly the killing of mental patients, mostly from 1939 to 1941 but afterward as well. A third group consisted of eight high-level Nazis who were involved in linking medical principles with racial ideology, both as theoreticians and as administrators. Another group of six held responsible positions in the Nazi medical hierarchy; their work became tainted by the various projects in which they took part. The three remaining doctors were for the most part engaged in traditional military medicine on the eastern front, but at the same time they were partly aware—and trying to avoid awareness—of the massive killing of Jews by Einsatzgruppen troops immediately behind the lines.

Introductions to the doctors were carefully arranged, largely by one person—a friend who as the director of a Max Planck Institute in Munich and a professor of psychiatry is a person of high standing in German medicine. He wrote an initial letter introducing me as a "prominent American researcher" who had worked on Hiroshima and Vietnam, which conveyed to those with whom I talked a sense of my concern with destructiveness in general.

About 70 percent of those approached in this way eventually agreed to see me, motivated in part by a sense of obligation to me as a "colleague" and in part by an inner inclination that included recognition of an opportunity to affirm their post-Nazi identity. They spoke with varying degrees of candor, indirection, and evasiveness, and I cross-checked much of the information against descriptions by others and various records, especially early ones. Still, I was surprised at how willing they were to see me and how relatively freely they talked. They had a need to explain themselves—to try to justify themselves. In the process they revealed a great deal, but none really confronted in a moral sense what he had done or been part of. In many cases, the doctor I interviewed would talk as if he were a third person, looking back at events as an observer.

I also interviewed a second group of former Nazis: twelve nonmedical professionals—lawyers, judges, teachers, architects, party officials and organizers—who gave me valuable background on the general Nazi project and how professionals fit into it.

Finally, I interviewed a third and very different group, eighty Auschwitz survivors who had been associated with medical work of some kind, most of them former inmate doctors. These interviews were held throughout Western Europe (Germany, Austria, France, England, Norway, Denmark), and in the United States, Israel, Poland, and Australia. Survivor physicians provided me with invaluable descriptions of the behavior of Nazi doctors and of the entire pattern of pseudomedical behavior in Auschwitz.

Most of the interviews in the first two groups were conducted with the help of an interpreter–research assistant, specially trained to facilitate communication (see Lifton 1975, 1969). All of these interviews were tape-recorded, which has permitted me to work from the original German. The surivor group differed in that many spoke fluent English (including some living outside of English-speaking countries), while others required interpreting from Hebrew, Polish, French, and German. I spent a minimum of two to four hours with most people in all three groups but had much more time with many of them, sometimes thirty hours or more during six or seven interviews, each lasting from a few hours to an entire day.

The psychological paradigm that I use in this study, as in others, departs from the classic Freudian model of instinct and defense and instead stresses the symbolization of life and death (Lifton 1979, 1980). Briefly, this paradigm includes both an immediate and an ultimate dimension. The immediate dimension—our direct psychological involvements—is understood in terms of connection and separation, integrity and disintegration, and movement and stasis. The separation, disintegration, and stasis are death equivalents, images that relate to concerns around death, while the experiences of connection, integrity and movement are associated with vitality and with symbolizations of life.

At the ultimate dimension I seek to account for larger historical experience. This concerns the struggle around symbolic forms of immortality: around a collective sense of being part of something larger than the self, which will—at least in one's imagery—continue indefinitely, beyond one's own limited life-span. This can be a human group, a set of social, political, or spiritual principles, a movement, nation, or institution. Symbolization of immortality was, of course, central to Nazi concepts of the "thousand-year Reich."

The general paradigm applies, I believe, to the widespread individual experience of separation, disintegration, and stasis among many Germans during the period following World War I. These feelings were described to me repeatedly in connection with general demoralization and confusion in association with military defeat, economic duress, and the threat of revolution. For many the Nazi movement held out the promise of new human connection, general social integration, and a sense of development and progress—all in the service of a vast national and cultural revitalization.

II

Many students of the Holocaust have rightly stressed the idea of a barrier that has been removed, a boundary that has been crossed: the boundary between violent imagery and periodic killing of victims (as of Jews in pogroms) on the one hand, and the systematic genocide in Auschwitz on the other. My argument here is that the medicalization of killing—the imagery of killing in the name of healing—is one important way of understanding that terrible step. At the heart of the Nazi enterprise, then, is the loss of a boundary between healing and killing.

In the sequence of psychological impressions of the killing process at Auschwitz and other death camps, early reports stressed Nazi sadism and viciousness. But as those attempting to understand the process realized that sadism and viciousness could not in themselves account for the killing of millions of people, the stress shifted to the principle of faceless, bureaucratized killing (Hilberg 1973; Rubenstein 1978; Arendt 1963). This remains a significant and necessary emphasis. Yet my belief is that neither of these emphases is sufficient in itself. We need also to consider motivational principles around ideology, and the various psychological mechanisms that contribute to the killing.

What I am calling medicalized killing certainly includes expressions of sadism, and it depends upon the elaborate bureaucracy and routinization of killing that prevailed in Auschwitz and other camps. But it also focuses upon the psychological motivations of specific individuals involved in the killing.

Medicalized killing can be understood in two ways. One is the efficient or so-called surgical method of killing large numbers of people by a controlled technology using highly poisonous gas. This method becomes a way of protecting the killers from the psychological consequences of face-to-face killing. Nazi documents reveal considerable concern with precisely those psychological consequences among Einsatzgruppen troops, a large number of whom apparently experienced incapacitating symptoms in response to their "work." I was able to explore that matter with a former Wehrmacht neuropsychiatrist, assigned to treat members of the Einsatzgruppen, who estimated that as many as 20 percent of those who did the actual killing had significant psychological difficulties. In other words, there were impediments—human impediments—when applying ordinary military methods to mass murder on this extraordinary scale. What I am calling surgical killing provided a means to overcome these impediments by minimizing the psychological difficulties of the killers.

But there is another dimension of medicalized killing, one that I believe is insufficiently emphasized: killing as a therapeutic imperative. This kind of imagery was dramatically revealed in the words of an SS doctor in response to a question posed to him in Auschwitz by a distinguished survivor physician, Dr. Ella Lingens-Reiner. Pointing to the chimneys in the distance, she asked: "How can you reconcile that with your Hippocratic Oath?" His answer was: "When you find a gangrenous appendix you must remove it."* The image here is of the Jews as a gangrenous disease, which has to be removed from the social or racial body of the German people in order to bring about a cure. Most SS physicians would not have answered that question so absolutely, would not have held such an extreme ideological position. But they were not likely to be entirely free of such "therapeutic" imagery, which was psychologically prevalent in the Auschwitz atmoshere and provided an important basis for the extermination camps in general.

Such imagery recalls the description of Turkey during the nineteenth century as the "sick man of Europe," and more specifically the similar

*Personal communication. Dr. Lingens-Reiner reported the same incident in her book slightly differently: Her question to the SS doctor, Fritz Klein, was, "Have you, as a doctor, no respect for human life?" His answer was: "Out of respect for human life, I would remove a purulent appendix from a diseased body. The Jew is the purulent appendix in the body of Europe" (1948, pp. 1–2).

attitude toward Germany at the end of World War I. Adolf Hitler, writing in *Mein Kampf* on the German state, said italicizing for emphasis: "*anyone who wants to cure this era, which is inwardly sick and rotten, must first of all summon up the courage to make clear the cause of this disease*" (1969, p. 396). Certainly many Germans felt that way, and one vision of cure involved the extermination of the Jewish people and the extermination or subjugation of Gypsies, Poles, Slavs, and others. That vision culminated in specific views of leading Nazi officials. For Hans Frank, jurist and *Generalgouverneur* of Poland, "the Jews were a lower species of life, a kind of vermin, which upon contact infected the German people with deadly diseases." Frank frequently referred to Jews as "lice," and when the Jews were killed in the area of Poland he ruled, he declared that "now a sick Europe would become healthy again" (quoted from Frank diary in Hilberg, p. 12). Himmler used similar language in cautioning his SS generals against tolerating the stealing of property which had belonged to dead Jews: "Just because we exterminate a bacterium we do not want, in the end, to be infected by that bacterium and die of it" (Hilberg 1973, p. 12).

Part of this vision includes a religion of the will, in which the will becomes "an all-encompassing metaphysical principle" (Stern 1975, p. 70).* What the Nazis "willed" was nothing less than total control over life and death, and, indeed, control of the evolutionary process. Making widespread use of the Darwinian term "selection," the Nazis sought to take over the functions of nature (natural selection) and God ("the Lord giveth and the Lord taketh away") in orchestrating their own "selections," their own version of human evolution.†

The therapeutic imperative was a biological imperative. One could call the Nazi hierarchy a "biocracy"—in the sense of the model of a theocracy, but with a very important difference. In a theocracy the rulers are the high priests, empowered by their tie to the sacred. In the Nazi

*The celebration of that religious impulse was epitomized by the gigantic Nuremberg rally of 1934, whose theme, "The Triumph of the Will," became the title of Leni Riefenstahl's celebrated film. Riefenstahl, in an interview with an assistant of mine, made clear that it was Hitler himself who provided that slogan for the overall Nuremberg rally.

†Stern (p. 77) makes a related point when he speaks of the Nazi and broadly fascist application of the doctrine of "the Will" as existing "within the framework of *Sozialdarwinismus* as that agency of Nature which acts in the social and political sphere with the same absolute validity as the principle of natural selection does among species of animals." But the Nazi version of fascism is unique in the extent to which its social Darwinism is bound up with racial theory—what I am calling the biomedical vision—to which the doctrine of the Will can be applied.

biocracy, the political and military leaders—Hitler and his circle—were the rulers, but they ruled in the name of what was held to be a higher biological principle. Among the biological authorities who gave credence to that principle—including physical anthropologists, geneticists, evolutionary and racial theorists of all kinds—it was mainly the doctors who became the activists, the practitioners. Doctors regularly function at the border of life and death. They, more than the other biological authorities, are associated with the awesome, death-defying, and sometimes deadly imagery of the primitive shaman, witch doctor, or medicine man.

Hence, manipulative political regimes or their clandestine agencies tend to call upon doctors to use their authority and skills—their shamanistic legacy—in support of the regimes' world views and against people perceived as threats to those world views. In the Soviet Union psychiatrists diagnose dissenters as mentally ill and incarcerate them in mental hospitals—a procedure that functions as political repression (Bloch and Reddaway 1977). In Chile, according to Amnesty International, doctors have been involved in torture for political purposes. In the United States physicians and psychologists have been employed by the CIA in unethical medical and psychological experiments involving drugs and mind-manipulation (Marks 1979). In the mass suicide and murder of more than nine hundred members of the religious cult known as the People's Temple in Guyana, in November 1978, the group's physician prepared the poison (Reston 1981; Lifton 1979).

To be sure, these examples differ fundamentally from the Nazi practices and are in no way to be equated with them. But their common principle is that of the physician as activist agent for some form of reality control or oppression.

The Nazis' unique intensity of focus on biological salvation gave special emphasis to this perverse use of the physician's power.

III

One may thus say that the doctor standing on the ramp at Birkenau—the division of Auschwitz where initial "selections" and most of the gassings were performed—represents a kind of omega point, a final common pathway of the Nazi vision of therapy via mass murder. In a sense the doctor takes on the mythical identity of a gatekeeper between two worlds—that of the dead and that of the living.

Doctors were not tried at Nuremberg for performing selections, partly because the full significance of this activity was not yet understood.* I believe, however, that the doctors' role in selections has even greater significance than their participation in medical experiments for which doctors *were* tried at Nuremberg.

The SS doctors made the initial large-scale "selections" of arriving Jewish inmates at the Birkenau ramp.† (Only Jews were systematically subjected to selections.) The task was performed quickly, massively, and often according to formula, so that old people, children, and women with children were all automatically selected for gas, while relatively intact young adults were permitted to survive, at least temporarily. The great majority of arriving Jews—most estimates are of more than 70 percent—were quickly sent to the gas chamber. Since no medical examination was done and no medical skill was required for this function, the Nazis apparently sought to invest it with medical authority and to represent it as a medical procedure.

After the selection, the presiding doctor was driven in an SS vehicle usually marked with a red cross, with a medical technician (one of a special group of "disinfectors" [*Desinfektoren*] from within the *Sanitaets-dienstgrade* or SDG) and the gas pellets, to a gas chamber adjoining one of the crematoria. There the doctor had supervisory responsibility for the

---

**United States v. Karl Brandt et al.*, Case No. 1, *Trials of War Criminals Before Nuernberg Military Tribunals* (1946–1949), vols. 1 and 2. See especially vol. 1, pp. 8–17, for the indictment, and pp. 27–74 for the opening statement of the prosecution. I was also able to discuss the issue with James M. McHaney, chief prosecutor of the medical trial, who confirmed the lack of full appreciation at that time of doctors' participation in the overall killing process. He stressed that the policy then was to prosecute high-ranking doctors (who were not likely to be at the ramp at Auschwitz), considered to have the greatest responsibility for overall medical crimes, and to do so on the basis of stark and convincing evidence, such as that associated with medical experiments on concentration-camp inmates.

†The description of doctors' activities is based on interviews with former Nazi Auschwitz doctors and with former inmate doctors, plus the following major sources: R. Hoess, *Commandant in Auschwitz* (World Publishing Co., 1960), including supplementary statement, "The final solution of the Jewish question in the Auschwitz concentration camp," Appendix 1; and "Die Nichtärztliche Tatigkeit der SS-Arzte im K. L. Auschwitz" (The Nonmedical Activity of SS-Doctors in the Concentration Camp Auschwitz), *Heft von Auschwitz*, no. 16, Auschwitz Museum, 1975, pp. 75–77 (the *Hefte* is a rich source of related materials). See also: materials of Frankfurt Auschwitz trial of 1963–65 in "Proceedings against Mulka and others, and English summary of that trial," B. Naumann, *Auschwitz: A Report on the Proceedings Against Robert Karl Ludwig Mulka and Others Before the Court at Frankfurt* (Praeger, 1966); *Przeglad Lekarski*, a journal published by the Medical Academy of Crakow (many articles have been translated into English by the International Auschwitz Committee and published in Warsaw); and H. Langbein, *Menschen in Auschwitz* (Vienna: Europaverlag, 1972).

correct carrying out of the process, though the medical technician actually inserted the gas pellets, and the entire sequence became so routine that little intervention was required. The doctor also had the task of declaring those inside the gas chamber dead, which in some cases meant looking through a peephole to observe them. This too became routinized, a matter of permitting twenty minutes or so to pass before the doors of the gas chamber could be opened and the bodies removed. The doctors' participation in selections, then, was the first of a series of tasks involving the whole sequence of the killing process.

SS doctors also carried out two other forms of selections. In the first, Jewish inmates were lined up on very short notice at various places in the camp and their ranks thinned in order to allow room for presumably healthier replacements from new transports. The other type of selection took place directly in the medical blocks. This is of very great significance because it meant, in effect, that the medical blocks—places where people were supposed to be treated for their diseases—became centers for camp "triage." This was not, of course, the usual triage, in which the doctor lets those beyond help die while giving full medical energy to those considered salvageable (this was the meaning given the term as originally used by the French military). Rather, it was triage plus murder, in which the Nazis killed those judged to be significantly ill or debilitated, or who required more than two or three weeks for recovery. That length of time was apparently set in conjunction with I. G. Farben, the firm that controlled and contracted for much of the work force. When some of the prisoners had typhus, the inhabitants of an entire block or even several blocks—sometimes hundreds at once—would be sent to the gas chamber in order to prevent further spread of the disease and the development of an epidemic. In their murderous practices, the medical blocks became microcosms of the overall Auschwitz process.

SS doctors were active as well in determining how best to keep the selections running smoothly—making recommendations, for example, as to whether women and children should be separated or allowed to proceed along the line together. They also advised on policies concerning numbers of people permitted to remain alive, weighing the benefits to the Nazi regime of the work function against the increased health problems created by permitting relatively debilitated people to live.

Doctors' technical knowledge was also called upon with regard to the burning of bodies, a great problem in Auschwitz during the summer of 1944, when the rapid arrival and destruction of enormous numbers of Hungarian Jews overstrained the facilities of the crematoria. These technical matters could include questions of physics—problems of maintaining great heat, of evaluating conditions for maximum efficiency in burning, and of overall function of the mechanical facilities of the crematoria.

Doctors also had to witness executions as part of their general function of declaring people dead, and had to sign various documents certifying that one could proceed with a punitive procedure. The latter function implied that an inmate could survive the particular punishment ordered—such as a certain number of blows with a whip.

Finally, doctors were involved in killing by injections, usually of phenol, into the heart or the blood system. These were widely employed prior to the complete functioning of the gas chambers, and were often used for very debilitated patients or for secret political murders. Doctors occasionally did these injections themselves, but more often they were performed by SDG personnel or brutalized prisoners.

All of these activities, of course, were manifestations of overall Auschwitz structure and function, as dictated from above. I am suggesting nonetheless that the doctors were given considerable responsibility for carrying out the entire killing process—for the choosing of victims, for the physical and psychological mechanisms of the process, and for the general equilibrium of killing and work-function in the camp.

IV

Although I have been emphasizing the doctors' role in medicalized killing, the medical experiments on human beings have their own importance, and can be understood as an aspect of the larger Nazi biomedical vision.* Generally speaking, in Auschwitz and elsewhere, medical experiments fell into two categories: those sponsored by the regime for specific

---

*Descriptions of experiments are based on interviews with former Nazi doctors and former inmate doctors; with survivors who had worked on medical blocks, including a physical anthropologist who had assisted Mengele in measurements on twins; and with other survivors who had themselves been subjected to these experiments and "research studies." See also, A. Mitscherlich and F. Mielke, *The Death Doctors* (London: Elek Books, 1962); M. M. Hill and L. N. Williams, *Auschwitz in England: A Record of a Libel Action* (Stein & Day, 1965); Y. Ternon and S. Helman, *Les Médecins Allemands et Le National-Socialisme* (Paris: Casterman, 1973) and *Historie Médecin SS* (Paris: Casterman, 1970); F. Bayle, *Croix Gammée contre Caducée: Les éxperiences on Allemagne pendant la deuxieme guerre mondiale* (Imprimerie Nationale a Neustadt (Palatinat), Commission Scientifique Francaise des Crimes de Guerre, 1950); and various Red Cross documents, published at Arolsen (West Germany) and Geneva, such as L. Simonius, "On Behalf of Victims of Pseudo-Medical Experiments: Red Cross Action," *International Review of the Red Cross* (Geneva, 1973).

ideological and military purposes, and those that were done ad hoc out of allegedly scientific interest on the part of the SS doctor.

In Auschwitz, the first category consisted mainly of sterilization experiments—injections of caustic substances into the uterine cervix of women by Carl Clauberg, and the use of X-rays on the genital organs of men and women by Horst Schumann, followed by surgical removal of testicles or ovaries to study the effects of the X-rays. These experiments were actively promoted by Himmler, who on the whole was somewhat deceived by the doctors in their claims that they were on the verge of achieving efficient and economic methods for large-scale sterilization of inferior peoples. Experiments were done at other camps on cold immersion and exposure to high pressure (as at high altitudes); on the effects of sulfonamides and other therapeutic agents on artificially created wound infections and gangrene; and on the effectiveness of various serums for typhus and yellow fever.

The second kind of experiment emerged from doctors' desire to do "scientific" work: many SS doctors found the enormous population of helpless victims irresistible from the standpoint of medical research. The largest ad hoc experiments of this category in Auschwitz were those undertaken by Josef Mengele and by Eduard Wirths, the chief doctor at Auschwitz. Mengele worked mostly with identical twins, but he also studied dwarfs, and to a lesser extent certain medical conditions, such as noma (tumorlike infectious ulcerations of the mouth and face, which can often become gangrenous). Because Mengele was known to be an ideological fanatic, it is frequently assumed that his study of twins was motivated by a desire to learn how to induce multiple births, in order to repopulate the world with Germans. The evidence, however, does not seem to bear out that assumption, even though his extreme focus on genetic factors did have a strong ideological component. Rather, I think, Mengele was continuing studies he had begun at the racial biology institute at the University of Frankfurt—studies of twins meant to confirm the overriding significance of genetic and racial factors. Mengele's dedication to the Nazi biomedical vision kept him always on the border between science and ideologically corrupted pseudoscience, a border very important to understand.

At times he stepped clearly over that border, as when he worked on prisoners with the rare condition of eyes of two different colors, injecting blue dye into a brown eye in order to see whether the eye could be rendered blue like the other one. But according to observations conveyed to me by several inmate doctors and by an inmate anthropologist who took bodily measurements for him, in much of his work he was apparently following standard practices of the physical anthropology of his time. His method was descriptive, the amassing of data, and I know of no evidence that he had any significantly original scientific ideas. On the whole, being a twin in his study had enormous survival value, as he tended to protect his research subjects. But it is also well established that on a number of occasions he had one or both twins—usually children—killed, because of interest in a possible post-mortem finding.

Eduard Wirths's experiments were meant to be a legitimate study of precancerous growths on the cervix in women. The most destructive aspect of these experiments involved the surgical removal of all or most of the cervix, although a small tissue biopsy would have been appropriate to this kind of study under ordinary conditions. But these were hardly ordinary conditions, and in the absence of anything approaching adequate care for the women so "studied," there were of course many complications and deaths. Wirths also became involved in a small experimental trial of a new typhus vaccine; inmates were first artificially infected with the disease, resulting in a few deaths. Such experiments with infectious diseases—especially typhus, because of its danger to German military and civilian personnel—were performed on a much larger scale in other camps.

Other kinds of experiments at Auschwitz combined official purposes with individual interests—such as the use of drugs (probably including mescaline, morphine, and barbiturate derivatives) for purposes of extracting confessions, and the use of poisons, including the development of poison bullets. Smaller ad hoc experiments involved tooth extraction around theories of focal infection, and there were relatively conventional bacteriological and microscopic studies. One borderline investigation involved the use of electroshock for mental illness, a project initiated by an Auschwitz inmate doctor with some experience in the procedure, with the approval and sponsorship of an SS doctor. Finally, as in many other camps, experimental surgery was done by SS doctors—that is, various operations were performed in order to gain experience in doing them, sometimes but not always under the supervision of more experienced inmate surgeons.

On the whole, experiments in Auschwitz were perceived as relatively limited, as compared to the extraordinary scope of what we are calling medicalized killing. But in another sense all of Auschwitz was sometimes viewed—by Nazi doctors as well as by inmates—as one vast "experiment."

V

In the sequence of medicalized killing, one can see a direct medical link between the official compulsory sterilization programs of 1933, the so-called euthanasia programs beginning in 1939, and the subsequent Final Solution, or concentration camp exterminations.* Many of the doctors I spoke to were in favor of the sterilization laws. These were broadly applied to people with conditions considered incurable, most extensively to mental defectives and schizophrenics. Some of the eugenic thought behind the laws extended far beyond Nazi Germany—there were at one time sterilization laws in a number of states in the United States—but no country, before or since, has imposed on its people so extensive and systematic a program of forced sterilization.

The key event, however, in the sequence from sterilization to Auschwitz was the program of direct medical killing—loosely and wrongly termed "euthanasia"—that operated in Germany, mostly from the winter of 1939–40 to late summer of 1941. This project was initiated on a direct order by Hitler and utilized large sectors of the German medical profession, especially psychiatry, to kill more than 100,000 German citizens who were defined as suffering from "incurable" mental disorders.

The killing function of Auschwitz-Birkenau was anticipated by that program in at least three ways. First, during that program the systematic use of deadly gas to kill large numbers of people was developed. The gas chambers were camouflaged as shower rooms to allay suspicions of the victims. Carbon monoxide gas was released into the chambers, with the number killed varying from a few to as many as seventy-five "patients" at a time.

Second, there was a direct "medical" and "psychiatric" link between "euthanasia" and concentration camp extermination in the form of the program known officially as 14f13. That program involved "physicians' commissions"—mostly psychiatrists, who were sent directly from the

*The most complete documentation of this sequence, and especially of the Nazi "euthanasia" project, can be found in the Heyde trial documents, compiled at Limbourg/Lahn and Frankfurt in 1959–60. See also K. Dorner "Nationalsozialismum und Lebensvernichtung" (National Socialism and the extermination of human beings) *Vierteljahrshefte fur Zeitgeschichte*, 15, no. 2 (April 1967): 121–152; G. Schmidt, *Selektion in der Heilanstalt 1939–1945* (Stuttgart: Evangeliches Verlagswerk, 1965); H. Ehrhardt, *Euthanasie und Vernichtung "Lebensunwerten Leben,"* (1965); G. Sereny, *Into That Darkness: From Mercy Killing to Mass Murder* (McGraw-Hill, 1974); Y. Ternon and S. Helman, *Le massacre des alienes* (Paris: Casterman, 1971); and F. Wertham, *A Sign for Cain: An Exploration of Human Violence* (Macmillan, 1966).

"euthanasia" program to some of the camps, including Auschwitz. There they "selected" "mentally ill" inmates to be sent to "euthanasia" killing centers. Selections soon came to include anyone who was sick, debilitated, or Jewish. The general principle of "life unworthy of life" was thus extended into the camps in this immediate way, to include not only medical but racial "unworthiness," as applied particularly to Jews.

Third, when the "euthanasia" program was officially halted in August 1941* program personnel were sent to occupied Poland to establish and administer the extermination camps in which millions of Jews were killed in gas chambers. The first commandant of Treblinka, the largest of these extermination camps, was Dr. Imfried Eberl, who had been an early participant in the "euthanasia" program and the director of the Brandenburg killing center, where the initial experiments and demonstrations of the use of gas chambers were undertaken. Eberl was the only physician ever to head an extermination camp, though his reign was very brief because he was considered too inefficient.

Auschwitz was planned separately from the "euthanasia" program, but there is a link in the person of Dr. Schumann, who came from a "euthanasia" killing center to Auschwitz, in order to conduct the sterilization experiments mentioned earlier.

Nazi political leaders and psychiatrists did not originate the idea of direct medical killing or "euthanasia." Arguments for killing mentally ill patients considered incurable had been put forward in previous writings, the most influential of which was a book by Karl Binding, a distinguished jurist, and Alfred Hoche, a distinguished psychiatrist, *The Release of* [Permission for] *the Destruction of Life Unworthy of Life,* published in 1920. While the Nazis extended their murder of mental patients far beyond the relatively restricted criteria prescribed in that book, it became a bible for their psychiatric argument, most particularly its malignant phrase "life unworthy of life" (*lebensunwerten Lebens*).

A special vocabulary was developed in connection with the "euthanasia" and deportation programs. Euphemisms for killing, such as "special

*The official termination of the program did not actually end the killing. With most of the "euthanasia" gas chambers dismantled, some doctors continued to kill adult mental patients by means of drugs (mostly morphine injections) or starvation. This "wild euthanasia," as it came to be called, was often encouraged by health authorities but also was sometimes done at the initiative of the doctors themselves. The killing of children—at first infants with birth defects, but then older children with less and less incapacitating deformities or illnesses—was done mostly after the official termination of the adult program. For children, drugs (often large oral doses of barbiturates) and various forms of neglect were used throughout.

treatment" (*Sonderbehandlung*) and "special action" (*Sonderaktion*), were very important, and quickly became the vocabulary of the genocidal process.† And the idea of "special treatment" for "life unworthy of life" became the realization of the Nazi biological imperative on a long-term basis. Soon the word "selection" was added, giving further verbal form to the spectacle of Nazi manipulation of the evolutionary process.

To understand these developments more fully one must look for their broader origins. The "euthanasia" program was not solely the whim of Hitler himself, although his direct order initiated it. Rather, it was the incorporation of eugenic principles then having wide currency into the broader Nazi biomedical vision. Also crucial to the medical killing was the merging of the two major strains of European racism (recently described by George Mosse [1978]): the older, mystical-medieval form of anti-Semitism and racism, to which Hitler was heavily exposed in Vienna and elsewhere, and the more modern, so-called scientific racism promulgated by various writers, including biological and physical-anthropological theorists, during the late nineteenth and the twentieth centuries. Mosse points out that early racism existed in sixteenth-century Spain, for instance, in the concept of "purity of blood" as a justification for victimization of Jews. But, ironically, it was the eighteenth-century impact of the new sciences of the Enlightenment that provided considerable grounding for European racism, along with the pietistic revival of Christianity (Mosse 1978, pp. xv–xvi).

The doctors, of course, always expressed themselves in terms of "scientific" racism. But there is evidence that the two strains merged in them as well: their claim to professional and scientific logic could cover over more primal impulses toward victimizing Jews and others, which they shared with much of the general population. Moreover, they could connect either or both currents of racism with what was, at least for them, a more fundamental vision of Nazi-linked national revitalization.

Perhaps the ultimate expression of this merger was the infamous collection of Jewish skulls begun in 1942 by an anatomist named Auguste Hirt for study and display at Strasbourg. While most of these skulls were eventually taken from Auschwitz, the original idea, as expressed in a letter to Himmler, was apparently to take the skulls of "Jewish Bolshevik commissars" to study a particularly evil manifestation of this disappear-

†The euphemism *Sonderbehandlung* was apparently taken from SS usage, where it meant killing outside of the ordinary legal process, essentially the same meaning carried over into the 14f13 program of "euthanasia" and subsequent mass murder in the death camps.

ing and despised race.* Hirt thereby brought together the two strains of anti-Semitism. On the one hand there is the mystical tradition of anti-Semitism and racism, for Hirt's plan recalls the *Protocols of the Elders of Zion*—the notorious forgery around the idea of a Jewish world conspiracy involving Jewish Bolsheviks and Jewish capitalists. On the other, his study of the skulls directly reflects "scientific" racism.

These patterns were all part of a general approach to the medical profession put forward by the Nazis as a national program. That approach was elaborated by Rudolf Ramm in 1943 in a very important book which became a standard guide for medical students and young doctors. In it, Ramm expresses great idealism about the physician's calling and conscience. He describes the new German physician as one who rids himself of materialistic concerns and embraces instead the new "National Socialist idealism"; who is no longer concerned primarily with the individual patient but is a "physician to the Volk" and the nation; who is a "cultivator of the genes.† While one cannot say that this perspective inevitably led to widespread sterilization, direct medical killing, and finally Auschwitz, it is at least consistent with those developments.

VI

In Auschwitz, too, killing was done in the name of healing. It is not too much to say that every action an SS doctor took was connected to some kind of perversion or reversal of healing and killing. For the SS doctor, involvement in the killing process became equated with healing. This, then, is what I call the "healing-killing paradox," which is the first of the Auschwitz psychological themes—or mechanisms—I want to suggest. These mechanisms help us to understand the kinds of self-process by which Nazi doctors could abrogate elements of conscience around commitment to life-enhancement, and thereby minimize their sense of guilt while participating in killing.

---

*M. H. Kater, *Das "Ahnenerbe" der SS 1935–1945: Ein Beitrag zur Kulturpolitic des Dritten Reiches* (Stuttgart: Deutsche Verlags-Anstalt, 1974). See also the Medical Case in note 4.

†R. Ramm, *Arztliche Rechts- und Standeskunde: Der Artz als Gesundheitserzieher* (Berlin, 1943). I do not mean to imply that German medical behavior can be understood simply in terms of this idealism. Indeed, the profession was profoundly corrupted at virtually all levels, and much that doctors did was associated with self-serving ambition of various kinds. But the idealistic claim of the biomedical vision had great significance nonetheless as a baseline that could combine with and facilitate other motivations, including those I will discuss in relation to Auschwitz.

Medical control of selections is a key aspect of this paradox, and Eduard Wirths was intent upon maintaining this control. He claimed that if doctors did the selecting, they would be more "humane" and save more people than would nonmedical Nazi personnel, a claim which sometimes had a kernel of truth. Wirths is a pivotal figure within the healing-killing paradox; prisoners who came into regular contact with him were impressed by his relative humanity and decency, but it was he who set up and maintained much of the overall program of medicalized killing in Auschwitz.

The consequences of this healing-killing reversal were also imposed on inmate doctors,* even though their position as prisoners was radically different from that of SS doctors. Many took Herculean measures to save lives—for example, pleading with SS doctors to let certain people pass in selections, warning inmates to leave the hospital when selections were imminent, replacing the identification numbers of living prisoners on the "selected" list with those of dead prisoners. But saving some prisoners in these ways usually meant that others would be killed in their place. The healing-killing paradox thus permeated all aspects of Auschwitz existence.

For SS doctors the integration into the healing-killing paradox involved a transition period, during which some became quite anxious and disturbed. Some of those I talked to or heard about had wanted to leave. Some were upset by selections, either expressing hesitation about them or temporarily (and in at least one case, permanently) refusing to do them. This reluctance could reflect fear, stemming from the whole scene of grotesque killing and dying, as much as it did moral restraint; in that kind of atmosphere the one may be difficult to separate from the other.

One of the doctors I interviewed who had had this kind of response, Dr. A, was well known in Auschwitz for his relative decency to prisoners—in fact, when he was put on trial in Poland he was acquitted on the basis of survivor testimony. When he first arrived at Auschwitz he was appalled and overwhelmed by what he saw and wanted to leave immediately. He approached his superior, who convinced him that he was needed, assured him that he would not have to do selections, and told him that by staying

*This material comes from interviews with physician survivors. See also E. A. Cohen, *The Abyss: A Confession* (Norton, 1953); O. Lengyel, *Five Chimneys: The Story of Auschwitz* (Ziff-Davis, 1947); W. Fejkiel, "Health Service in the Auschwitz I Concentration Camp/Main Camp," *Przeglad Lekarski,* English translation (Warsaw: International Auschwitz Committee Anthology, vol. 2, pt. 1, 1979, pp. 4–37); R. J. Minney, *I Shall Fear No Evil; The Story of Dr. Alina Brewda* (London: William Kimber, 1966); G. Perl, *I Was a Doctor at Auschwitz* (International Universities Press, 1948); and Lingens-Reiner *(Prisoners of Fear).*

he would help strengthen their unit, which was separate from the main medical division. He decided to stay and struggled through the next three weeks—the all-important transition period—during which he made a concerted, conscious effort to overcome his anxiety and traumatic dreams, including guilty dreams about a former Jewish school friend. As part of his struggle to get over some of these symptoms, he succeeded in integrating himself with SS doctors. He also managed to integrate himself to a considerable extent with the inmate doctors who worked under him. Dr. A was psychologically functional until the chief camp doctor, because of the extraordinary numbers of Jews arriving in transports, decided to ignore administrative distinctions and ordered him to "ramp duty"—i.e., selections. He again became very upset and went immediately to Berlin to speak to the highest medical officer of his own administrative unit. He said that he was unable to do selections, stressing psychological incapacity rather than an ethical objection. The officer listened sympathetically, said he could understand as "I am a family man myself," and arranged for Dr. A not to have to do any selections.*

Dr. A went on to describe how a younger man, Dr. B, fresh from an SS Medical Academy, was then brought in and assigned to do selections instead. Dr. B also became upset, virtually collapsing at the first selection he witnessed. He was then put through a "rehabilitation program" to ease his transition. One component of the program placed him under the guidance of Josef Mengele, who taught him that he would be "saving lives" through selections, and that it was necessary to do these things in order to solve the "Jewish problem." He was also permitted to have his wife stay at the camp, which was very unusual, especially for a young doctor. Further, and most ironically, an older, Jewish inmate doctor, a distinguished professor from Eastern Europe, was assigned to tutor him for his medical thesis, which he had not yet completed. He formed a close relationship to the Jewish doctor, who became, in the opinion of Dr. A, more or less a father figure to him. After several weeks Dr. B was "strong enough" to perform selections, continuing to do so until the end of the war. When taken into American custody, he killed himself.

Dr. A feels more guilt, I think, toward Dr. B than he does about the massive number of Jews killed in Auschwitz. The Jews are more impersonal to him, and he is able to separate himself psychologically from the killing process.

Another mechanism contributing to Nazi doctors' behavior was their

---

*That senior figure was himself extensively involved in human medical experiments, for which he was eventually convicted and hanged.

relationship to ideological fragments. The great majority of doctors I interviewed, and, I believe, of Nazi doctors in general, were not ideological fanatics. Mengele and a few others were undoubtedly exceptions. Most seemed to believe only in fragments of ideology. These, however, could be very important. For example, the doctors could believe such ideological elements as the importance of the Nazi movement for revitalizing Germany, and the existence of a "Jewish problem" that required a "solution." These ideological fragments could become a basis for resolving ambivalent feelings in the direction of prescribed beliefs and actions. As one former Nazi doctor told me: "It is a lot easier if you either totally believe in them [the Nazis] or you are against them. It is very tough when you are somewhere in between."

A third mechanism was Nazi doctors' contradictory sense of themselves as physicians. Doing virtually no medical work themselves, they could at times take pride in having distinguished inmate physicians working under them. They would sometimes introduce the latter as "the professor from Prague" or "the professor from Budapest." Although these introductions contained an element of sarcasm or irony, they also served to provide a sense of medical presence and thereby to ward off suppressed shame and guilt at being involved in killing instead of healing.

The doctors could also reinforce their medical self-image by what they understood as "scientific" discussions of racial issues. In another manifestation of the inner struggle to continue to view themselves as physicians, they tended to become involved in what one SS doctor described to me as "hobbies"—such as the medical experiments on inmates, or special small-scale medical units or laboratories.

Within these struggles around professional identity, the strongest single pattern was the technicizing of everything. As an SS doctor said to me: "Ethics was not a word used in Auschwitz. Doctors and others spoke only about how to do things most efficiently, about what worked best." There can be no greater caricature of modern tendencies toward absolute pragmatism and technicism in place of ethics.

A fourth mechanism involved psychic numbing, diffusion of responsibility, and "derealization." At the heart of this mechanism is diminished capacity and inclination to feel, so that one need not experience oneself as in any way related to cruelties and killings.* When doctors killed, they

*Alexander and Margarete Mitscherlich discuss overall Nazi tendencies toward derealization (1975). For general explorations of psychic numbing in extreme situations, see also Lifton (1980, 1975).

generally did so from a distance. It was usually someone else who injected the phenol, and always someone else who inserted the gas pellets.

Heavy drinking—virtually every night and for some during the day—contributed importantly to the numbing. Discomfort felt by newcomers was often expressed, and vaguely put aside, at these drinking sessions, as were questions about Auschwitz in general. This was part of the transition period for newcomers. Their psychic numbing was encouraged—one may say demanded—by virtually everything and everyone around them. Powerfully contributing to that numbing, and to the relatively quick adaptation of most Nazi doctors, was the routinization of all phases of the "death factory." At the same time, the very extremity of Auschwitz transgressions—the sense that one was on a separate planet—contributed to the process of derealization, to the feeling that things happening there did not "count" in terms of the "real world."

A fifth mechanism was a bizarre form of construction of meaning. Auschwitz reminds us that man is so meaning-hungry a creature that he will render in some way significant and justified virtually anything he finds himself doing. Auschwitz doctors went to work in the morning, joked with their secretaries, exchanged greetings with "colleagues," engaged in daily backbiting of their "enemies"—in other words, behaved as though they were in an ordinary place, an ordinary institution devoted to some life-enhancing purpose, instead of a vast killing machine.

The construction of meaning was enhanced by the well-known process of blaming the victim (Ryan 1976): the Jews did not look human, the Gypsies did not distribute their food equitably, people died in the hospital block because of inmate doctors' poor treatment. Even Mengele's sartorial elegance and cool pointing of the finger at selections were, in their dramatic staging, part of this extremely important quest for inner significance.

Two additional important mechanisms that I will mention only briefly involve omnipotence and impotence. SS doctors, in their literal life-death decisions, experienced a sense of omnipotence that could protect them from their own death anxiety in the Auschwitz environment. That sense of omnipotence, along with elements of sadism with which it can be closely associated, contributed to feelings of power and invulnerability that could also serve to suppress guilt and enhance numbing.

Yet doctors could feel powerless, consider themselves pawns in the hands of a total institution. That feeling was described to me as follows: "I'm not here because I want to be—but because prisoners come here. I can't change the fact that prisoners come here. I can just try to make the best of it." While doctors in most cases could probably have arranged to leave Auschwitz if they felt strongly enough about doing so* they had no capacity to interfere with the basic functioning of the institution. But that claim of powerlessness was also a means of renouncing individual responsibility and fending off a sense of guilt.

An eighth mechanism was the feeling of these medical victimizers that they *themselves* were undergoing an ordeal. They believed that they were faced with a very tough, unpleasant job that they simply had to do, while in the process they could feel sorry for themselves for having to do it. That attitude was encouraged by Heinrich Himmler, who appeared at Auschwitz several times and made speeches similar to his famous declaration to Einsatzgruppen leaders about the enormous demands made upon Nazi killers ("Most of you must know what it means to see a hundred corpses lie side by side, or five hundred, or a thousand") and their heroic achievement ("to have stuck this out—and except in cases of human weakness—to have kept our integrity . . . is an unwritten and never-to-be written . . . glory") (Dawidowicz 1975, p. 149).

Still another mechanism was the attraction of order—the overall appeal of what Eliade calls the movement "from chaos to structure and cosmology" (1959). To Nazis, doctors included, it was important to keep Auschwitz a coherent, functioning world. If things got difficult, doctors could point out how much worse they were before an orderly routine had been established in Auschwitz—or at other camps where no such order existed.

Finally, there was one overall mechanism, that which I call "doubling," within which all the others operated. It includes compartmentalization, or "splitting," of various elements of the psyche, so that one could both participate actively in the killing and remain tender in one's family relationships and even occasionally in certain relationships in Auschwitz. Use of the term *doubling,* rather than mere splitting, calls attention to the creation of two relatively autonomous selves: the prior "ordinary self," which for doctors includes important elements of the healer, and the "Auschwitz self," which includes all of the psychological maneuvers that help one avoid a conscious sense of oneself as a killer.† The existence of

---

*The problem about leaving was that the alternative usually was serving on the eastern front, which during the last years of the war often meant death. Most preferred to stay in Auschwitz.

†In his valuable study, Henry V. Dicks stresses "splitting" in connection with other Nazi killers (1972). My emphasis on "doubling" is more consistent with contemporary focus on holistic function, including focus on the self and on individual and group identity. See, for instance, Erikson (1968), Kohut (1977), Guntrip (1971), and Lifton (1980).

an overall Auschwitz self more or less integrated all of these mechanisms into a functioning whole, and permitted one to adapt oneself to that bizarre environment. The prior self enabled one to retain a sense of decency and loving connection. The extraordinary demands of functioning in Auschwitz seemed to require doubling of this kind and at the same time sufficient integration of the two selves for general psychic functioning. To an important degree, ideology can serve as a bridge between two such selves. For instance, the strongly held image of national and personal revitalization associated with the Nazi movement could be compatible with both the prior self and the Auschwitz self, and could thereby provide the necessary psychic common ground.

VII

By way of conclusion, I would like to mention three general areas of concern suggested by the study.

First, the study of Nazi behavior forces us to reexamine relationships between healing and killing. When we do, we find that the distinction—the barrier—between them has always been more fragile than we wish to believe. That fragility is revealed in primitive mythology and ritual, as described in the works of Joseph Campbell, Otto Jensen and James Frazier. Whether the killing is done by mythological gods, by human medicine men, witch doctors, or shamans, specifically as religious ceremony (as in various forms of human sacrifice) or in connection with hunting or warfare, it is done in the name of a higher purpose—on behalf of a healing function for the tribe or people.

In modern experience, the use of advanced technology radically alters whatever balance might have been maintained between healing and killing in the past. As the Nazis demonstrate, science in general, and biology in particular—however distorted or falsified—can be mobilized on behalf of a murderous claim to healing. So while focusing on what is specific to the Nazi project, we must also begin to raise more general questions about the significance of breakdown, or threatened breakdown, of distinctions between healing and killing—for physicians, scientists, and professionals everywhere, and for the institutions they create and maintain. We must raise the same questions concerning current projections of "triage" policies for combatting starvation and disease.

Second, healers—even the highly imperfect healers of modern medicine—did not automatically turn into killers overnight without some kind of ideological justification and motivation for doing so. Men and ideology can perform strange and deadly dances, using incomplete choreography as a basis for endless inventive steps. The fact that men embrace only fragments of ideology rather than the total system does not mean the ideology is any less dangerous—especially when it involves the reversal of healing and killing. It can be all the *more* dangerous because one can embrace these fragments in the name of absolute consequences. The Nazis mobilized a peculiar combination of partial, often fragmented ideology and total (comprehensive) ideology, which individuals—here, doctors—lived out. This Nazi blend was never fully coherent, yet held out something for everyone but its victims. The Nazi way of combining political and biomedical imagery suggests the flexibility and intricacy with which ideological elements can be held. If these elements can evoke collective imagery of revitalization, their destructive and contradictory components can be absorbed. Ideological systems can then have even greater significance than previously realized in motivating and supporting murderous behavior.

Third, I believe that a deeper exploration of the Nazi practice of medicalized killing—and of the ideological, historical, and psychological currents around it—takes us closer to an understanding of Nazi genocide. This is not, of course, the only emphasis that can be made in the approach to the terrible question of Nazi mass murder. Rather, it provides an additional dimension to our understanding of how such a program could be instituted, and how individual people could help carry it out. I am suggesting that the elements contributing to mass murder, including extensive sadism and technicized bureaucratic killing, were contained within an overall Nazi biomedical vision of mass murder as a healing process. More generally, we do well to understand much collective violence in terms of a perverse quest for the vitality and immortality of one's own group. We thus encounter the impulse toward mass murder in the name of "more life" (Becker 1975; Lifton 1980).

We need to understand that impulse, wherever it occurs, if we are to renew the meaning and spirit of healing, and in the process renew ourselves.

REFERENCES

Amnesty International. "Violations of Human Rights: Torture and the Medical Profession," report of a Medical Seminar. London: Amnesty International, Index CAT 02/03/78.

Arendt, H. 1963. *Eichmann in Jerusalem: A Report on the Banality of Evil.* New York: Viking.

Becker, E. 1975. *Escape from Evil.* Free Press.

Binding, K., and Hoche, A. 1920. *The Release of* [Permission for] *the Destruction of Life Unworthy of Life (Die Freigabe der Vernichtung lebensunwerten Lebens).* Leipzig.

Bloch, S., and Reddaway, P. 1977. *Psychiatric Terror: How Soviet Psychiatry Is Used to Suppress Dissent.* New York: Basic Books.

Dawidowicz, L. S. 1975. *The War Against the Jews 1933–1945.* Holt, Rinehart & Winston.

Dicks, H. V. 1972. *Licensed Mass Murder: A Socio-psychological Study of Some SS Killers.* New York: Basic Books.

Eliade, M. 1959. *Cosmos and History: The Myth of the Eternal Return.* New York: Harper Torchbooks.

Erikson, E. H. 1968. *Identity: Youth and Crisis.* New York: Norton.

Guntrip, H. 1971. *Psychoanalytic Theory, Therapy, and the Self.* New York: Basic Books.

Hilberg, R. 1973. *The Destruction of the European Jews.* New Viewpoints–Franklin Watts.

Hitler, A. 1969. *Mein Kampf.* London: Hutchinson.

Kohut, H. 1977. *The Restoration of the Self.* New York: International Universities Press.

Lifton, R. J. 1969. *Thought Reform and the Psychology of Totalism: A Study of "Brainwashing" in China.* New York: Norton.

———. 1975. *Death in Life: Survivors of Hiroshima.* Touchstone Books.

———. 1979. "The Appeal of the Death Trip." *New York Times Magazine,* Jan. 7, pp. 26–27, 29–31.

———. 1980. *The Broken Connection: On Death and the Continuity of Life.* Simon & Schuster: Touchstone Books.

Lingens-Reiner, E. 1948. *Prisoners of Fear.* London: Gollancz.

Marks, J. 1979. *The Search for the "Manchurian Candidate":The CIA and Mind Control.* Basic Books.

Mitscherlich, A., and Mitscherlich, M. 1975. *The Inability to Mourn.* New York: Grove Press.

Mosse, G. 1978. *Toward the Final Solution: A History of European Racism.* New York: Howard Fertig.

Reston, J., Jr. 1981. *Our Father Who Art in Hell: The Life and Death of Jim Jones.* New York: New York Times Books.

Rubenstein, R. 1978. *The Cunning of History.* New York: Harper-Colophon.

Ryan, W. 1976. *Blaming the Victims.* New York: Vintage Books.

Stern, J. P. 1975. *Hitler: The Führer and the People.* London: Fontana/Collins.

INTRODUCTION

This essay, by Dr. John Hanson, is a psycho-historical examination of the origins, nature, and purpose of Nazi culture. Hanson's central agrument is that sociopathic tendencies and genocidal inclinations were socialized in Nazi Germany; cultural imagery both denied and reflected a society in the process of dissolution. The Nazi social fantasies swallowed up by the masses, Hanson maintains, kept the populace in a state of repression. That is to say, Nazi culture incited the masses to participate in war and the elimination of "racially-impure" non-Aryans and simultaneously helped to block awareness of despair, self-hatred, and crushing feelings of inferiority. Nazi culture with its psychopathic symbols succeeded in placing the majority of Germans in a "pseudo-aesthetic trance" in which they no longer knew who they were or what they had become. The Nazi propaganda effectively infiltrated the German collective psyche; the need to feel heroic and their millennial hopes hastened the Germans' entrance into the bloody, phantasmagoric world of Nazi culture.

Official Nazi art and culture originally reflected the "Nazi myth" of racial superiority, the Thousand Year Reich, and world domination. As the Nazis began to lose the war, and defeat became a nearing reality, symbols and cultural imagery reflected the war of extermination against the Jews and the general transformation of Germany into a death factory. To the very end, Hanson maintains, symbols replaced reality. The Holocaust, the apex of the Nazi delusional system, was reflected in its own set of group fantasies, and when these were acted out, they left millions dead and Germany in ruins.

Hanson's interest in totalitarian culture and propaganda stems from an examination of the role of unconscious processes in society. Such processes spur political symbolism, which he views as the manifestation of a romantic aestheticism. People isolate and fasten upon fragments of these aesthetic illusions, and seduced by the power of myth and fantasy, they remain blind to their needs and fears and their dehumanization and self-destruction. Hanson's survey is an attempt to heighten our awareness of the potentially lethal combination of "mythic nationalism empowered by amoral machinery." Modern German history evinces a perplexing intertwining of transcendent and bestial thought and deed, and warns of the dangers inherent in the collective search for symbols of power and immortality by those who feel powerless and are riddled with impotent rage.

Nazi Culture: The Social Uses of Fantasy as Repression

JOHN H. HANSON

As we contemplate the murderous process of modern history, the Holocaust emerges as its most horrifying manifestation. The gulags and mass starvations under Stalin, the pogroms throughout central Europe, the violent civil wars and colonialist invasions—all are overshadowed by the orgy of technologized killing that took place in the Third Reich. After the sight of thousands of emaciated bodies bulldozed into trenches at Bergen-Belsen and the display of shrunken heads and patches of tattooed skin from Auschwitz, we seemed to have reached a state of imaginative paralysis, a glut of horror that makes it impossible for us to even come to grips with the threat of universal nuclear holocaust. For Westerners, the horror of the Holocaust lies in a horror of recognition: that the crimes were committed by our *Doppelgängers,* our doubles, and that the monstrosities were committed by Europeans in the name of *Kultur.*

The murder took place because it was nurtured by European fantasies acted out by Germans who were able to merge technology and primitivism as delegates of European anti-Semitic and antiethnic feeling. The literature of modernization makes the point over and over: mythic nationalism empowered by amoral machinery is lethal. Historians have documented hatred just as virulent in Rumania, Bulgaria, and France, to mention just a few of the hotbeds of European anti-Semitism—it was the Germans, in a combination of aberration and expertise, who acted on those hatreds and were consistently abetted by their allies and collaborators. It was among the hypercivilized—as Freud was to ruefully notice in his own Vienna—that the impulsiveness of the pogrom was systematized by a bureaucracy into a liquidation.

It is the relationship between cultural imagery and genocide-enabling fantasies that is the concern of this essay. Specifically, I am interested here in the socialization of sociopathic tendencies, in the generalization of disturbed thought that made the Holocaust possible. While *suppression*—the sheer authoritarian weight of the Nazi state—was essential to its rise and continuance, the battle for total power was fought in the minds of the German electorate long before the actual machinery of power had been expropriated by the Nazis.

Repression—a combination of historical amnesia and selective excitation and disguise of primal anxieties—enabled the tenets of Nazism to be internalized as a social fantasy, a shared set of psychopathic symbols that blocked introspection and enabled the average citizen to soar to the delusional heights of group heroism. Nazism was a masterpiece of what Jacques Ellul has called "social partitioning"—it was a fragmented system of thought united only on the level of fantasy. Its violence, its paranoia, its total devaluation of the individual—were all facets of a generalized social and psychological collapse that swept over Europe at the height of the depression. A manifestation of the problem, Nazism posed as its solution; a breakdown of historical consciousness, it portrayed its antihistorical fantasies as the voice of History itself. This facade of unity quelled the cognitive dissonance of the individual and neutralized the struggle between rival classes and groups within German society. This "Manichaean universe of propaganda" (Ellul) was a tense world of manipulated symbols overlaying not only systematic social violence but a world of antitypes that lurked behind the surface of Aryan "health." These displaced affects—the fear of disorder, modernity, sexuality—were allowed to emerge only when they were attributed to an enemy of the state. Thus the familiar pattern of modern totalitarian societies: total power in the name of total menace, total authority invoked in the name of total anxiety.

Nazi culture, like the culture of imperial Germany, arose to provide a mystique for a ruling elite in an age of masses. Wilhelmine Germany may have allowed a good deal of avant-garde experimentation, but under the tutelage of Wilhelm II, state culture was monumental, escapist, operatic. The Kaiser, afflicted from birth with a withered arm, followed a classic Adlerian pattern of compensation in his taste for the grandiose. All these monuments to the state assured the citizen of one fact: that Germany was eternal, that it was rooted in myth, not history. It assured the timid middle class and the anxious nobility that their places on the stage of time would not be rudely taken over by the working class, and it refuted Marxist materialism and the secular religion of progress alike in insisting on the transcendental qualities of the nation. By invoking the formal language of neoclassicism and the slick, often erotic allegorical realism of the *fin-de-siècle,* the old elites around the Kaiser chose a symbol set that glorified the military violence and baroque sensuality of the *ancien régime*. These fantasies of empire formed a national myth that enabled the old ruling class to mystify the sources of its power and to project a theater of supermen onto which the bourgeois functionary or the small shopkeeper could project his ideals, and at the same time, this anachronistic culture served to neutralize the influence of the new working class and the new elites centered on the great cartels which were pushing aside the landowners and individual entrepreneurs. Imperial culture served the forces of antimodernism.

To a great extent, German culture of the late nineteenth century was anachronistic, because industrialization—the migration to manufacturing centers, the emergence of new monied classes—had occurred so rapidly that symbols of the new order had little time to evolve. The "dream screen" of Wilhelmine culture conveniently skirted the present and its contradictions, and presented a heroic society based on sacrifice and subordination. To the power of change, it opposed a selective vision of the past, a Heroic Age, based on a combination of Homer and Tacitus, a Bismarckian melodrama that left out the French Revolution, the 1848 revolts, the rise of Marxist thought, suffrage, machinery, and atheism. Like the protypical American commercial with its all-white 3.5-size family, its two cars and preinflation mortgage, German official culture excluded what contradicted it, just as the Formica paradise concocted for the upper middle classes of white America is purged of anyone poor, black, blue-collar, or dissident. Just as the smiles of commercial portraiture look onward beyond the viewer into a cloudless future, the glowering statues and frigid palaces of imperial Germany looked backwards—and beyond—the new Germany of inflation, class warfare, enfranchsied Jews, socialists and new money. What Herbert Marcuse called "repressive desublimation" in *Eros and Civilization* aptly describes the conditions initiated by the old elites in Germany and raised to a frenzy by the Nazis. The phenomena that Marcuse noted in advanced industrial societies—the combination of autocracy and tribalism—produced ritualized behavior joined with ego collapse. Fantasy in the service of repression—state-incited violence and state-aroused sadomasochistic eroticism—these were the undercurrents of German society that were able to emerge uninhibited in the Nazi psyche. Official culture was used as a tool of social integration by offering a collective ego ideal in the form of anachronistic historical romances and a collective antithesis in the form of all those forces and figures that disrupted the official picture of reality. Thus sociopathic tendencies could be sanctioned in the service of simplifying social reality: extermination could be transformed into chivalric quest, and art, deprived of its own imaginative mission, could be used to infiltrate the collective psyche.

Because of our often liberal/psychologistic prejudices, we tend to think of aesthetic experience as predominately private. Indeed, many aspects of culture since the Enlightenment support that view of art, and the privacy—the subjectivity—of art (and religion, and morality, and civil rights) is all a by-product of the modern ascendancy of the middle classes. As a political/cultural world view, bourgeois culture has given us the novel, empiricism, the easel picture, the hermetic tradition in romanticism and symbolism, capitalism, and an entire set of individual-centered institutions and modes of relating to the world. The middle-class revolution in Europe replaced the epic with the novel of manners and "arriving" in society; it replaced the ethico-religious view of life by the pragmatic and experimental (Weber's classic thesis); it replaced the mural, the history paintings, busts, and palaces with an uneasy mixture of *Kitsch* (of which *Victoriana* is a prime example), nationalism, and egoistic self-celebration. The ascendant classes replaced the epic hero with the bohemian and cryptic prophet, the disjunct and alienated artist whose very displacement reflected his dynamic society. Above all, the new classes were the agents of capitalism, replacing the agrarian economy and hierarchy of old Europe with the centripetal forces of industrial nationalization and the concentration of capital. The older culture had been based on the wheel of nature, heroic sacrifices to the gods, and the piety and security of the church. The new social order was secular, antimythic, pluralistic, and imaginatively vested with the linear belief in progress rather than the cyclical concepts of "fate" and blood. There arose in Germany not only a system of competing values but a clash of fantasy systems, a war of unconscious images. The new ethos of progress and plenty was not only fatally democratizing, it was guilt-arousing on the deepest level—it replaced feudalism and its sacred bonds with universal Oedipal struggle. The gods, in Socratic fashion, were ignored or, worse yet, debunked. This crisis of values and identity was particularly threatening to a society that wished to see itself as an organic whole. The life-affirming implications of this fundamental thought—that all living organisms must change or become moribund—was lost on the rightist Hegelians who were the theoreticians of the Reich.

These internal tensions emerge in Frank Wedekind's famous play of pubescence, *Spring Awakening* (1891); they surface in the violent domestic dramas of the expressionist dramaturges, and they help to explain the oft-noted manic release that followed Germany's entry into war in 1914, a Dionysian intoxication that swept along even the skeptical Thomas Mann and Sigmund Freud. Both of these veteran skeptics and "outsiders" (as they have been called by Peter Gay in his *Weimar Culture*) succumbed to nationalist fervor in the first days of the war, a response shared by many adversaries of the regime. If capitalism's inherent innovations had seemed on the verge of immersing the old order, in war the contradictory philosophies of hyperproduction and heroic holocaust could be reconciled in the *Burgfrieden,* or party truce, declared by the Kaiser. Briefly, the nation seemed to be one body. Cubist painters rushed to design camouflage nets; a huge statue of General Hindenburg was erected in Berlin, and each contributor to the war effort was permitted to drive a nail of iron into the oak totem. For the moment, the religion of the nation was the dominant cult, its icons the incredibly crude images of World War propaganda which saturated the German home front, its liturgy the delusional war economy free of strikes, its icons the returning wounded soon to change from a trickle to a flood, and after the war a reproach in the form of mutilated pencil vendors on every corner. German society was submerged in myth; the heroic cult of Hermann (the legendary Arminius, conqueror of the Roman legions) was revived, the Junkers now gave orders to the capitalists and, indeed, to the entirety of German society. The bodies of rebellious German youth were cast into the flames; the smoke rose to the gods and they were nourished.

War allowed Germany to return to the neoromantic titanism and samurai mentality of its nationalists and conservatives. The war's end in defeat and the imposition of the infamous "war guilt" clause of the Versailles treaty (a guilt no less stinging although assumed by civilian signatories) left the nationalist myth in a shambles and the brief, spurious reign of unanimity in 1914–1918 another dream to join with nationalist utopias like the Germanic tribe, the Prussian drill squad, and the feudal village. With defeat came feelings of morbidity and a squabble over who was to blame for the national humiliation. The postwar inflation sparked an orgy of speculation, and the defeated army was joined by the divested middle class, its savings destroyed. The avant-garde renewed its aggressive attacks on German pomposity, a 1919 art show even featuring a pig suspended from the ceiling in a German officer's dress uniform. German soviets sprang up in imitation of the Bolsheviks, and in a well-known sequence, the Right, old and new, recouped its losses and violently began to reestablish its power bases in the heart of the shaky Weimar Republic. To the conservatives, jazz, Jews, and juveniles seemed to be the face of the new society, and they vowed to destroy it and reorder Germany. Saturated with familiar *Nibelung* violence, the new *Kulturkampf* was eventually taken up by the Nazis and carried to its illogical conclusion: a new Holocaust, fueled first by books and paintings, then by authors and artists themselves.

Much has been made of the historical regressions of the Nazis, most cogently in Rudolph Binion's *Hitler Among the Germans;* it is clear that Hitler's entire career was a set of conversion symptoms, a sociodrama acted out with a cast of willing millions. Before the war and his final lapse into the role of barbarian, Hitler fantasized building the Thousand Year Reich as a crowning *Gesamtkunstwerk,** a monument to his vision of himself as *Kunstpolitiker,*† the artist leader who would mold the inchoate masses into a supreme symbol of authority. In this role fragment, too, he was able to draw on deep-seated German fantasies, and the same concerns with disease and regression that Binion so brilliantly analyzes in Hitler's political vision appear in his vision of culture as well. These bodily metaphors for social anxieties (at the unconscious level all societies are bodies politic) have also been systematized by Richard Koenigsberg in his *Hitler's Ideology*. Both Binion and Koenigsberg show that the alleged political concerns of Nazism—with the nation, ideals, authority—are actually fantasized *visceral* fixations.

While Oswald Spengler is often cited as the modern voice of decay in German cultural circles, and Gobineau, Chamberlain, Langbehn, and others as his harbingers, the disease metaphor as critique of modern art was most powerfully (and popularly) articulated by Max Nordau (ironically a Zionist leader and physician horrified by the sensuality of decadent *fin-de-siècle* Viennese culture) in his mid-nineties bestseller, *Degeneration*. Here the "parasitology" later evolved by Hitler is presented with full-blown pedantry and with the same kind of logic that no doubt motivates Soviet psychiatrists who commit poets to padded cells. Worse, Nordau's quasi-biological language invited, ultimately, the kind of social "surgery" the SS undertook. Nordau associates modernism with death—"Forms lose their outlines, and are dissolved in floating mist. The day is over, night draws on."[1] In this "dusk of the nations," the impressionist is

*"A total work of art" (eds.).
†"The artist-politician" (eds.).

suffering from hysteric glaucoma, the symbolist poet from "graphomania," Wagner himself is "alone charged with a greater abundance of degeneration than all the degenerates put together."[2] Avant-garde schools are like "criminal bands"; the new artist is an "ego maniac," the decadent movement the expression of a shared physiological decay. In fact, notes Nordau, "This desparate cry towards the 'new' is the natural complaint of a brain which no longer feels the pleasures of action, and greedily craves a stimulation which his powerless sensory nerves cannot give him."[3] Ultimately, the artist's sickness makes him different, and in a *tour de force* amply applied by the totalitarians, his difference is his sickness: "they cease to subordinate their energy to the total energy" because they are ego-maniacs, and their stunted development has not attained the height at which an individual reaches his moral and intellectual junction with the totality, and their ego-mania makes the degenerate necessarily anarchists, i.e., enemies of all institutions.[4]

To be fair to Nordau, his closing lines in *Degeneration* contained a call for a renewed commitment to "enlightenment" and "consciousness," but his dismissal of modernism as organic aberration helped strengthen the body metaphor behind right-wing thought. Nordau's vision of social morbidity came at a time when venereal disease, and syphilis in particular, had been classed along with alcoholism, social displacement, and speculation as a hereditary disorder. It was the age of the clitorectomy and phrenology, the prologue to fascism's elevation of "racial science" to the level of a political vision. Combined with political reaction, the Schopenhauerian mystique of the will, and the vague, vitalist philosophies of the close of the century, the positivist doctrine of progress as health became a neofeudal battle for "the death of death" and the apocalyptic renewal of "life forces." Social Darwinism, combined with German cultural megalomania and militarism, was a prime example of the Nietzschean nationalism of this period.

Abstraction, dynamism, and internationalism were the forces of disease represented in Weimar culture according to the conservatives. The skyscraper, the automobile, the city itself, and what Rosenberg called its "men of asphalt" were seen as symbols of the new Sodom. The Bauhaus aesthetic of industrial design, the new novels influenced by Joyce, the anticlassical poetry, and atonal music were all symptomatic of social degeneration for the conservatives. The new socialist government patronized the avant-garde, although it had inherited virtually intact the entirety of the Wilhelmine judiciary, civil service, police, and military officialdom.

While the radical left enjoyed lampooning Weimar President Ebert's ursine looks and moderation as ineffectual and indeed "antiheroic,"* for the conservatives, the new republic was pro-industrial culture unchained. A Jew, Walther Rathenau, was made one of its chief ministers, and although he reorganized Germany's debt structure, this electrical-products executive became one of many Weimar officials assasinated with impunity in the postwar period. And although even the right, despite itself, had to recognize the inevitability of industrialization, its social implications were anathema. Old money operating behind an archaic heroic facade was what they wanted—a "Third Reich" in Van den Bruck's words, not a socialist phalanstery. In many ways, the socialist reign of reason was one that Nordau would have approved, and it was the very core myth of progress and reason that the rightists attacked in the "alien" republic.

While many of the fine cultural achievements of the Weimar period served to redeem the image of a militaristic, insular Germany in the eyes of international circles, and while between depressions the republic enjoyed a five-year period of stability before its fall in 1933, a return to cosmopolitan greatness along Goethe's lines held little attraction in conservative circles. Autarky, protectionism, and the conquest of other nations as sources of cheap (slave) labor and natural resources loomed in the reactionary imagination. Basically, the rightists wanted to replay the late nineteenth and early twentieth century, resume colonialism, prosecute a war to victory, reclaim "Germany for Germans." To an unusual degree they were concerned with aesthetics and cultural politics, and they came to lump all of the avant-garde from architecture to psychoanalysis under the term *Kulturbolschewismus,* "cultural Bolshevism." Kleinman points out that "this impulse to aestheticize reality was itself a basic element in the meaning of German history, even before the emergence of Hitlerian propaganda."[5] German politics truly was a psychomachia, a struggle between strata of imagery in the national mind. At stake was the structure of national identity: "One way to understand Germany's history and its fascination with borders, frames and boundaries is to see this search as a series of aesthetic operations in which limits (that is, forms) were continually being drawn. The object of all this 'drawing' was to exclude that which was not German and, therefore, create the perfect

*Ebert had the misfortune of being a thoroughly ordinary-looking man, a union leader, and a good papa. The romantic left found him totally unromantic and tainted by political compromise.

outline of the 'true German.' "[6] In the eyes of the right, the "true German" was the serf, ready to die *en masse,* the burgher, solid, sober, and apolitical, the selfless knight, the nurturant mother or pure maiden, the craftsman, productive and unambitious. To this Christian cast was opposed the rootless peasant migrating to the cesspool of the city, the vulgar *nouveau riche* (seen as "Jewish"), the Red soldier, the abortionist whore, and the sullen proletarian—the demonic forces of democracy. At stake in this psychomachia was control of the process George Mosse has called "the nationalization of the masses."

The Nazis were able to meld an inchoate protest into a temporary coalition that they were able to allow to disintegrate or purge after their acession to power. Nordic mystics, disgruntled leftists, lunatic anti-Semites, ruined shopkeepers—the composition of marginalized men who made up the movement is familiar. While the Marxists could only see a fascist party subservient to traditional nationalists, and many psychohistorians could initially only vilify the *petit bourgeois* in brownshirt, the mass appeal of the Hitler movement lay not in its ability to mobilize merely the unemployed lumpenproletariat or the old elites or the casualties of inflation alone. As Fred Weinstein has recently pointed out in his *The Dynamics of Nazism,* Hitler's electorate was not a splinter group but represented sections of every class stratum of the voting public. The appeal that the National Socialists were able to make was not on the level of doctrine but on the subliminal level of unconscious imagery. At this level, the strains of the masochistic desire to be dominated, the destructive disease fantasies, and the dreams of aesthetic reintegration could be reached, and the failed painter/architect Hitler and the novelist *manqué* Goebbels were themselves immersed in the very fantasies they exacerbated. As Hugh D. Duncan has pointed out,

> Superiors must *persuade* inferiors to accept their rule. This is done through the glorification of symbols of majesty and power as symbols of social order in many kinds of social dramas wherein the glory of the ruler as a "representative" of some transcendent principle of social order is dramatized. Such dramatization is intended to create and uphold the dignity of the office as a representation of a principle of social order, not the man himself. Hitler did not rule as a man, but as a "savior" of the German people. His life was an allegory of every German life. His mandate, so he taught, and so his followers believed, came from some supernatural "historic" source. He was an agent of a "higher power," whose mystery could be penetrated only

by semi-divine heros who did what they "had to do" because they were moved by a divine historic will. Yet no one in modern times was more careful than Hitler to stage great community dramas in which the German people were persuaded to believe in laws of destiny which were immutable and "beyond" reason.[7]

The Nazis were able to tap the fear of freedom, the self-hatred, the anxiety over disorder experienced by the postwar Germans and to devise a liturgy of healing and resurrection that guided the populace out of history and into unconsciousness.

It was precisely because they offered a *Kultur* rather than an ideology that they were able to so easily defeat their more consistent opponents. By now, the image of "folksy" monopoly capitalism, billing itself as a "way of life" rather than a system, is familiar, but the Nazis were the first to combine *volkisch* nostalgia with high-tech propaganda. The Nazis intensified this fragmented style of thinking that had frustrated German social unification by building their system on just that fragmentation. Outside the magic ring of the Reich lurked the institutionalized enemies of the German biosphere: the Jews, the anarchists, the Communists, all race-polluters whose ideas wrought actual genetic damage. The Night of the Long Knives and Hitler's rule by faction acknowledged the mythic principle even within the party; the Holocaust and the defeat after Stalingrad transferred the social drama to a world stage, a mythic cosmos. Symbols replaced reality.

While Stalin and Mussolini were far from insensitive to the need for the control of mass culture and the artist, Hitler's inner imago, as Speer's memoirs so amply attest, was tied up in his artist/destructor drama. While he created an overblown official culture that was a monument to terror, he assured the German people that this all was done to cleanse and rejuvenate their society: "My fellow citizens, I believe you have no doubt already heard that I still have some rather significant plans, large and beautiful plans, for my people. My aim is, I say to you, to make my German people rich, the German nation beautiful. I want to see the standard of living raised for each individual. I want us to have the best and most beautiful culture."[8]

What Hitler was promising was that art would emerge from the private subjectivity of the artist and become life itself. All reality would become a living symbol of National Socialism, each individual existing only in the superorganic *Gesamtkunstwerk*, the total state. Long before they dominated the museums, the academies, and the state organs of culture, the

Nazis practiced their aesthetics in the mass rally, which the Nuremberg rallies of Speer were to raise to their ultimate, crushing expression. The operatic fascism that Wagner had imagined in his writings was realized by his ardent follower—the sublimation of self, the death of the ego in the chorus of the group, the replacement of vulgar, dissonant reality by *mythos*—Hitler had learned the lessons of Bayreuth well. The expressionist dream of a New Man, reborn in the crucible of a passionate creation, was travestied in the Nazi state. Hitler's world stage was

> dependent on the stability of an aestheticized, ritualized public sphere. . . . Where free art should be, politics reigns, namely terror, proscription, repression. Where emancipatory politics should be, pseudo-art reigns, namely the illusions of beauty, harmony, sensual joy and sublimity. . . . the political formation of the world was thereby ignored. It was replaced by the formation of the world in accordance with the laws of beauty. By having everything political—that is, all those forces which were dedicated to the interests of the masses and pressed for social change—disappear from the publicly established aesthetic illusion, then that illusion became usable in the machinery of rule.[9]

Behind the facade of a Thousand Year Reich, a chaotic, violent society in a state of perennial struggle was ruled by "Night and Fog" orders and a host of other infamous bureaucratic euphemisms for death.

Once officially in power, Hitler began his *Gleichschaltung,* the Nazification of the state. A long debate among Hitler's supporters ensued as to the nature of National Socialist culture. Alfred Rosenberg, the self-proclaimed leader of the vitalist, *volkisch* factions of the movement, articulated a variant of apocalyptic pessimism, a vision of a diseased landscape redeemed by a heroic race. In Rosenberg's vision, aesthetics functioned as a romantic tribalism.

> The Nordic soul is not comtemplative, and . . . does not lose itself in individual psychology. . . . it willfully experiences cosmic-spiritual laws.[10]

> All political formations express a new life-feeling and come to an end only when the life-feeling no longer serves the general good of the people or the group. Thus every great period and every great national conception take their departure from the same source [the depths of

> the "Aryan soul"] that gives rise to cultural creations. National Socialism therefore regards the unity of culture and the state as being based on and directed by a definite attitude towards life.[11]

This occult view of the state saw Nazism as the fulfillment of a mythic cycle of group life, and Rosenberg's Nazism helps explain the attraction the movement held for Martin Heidegger and Carl Jung. In the course of the twenties, Rosenberg had gathered around him an umbrella group of like-minded theosophists, racists, and antimodernists that he called the "Combat League for German Culture." With Hitler in power, the astrological archetypes seemed to be aligned for a triumphant return to Teutonism, and Rosenberg helped spearhead the purging of German cultural officialdom. "The German people has found its style," he declared. "It is that of the marching column."

Although Rosenberg received an appointment as a monitor of sorts of German cultural life, his interests conflicted directly with those of Josef Goebbels, whose ambitions for the Ministry of Propaganda were global. Goebbels's youthful fling with literary expressionism, his Berlin cultural and political connections, his interest in the new mass media, and his sympathy with the Nazi "Nordic" modernists and overwhelming contempt for the theosophical babbling of Rosenberg's *Schwarmerei** made conflict between the two factions inevitable. Goebbels's "steely romanticism" drew on a revolutionary dynamism that was alien to Rosenberg's vision of the return of the Aryan deities, and their rivalry was exemplified in Rosenberg's 1934 denunciation of an Italian futurist art show that visited Germany with Goebbels's support. The fascist exhibition was denounced as "degenerate," and the controversy was only quelled when Hitler denounced both factions in his 1934 Nuremberg party address.

The Nuremberg speech made it clear, at the same time that Stalin was purging his own cultural cliques, that no one faction would represent the National Socialist vision. In 1935, Julius Streicher, the bestial editor of the anti-Semitic newspaper *Der Stürmer,* was allowed to mount an exhibition of "degenerate art" *(Entartete Kunst),* and two years later, the major cultural festival of the Third Reich, the opening of the massive "House of German Culture," took place in an explosion of Nazi pageantry. Hitler oversaw the ceremony himself and permitted the simultaneous opening of a huge exhibition of officially condemned modern art to

*A German Enlightenment insult directed against the religious enthusiasm of Germany's pietists—thus all "enthusiasts" (eds.).

effectively underline the difference between the stallions, warriors, and sturdy mothers and babies set in rural landscapes of Nazi art and the "nigger art" (Rosenberg) of the avant-garde.

In the "House of German Culture," the grotesquely muscular, monumental nudes of Arno Breker, the faintly obscene "allegorical" maidens of Adolf Ziegler, and a constellation of other art works celebrated the new "heroic" culture of violence and eroticized sentimentality. The building itself bore Hitler's dictum: "Art is a noble and fanatical mission." The juxtaposition of neoclassical "nobility" and destructive frenzy characterizes Nazi culture as a whole, where romanticized "death was the fountain of youth."[12] The sheer size of the works dwarfed the viewer in a kind of primal-scene vision of authority. In Karl Mannheim's analysis, this "spiritualization of politics," so frequently evoked by the Nazis, was a derealization of political life and in Nazi culture: "orgiastic energies and ecstatic outbursts began to operate in a worldly setting, and tensions, previously transcending day to day life became explosive agents within it. The impossible gives birth to the possible and the absolute interferes with the world and conditions actual events."[13] The exhibition represented not so much a new "aesthetic" as the politicization of mental life, and across Munich, the much-decried "degenerate art" exhibition hosted overflow crowds as thousands came to view examples of Nazism's "other," the amalgamated-chaos beast of Jewish, Bolshevik modernism. Included in the show were examples of nearly every internationally known German modernist: expressionists, dadaists, surrealists, and constructivists. Each picture was framed by denunciatory slogans, and the paintings and sculptures were often juxtaposed with photographs of anatomical abnormalities or captioned with fragments of avant-garde poetry in order to highlight their illogicality. These works were created, the exhibition pamphlet shrilled, "in the cultural service of the Bolshevist plan of anarchy."[14] They attested, in language that was a direct descendant of Nordau's *Degeneration,* to "the progressive deterioration of perception of form and color"; they were "voodoo objects"; they depicted German soldiery, for example, "as cretins, common erotic libertines and drunks"; they held up "the Negro as the racial ideal."[15] In his dedicatory speech, Hitler called for a "new human type" and eugenic measures "to prevent further inheritance of such a ghastly defect of vision."[16]

From 1937 until the end of the first easy triumphs in Russia, cultural proselytization continued in the Third Reich. Traveling exhibitions were organized, the *Gleichschaltung* was extended to all Europe, the few massive public building projects were completed, and Goebbels oversaw the production of miles of propaganda films. As the war moved toward Germany's defeat, the war of extermination replaced the war of conquest, and the Reich, under the direction of Himmler and Speer, became a death factory. Wartime art became preoccupied with the vanished rural world, echoes of the First World War front, and the face of the universal enemy. Nazi architecture, including the Berlin Reich Chancellery, which stood over Hitler's bunker, furnished a new crop of neoclassical ruins for the Nazi vision of antiquity. The victory columns and mortuaries, never erected, were replaced by the death camps, and the return to Hellenistic empire became instead a Germanic twilight of the gods. After his famous 1943 call for "Total War," Goebbels exemplified the shift in Nazi thought from a surface commitment to restoration to the final emergence of what Hermann Rauschning had called its "revolution of nihilism." Rauschning's early denunciation of National Socialism centered on its destructive instability—an element that became evident to outside observers only with the Reichstag trial and the 1938 pogroms. In 1945, Goebbels returned to the language of expressionist cataclysm, the language of the *Spiesserschrecker,* or scourge of the bourgeois.

> Under the debris of our shattered cities the last so-called achievements of the middle-class nineteenth century have been finally buried. . . . Together with the monuments of culture there crumble also the last obstacles to the fulfillment of our revolutionary task. Now that everything is in ruins, we are forced to rebuild Europe. In the past, private possessions tied us to bourgeois restraint. Now the bombs, instead of killing all Europeans, have only smashed the prison walls which held them captive. . . . In trying to destroy Europe's future, the enemy has only succeeded in smashing its past; and with that, everything old and outworn has gone.[17]

The facade of *Kultur* had finally fallen, revealing the destructive rage and psychic disintegration that passed itself off as a "New Order."

Psychohistory, as Peter Loewenberg has recently shown, has moved away from an exclusive concern with leadership and familial pathologies to the study of National Socialist society as a group experience, a shared fantasy rather than a charismatic conspiracy or a berserk patriarchy.[18] Lowenberg has cogently demonstrated the genesis of Nazi thought within the age cohort that witnessed the dethroning of the father in postwar Germany. Thus fantasy in this case is historically articulated during a common national experience. Group fantasy structure explains the emphasis on symbolic/aesthetic manipulation in Nazi thought and the destructiveness that it released and camouflaged at the same time.

David Schoenbaum notes, in his study of Nazi social dynamics, that "the basic problem was not political or economic, but social, the problem of an arrested bourgeois-industrial society, convinced by its guilt feelings and its impotence of its own superfluousness, and prepared to destroy itself with the means of the very bourgeois-industrial society it aimed to destroy."[19] Nazi culture was a straitjacket for a suicidal society. The images served to displace aggression both in time and in space, to anesthetize and incite. As a system of thought, Nazism was an intellectual babble held in place by armed terror; its central emphasis on beauty was a means of eroticizing authority. In the vision of *Kultur* invoked by Hitler, Goebbels, Rosenberg, Streicher, and Speer, art and chaos were inseparable, "degeneration" was the real force behind history.

In his striking reassessment of Eichmann's Rorschach tests, Robert McCully goes beyond the critique of nazism as hypernormalcy or "banality."

> By definition, a banal mind lacks the capacity to transform what is ordinary into the unusual. Eichmann's imagery looks ordinary at first glance . . . [but] his personal or imagined material reveals complex mechanisms and fantasy, fragments from an inner world sharply contrasting to his outer facade. . . . [Eichmann's associations] . . . suggest an inner state of *partitioned violence*. . . . Transition in the imagery suggests that partition around violence *dissolved easily*.[20]

Analysis of Eichmann shows, then, not mere banality, as Arendt contended, but a much more complex inner partitioning and an inexhaustible supply of sadistic rage. The same dualism was detected by Gregory Bateson in his discussion of Nazi cinematic imagery: the face of the enemy "is in a sense a self-portrait of Nazism. It represents what the Nazis themselves would be without their discipline or—psychologically speaking—what they *are* under the veneer of the discipline."[21]

The Holocaust happened because Western Europe's most industrially advanced nation became powerful enough to act as a delegate of European anti-Semitism and racist nationalism. Its monstrosities were systematized by the German forebrain and rationalized—even "beautified"—by a conservative, antimodernist culture that Germany had evolved to mask its own social and psychological fall into modernity. Self-hatred, inferiority feelings, and a masochistic identification with authority were externalized in a war on "enemies" who had to be big enough to inflate the devalued ego of the aggressive followers of Nazism.

At its heart, Nazi culture, with its knights and demigods, was an idealized act of destruction. Projected self-destructiveness returned in the form of cosmic enemies. "Very often the apparent content of the ideological system makes way for the persecutory objects," indicates Willy Baranger; an underlying nihilistic despair sets in, in which the ego is "overcome by the feeling of its own destructiveness or of its own incapacity to restore its objects."[22] Nazi cultural ideology helped to isolate its proponents from their own self-hatred. Its inconsistencies made it not banal but magical. As Robert J. Lifton says in his recent study of the Nazi doctors, "The fact that men embrace only fragments of ideology rather than the total system does not mean the ideology is any less dangerous. . . . It can be all the *more* dangerous because one can embrace these fragments in the name of absolute consequences."[23] This fragmented ideology functioned as a pseudo-aesthetic trance, a figment of unity dependent not upon the enhancement of reality but upon its destruction by managed group fantasies. The human ability for abstraction and aesthetic isolation served to protect the Germans not only from a knowledge of who they were but from a sane appreciation of what they had become. It is in the triumph of Nazi culture that we can see the modern reduction of everything to means and the victory of propaganda over even the human love of life.

REFERENCES

1. Max Nordau, *Degeneration,* with an introduction by George L. Mosse (New York: Fertig, 1968), p. 6.
2. Ibid., p. 171.
3. Ibid., p. 288.
4. Ibid., p. 289.
5. Bill Kinser and Neil Kleinman, *The Dream That Was No More A Dream: A Search for Aesthetic Reality in Germany, 1890–1945* (Cambridge, Mass.: Schenkman, 1969), p. 6.
6. Ibid., p. 23.
7. Hugh D. Duncan, *Symbols in Society* (New York: Oxford University Press, 1968), p. 53.
8. Cited in Rainer Stollmann, "Fascist Politics as a Total Work of Art: Tendencies of the Aesthetization of Political Life in National Socialism," *New German Critique* 314 (Spring 1978): 46.

9. Ibid., p. 51.
10. Alfred Rosenberg, "Kultur: The Volkish Aesthetic," in *Selected Writings*, edited by Robert Pois (London: Jonathan Cape, 1970), p. 138.
11. Dorothy Thompson, "Culture Under the Nazis," *Foreign Affairs* 14 (1936), p. 409.
12. James McRandle, *The Track of The Wolf: Essays on National Socialism and Its Leader, Adolf Hitler* (Evanston: University of Illinois Press, 1965), p. 77.
13. Karl Mannheim, *Ideology and Utopia: An Introduction to the Sociology of Knowledge* (New York: Harcourt, Brace & World, 1936), pp. 212–213.
14. National Chamber of Propaganda, Bureau of Culture, *Guide Through the Exhibition of Degenerate Art*, trans. William C. Bunce (Redding, Conn.: Silver Fox Press, 1972), p. 2.
15. Ibid., pp. 6, 8, 12, 19.
16. Ibid., p. 28.
17. J. P. Stern, *Hitler: The Fuhrer and the People* (London: Fontana/Collins, 1975), p. 34.
18. Peter Loewenberg, "Psychohistorical Perspectives on Modern German History," *Journal of Modern History* 47 (1975): 229–279.
19. David Schoenbaum, *Hitler's Social Revolution: Class* and *Status in Nazi Germany 1933–39* (New York: Doubleday Anchor, 1967), p. 287.
20. Robert S. McCully, "A Commentary on Adolf Eichmann's Rorschach," *Journal of Personality Assessment* 44, no. 3 (1980): 315.
21. Gregory Bateson, "An Analysis of the Nazi Film *Hitlerjunge Quex*," in *The Study of Culture at a Distance*, ed. Margaret Mead and Rhoda Metraux, (Chicago: University of Chicago Press, 1966), p. 311.
22. Willy Baranger, "The Ego and the Function of Ideology," *International Journal of Psycho-Analysis* 39 (1958): 193–194.
23. Robert J. Lifton, "Medicalized killing in Auschwitz"; in the present volume, above p. 32.

INTRODUCTION

Professor Moses is concerned with understanding the impact of both the historical and psychological reality of the Holocaust and of its survivors on the psychosocial and psycho-political development of the State of Israel. He begins his essay by describing his evolving personal and professional interest in the survivors who emigrated from Europe to Israel. He suggests that the changes in his attitude toward the survivors were part of a more general social trend in Israel: from initial denial and avoidance in the late forties, through awareness of the survivors' suffering in the sixties, to empathy and identification in the seventies. He discusses the question of the centrality of the Holocaust experience for survivors and others. Professor Moses also deals with the psychological problem of Jewish passivity during the Holocaust and its relationship to Israeli activism and patterns of self-defense. He points out the implications of the use of Holocaust imagery by Israeli political leaders to describe their enemies; specifically, that such attitudes may psychologically be indicative of a tendency to a repetition of Jewish victimization. He concludes his essay by suggesting how the community might facilitate greater adaptation of the survivor to Israel and of Israel to the survivor; and how individual, group, and national attitudes to the Holocaust may influence current political and social policies.

An Israeli Psychoanalyst Looks Back in 1983

RAFAEL MOSES

PERSONAL CONTEXT

It is particularly important that anybody who wishes to express opinions about the Holocaust, and even more so a psychoanalyst, state something about his own history in relation to the event. It is important to strive for awareness of the roots of our attitudes to such emotionally laden topics; a person's attitudes and therefore views may well be influenced by his life history and experiences. My own experience in relation to the Holocaust has been shaped by my having been born in Germany to Zionist parents, who as Zionists since at least World War I never had any question in their own minds that they wanted to leave Germany in order to move to Palestine. In the summer of 1937, I came to Palestine with my parents and began to settle down to a reasonably stable and ordinary life after having spent time in Germany, Italy, and England. In 1942, I enlisted in the British Army from Palestine, first the Palestine Regiment, later to become the Jewish Brigade Group.

The Jewish Brigade Group had much contact with Holocaust survivors in Europe, or as they were called then, "people from the camps." It was the Jewish Brigade Group that helped many of them to find refuge in different way stations, from Germany down toward Italy, on their illegal way to what was not yet Israel. In spite of this historical fact, my own remembered contact with camp survivors was minimal. I must have seen some from a distance, but I do not recall any direct personal contact or any significant impact related to their experiences.

I say this not only because I feel that it is relevant to my subsequent development but also because it indicated a phenomenon of the times: namely, the fact that the personal lot of the Holocaust survivors did not reach the consciousness of the Israelis until much later. Holocaust survivors were being absorbed in Israel in ways which served the needs of the collective, the group, the Yishuv in Palestine and later the State of Israel, and not the individual needs of the immigrant Holocaust survivor.

Obviously, somewhere in my mind I had known that there were people who had been in extermination camps in Europe and were now living in Israel. However, I did not have any real conception of what this meant or what the experience was which they had gone through, or how they were managing to live their lives subsequently in Israel or elsewhere. Personal contacts with Holocaust survivors were few, and were kept at a safe psychological distance. In 1957, I was asked to give psychiatric medical opinions about Holocaust survivors for German restitution courts. The suggestion interested and appealed to me. From then and until today I have seen about three hundred Holocaust survivors for this purpose.

This then was my first professional contact with Holocaust survivors. What stands out in my mind are those survivors whose stories were most difficult to listen to. I remember in particular a man in his fifties, seen early on in my experience as a psychiatric "expert" in this field. He arrived together with his wife. Both were dressed shabbily, and exuded an air of misery. My attempt to separate the man from his wife ended quickly when I felt his strong need not to be alone with me. He told me of four years in one of the major concentration camps. His wife had undergone a similar fate in another camp. The details which I felt I had to elicit in order to both comprehend and report on what happened to him were almost unbearable to me. I was dimly aware of emotional distancing, which I tried to fight against. What made such experiences a little easier was my conviction that I was doing my best to help survivors attain some compensation for experiences which were indescribable and unimaginable. Yet when the first interview came to an end, I felt some relief, as though I had been reprieved, at least for a while. I ended the session, and as I accompanied the couple to the door, the wife turned to me and asked: "And Doctor, tell me, where were *you* during the war?" I sensed the hostility of this question addressed to someone who spoke not their native Yiddish but the German of the Nazis. I reacted mainly with guilt that I had not suffered any of the horrors to which they had been subjected.

This is perhaps an extreme example of an examination, yet it is indicative of the intensity and quality of reactions which were ubiquitous both on the part of the Holocaust survivors who came to me and of myself. In order to be able to allow myself to become involved emotionally with what they had been through, I needed to become aware of my own feelings in the course of such an interview, and therefore of my own feelings about their experiences as compared to mine during the war. I had to come to terms with my own reactions both to the Holocaust and to not having gone through it. Gradually, I became convinced that for a Holocaust survivor, going through this kind of interview invariably had a therapeutic aspect. To open himself up, to review his life history and his specific Holocaust experiences, which so often included the loss of close members of the family, was very painful yet helpful. This is particularly true because for almost all survivors it was the first time in their life that they were talking openly about their Holocaust experiences. As for myself, I began gradually to see myself as a committed advocate of Holocaust survivors.

I have briefly described my personal involvement with Holocaust survivors to demonstrate my reactions, which paralleled those of Israeli society at large. That is to say, the fate and experience of Holocaust survivors became something to be recognized, talked and written about, only in the early sixties. This means, in fact, that for almost twenty years Holocaust survivors had been coming to Israel, had been living and interacting with other Israeli citizens without a mutual recognition and dialogue about what they had gone through.

SOME CLINICAL OBSERVATIONS

Before dealing with some of the social-psychological aspects of this particular phenomenon in Israel, I would like to make a few remarks based on my professional contacts with survivors and children of survivors in psychotherapy or psychoanalysis, whether directly or by way of regular supervision of such treatment cases.

I believe that there is a difference between a brief contact of one or two interviews around a medical opinion and an ongoing treatment situation, not only in the nature of the relatedness but also in the therapeutic work done on the impact of the Holocaust experience on the patient. In the brief contact, although the relationship is less deep, it tends to focus more on the specific Holocaust experience, whilst in an ongoing therapeutic relationship the Holocaust experience tends to become one of many emotionally laden events and not necessarily an overriding one.

I would like to report an unusual psychotherapy case with a thirty-year-old patient who had previously been in both psychotherapy and psychoanalysis. When he was a young boy of three, his parents were in hiding from the Germans. One night, when the German soldiers were close by and he was crying, his parents considered choking him to ensure they would not be discovered. Soon after, both his parents were killed, and he grew up for the first few years with his grandparents and then with his uncle. He came to me complaining of dissatisfaction with his job and also in his marital relationship. I felt that he had not worked-through his separation from his previous therapists. I feared long-term treatment would allow him to settle down for more dependency gratification, and therefore I suggested time-limited psychotherapy for three months, two or three times a week, which he accepted.

What was striking about this treatment, and I believe in part a function of my imposed time limitation, was that the patient focused time and again on the period of his childhood when he and his parents were in hiding from the Nazis. He relived and worked-through, in the tranference relationship, the shock, anger, and rage that he had been a hindrance to his parents and that they had nearly killed him. These feelings paralleled similar feelings he had later experienced toward his grandparents, uncle, and wife.

It was as if the time limitation directed the patient to elicit experiences, symptoms, or inhibitions which were directly related to the Holocaust experience. This probably would not have been the case with long-term treatment. Thus, the type of therapeutic intervention seems to affect how and to what extent the Holocaust experience is brought into treatment. Further investigation of the effect of different types of interventions would be useful.

The Holocaust has become an important focus of the lives of several groups of persons. These include not only persons who directly experienced the Holocaust but also the children of Holocaust survivors and those survivors who did not experience long-term Nazi persecution. The latter are usually persons who left Europe by 1939 or 1940 at the latest and thus were exposed to some milder degree of Nazi persecution.

A major damaging influence that is found in those with long- or short-term exposure to Nazi persecution, as well as those indirectly affected by the Holocaust, is the loss of security in their interpersonal world. This results from the persecution of their parents and of their group, that is, of the authority figures who conventionally provide security. Von Baeyer et al. (1961) described two aspects of this major traumatizing effect. The first is the loss of safety and security in relation to the larger social world when one's own group, the Jews, has become the target not only for verbal hostility but also for physical extermination.

The second aspect is the loss of safety transmitted to the children and young people by the adults' loss of confidence in themselves and in their world. For example, a father who returned after only a week of being interned may appear a different person to the child. Whereas before he seemed reasonably sure of himself and well functioning, he now appears, if not broken, at least despondent. This will affect the child's perception of himself and his family, and will shake his world to its foundation.

A particular difficulty was experienced by Jews who grew up in an assimilated environment. They had come to believe that they were part and parcel of the society in which they lived. They were equals and could trust their standing in society. With the Holocaust came the shock of being displaced, of being forcibly evicted from a social position of equality and safety. Such a shock was often the more traumatizing, the more they had believed themselves to be so secure.

A further traumatizing influence was the difficulty in adapting to a new environment. This was particularly so if there was no wish to emigrate to the new country, but a sense that emigration was an enforced one.

The point I wish to make is that the intensity and the widespread nature of the persecutory events were of such a magnitude that they resulted not only in primary effects. They could and did cause a large group of secondary effects which often served as important influences in people's lives, even in people who had not been directly persecuted. I wish to draw attention to this phenomenon.

The children of survivors are a group that we now recognize as being significantly influenced by their parents' Holocaust experiences. We are now aware of the effect on their present-day adjustment and on their intrapsychic and interpersonal equilibrium. This awareness may lead psychotherapists and psychoanalysts to actively explore and ask questions which point in this direction. However, this new awareness and focus in treatment is perhaps the more interesting in that it was conspicuous by its absence in the past. It is generally known today that one of the most striking findings in most families of Holocaust survivors has been an unwillingness to talk about Holocaust experiences. As a result these experiences have become linked with an aura of something unspeakable and untouchable; they have created a vacuum around which people moved. We do not know the comparative results between a treatment technique that has not actively sought out the influence of the parents' Holocaust experiences with one that has. We do know that when the Holocaust experience is focused on, this becomes a very meaningful and emotionally laden issue for the patient. However, if this material is absent we do not know enough about the consequences. For example, does the treatment then lead to less of an improvement in functioning? Are there some patients who do equally well. If so, what are the reasons?*

What conclusions of a more general nature could I draw from my clinical experience with Holocaust survivors? Firstly, we have not yet clarified for ourselves whether Holocaust experiences can be viewed within the spectrum of known human experience or whether they need to be seen as a totally different category of experience. My answer at this time would lie in between these two possibilities: While different from many if not most human experiences, they can only be approached, understood, or mastered—even partially—if they are viewed as lying within the span of human suffering.

Secondly, the very existence of the Holocaust and of its aftereffects has required us—psychoanalysts, psychotherapists, Jews, or citizens of the world—to come to terms, each one for himself, and to a lesser extent certain social groups, with the meaning of the Holocaust. We must deal actively with our own more or less conscious emotional reactions to the Holocaust. I am thinking here of denial and of guilt—the guilt of having survived, perhaps without even having been there at all—but also of the various forms of aggression which are sometimes engendered by guilt (Moses 1983*c*).

Thirdly, therapy with Holocaust survivors raises a question of general interest: How differently are some central aspects of a person's emotional problems dealt with in short-term or focused psychotherapy compared with long-term psychotherapy or analysis? Are other problem areas analogous to Holocaust experiences in this respect? Are there individual ways of dealing with trauma which make it become more part and parcel of our general psychic conflicts, as opposed to maintaining highly charged isolated areas of disturbance? Can this take place only after a long interval of time? Or does it depend on the personality structure of the individual? Or on the conscious attitude or the unconscious conflicts of the therapist/analyst? Moreover, how can we understand the fact that the impact of the Holocaust on the parents is sometimes strangely muted or even absent in the psychological treatment of their children? And that it can, through the therapist's awareness, as well as through a more general social awareness, become more of a focus in such a treatment? Perhaps we should consider other problem areas in the human psyche that might similarly

---

*This phenomenon perhaps parallels the problem of the conflicts unresolved in a first psychotherapy or psychoanalysis—be it because of the readiness of the patient or the fit between patient and therapist.

come into unexpected focus once either the social fabric or the therapist pushes the topic to the fore.

Fourthly, and now we are already one step further within the sociopsychological realm, I think that there is an interesting parallel in the increased emotional distance between therapist and patient in the late forties as compared with the seventies. In the Psychiatric Service of the Israel Army Medical Corps, we related to the battle-fatigued soldier during the War of Independence in a way very different from how we related to the soldiers suffering from combat reactions during the Yom Kippur War in 1973. The emotional closeness, the echoing of the soldiers' experiences in the therapists, and the degree of identification and empathy with our patients were significantly greater in 1973 (and in the Lebanon War in 1982) than in 1948. I see this as the development of an overall social trend in Israel. As such, it can also serve to explain some of the differences in the attitudes of Israelis to Holocaust survivors: the lack of interest and empathy in the late forties and fifties, followed by the gradual awareness of their existence and suffering in the early sixties, leading to more identification and empathy in the seventies.

THE HOLOCAUST AND ISRAELI SOCIETY

I shall now focus on the social-psychological impact of the Holocaust and its survivors on the Israeli scene.

Holocaust survivors began arriving in Israel in 1942. They arrived in large numbers from 1945–46 to the mid-1950s, to a total of several hundred thousands. The immediate response by the public was avoidance and denial of the unpleasant reality that they were different. We might try to explain this denial on the basis that such overwhelmingly horrible experiences could not be directly faced or met by most average Israelis. It is easily credible that we did not want to be bowled over by these unimaginable experiences and by the reactions they evoked in us: first of incredulity, then of intense anger, shame, pity, and guilt. On a deeper level, it seems reasonable to assume that wishes and fears were here stirred which we ordinarily want and need to leave repressed. These wishes and fears are stirred up less intensively when external events, such as far-off wars, natural disasters, and children starving in Biafra, are encountered. With the Holocaust, however, the threat of setting loose dangerous forces within us was indubitably perceived as much greater. It is for this reason that Israelis needed to deny the outer realities of what Holocaust survivors had been through, and as a result also its psychological aftermath. This view seems to be corroborated by the fact that in the United States, too, it was only in the late 1950s and early 1960s that the first papers on the subject were published, such as Niederland's now classic paper on survival guilt (1961). This term has by now become a household word and a real and almost graspable affect. Previously, it had been only a dry and theoretical concept.

There is at least one other factor in the history and development of Israel which is relevant to our reaction to the Holocaust and to the survivors at the time. In Israel, as in the Yishuv of Palestine before the state was established in 1948, the group was much more important than the individual. It was felt that we needed to act first and integrate afterwards. Introspection, looking at what happened within oneself, was disdained as behavior which might paralyze action. This mode of being was deemed inappropriate for pioneers who were viewed as building the country with a hoe in one hand, and defending themselves with a gun in the other. As a result, people were discouraged not only from introspection but also from awareness of their feelings generally, and particularly of certain negative feelings, like fear and anger. Yael Dayan, the daughter of Moshe Dayan, wrote a book called *Envy the Frightened* (1960). Here she described a young boy growing up in a moshav, a collective village, in the north of the country, who was not allowed to be afraid. Both his parents and the other adults around him gave him the unequivocal message that fear was not acceptable. Attitudes and feelings like this also shaped the policy of the Yishuv and then of the State of Israel toward the immigrants.

It is also of interest to briefly consider the antecedents to such attitudes and feelings in the culture of the shtetl, the East European Jewish small town (Moses and Kligler 1966). Not only were all immigrants to Israel exhorted to come to the land of milk and honey, but everybody was convinced that this must be what they wanted, because it was best for them! In fact, they arrived in a harsh land, where a living had to be eked out with difficulty. The discrepancy between the expectations created by the myth and the harsh realities found was thus considerable. Immigrants to Israel were viewed not as individuals who needed help to adapt to the new environment but rather as tools required for the building of the country. On their part, the immigrants supported this through their idealization of the "land of milk and honey," and because their self-esteem was bolstered through being part of a Jewish state. As a result, for example, they were assigned places to live on the basis of the needs of the country and were not allowed to choose to live where they wanted. Similarly, they were dispersed in the country, so that cultural groups could not band together to provide mutual support for their individual members. The prevalent ideology prescribed that the ingathering of the exiles required a melting-pot mentality, where differences had to be pushed aside so that people could merge into what was seen as the unified whole which existed ready to absorb immigrants. The melting-pot theory, however, was in practice soon referred to as a pressure-cooker mentality (Eisenstadt 1967). In other words, it was clear to everybody that intense pressure was being exerted on the immigrants to make them adapt to the needs of the group, of the collective, of the state. Their own individual and emotional needs were to a large extent ignored.

These basic cultural values were prevalent in Palestine and Israel. They clearly must have influenced the attitude of the absorbing society as a social unit, and of its members who served as its representatives to the Holocaust survivors who came to Israel in large numbers during those years. These attitudes must have affected the survivors—both in their already low and guilt-ridden self-image and in their view of the absorbing society and their possible place in it. One would expect such a view, by and large, to negatively affect their absorption and their adaptation.

A further factor which influenced the attitudes toward the Holocaust and the survivors is related to the reaction of the Israeli, particularly of the younger generation, to the view that European Jews during the Holocaust had been "led like lambs to the slaughter," a view put forth with much abrasiveness by Arendt (1963) and Hilberg (1961). I am referring to the apparent passivity and willingness to go along with the Nazi extermination machine with an apparent minimum of serious attempts to fight it, in stark contrast to the attempts which took place in some of the ghettos, such as Warsaw.* The argument raged in Israel at the time of the Eichmann trial in 1961, especially among the Sabras, who could not understand how their parents' generation could have allowed these terrible events to take place without even attempting to resist in some active way. It was the passivity, then (Zborowski and Herzog 1962), which ran counter to the current Israeli need to actively defend oneself, to not allow oneself to become the passive object of the Gentiles' cruel and barbaric assault, as had been wont to happen in the shtetl of yore during the pogroms in Greater Russia and Poland. In this sense, a countershtetl mentality has become an intrinsic part of the Israeli mind-set.

I think that the need to be active was thus another factor furthering the

---

*See question no. 7 in "Psychoanalysis and the Holocaust": A Roundtable" (below, pp. 221-224) for a discussion of contribution of the Jews, if any, to their own destruction by the Nazis (eds.).

avoidance of dealing with the Holocaust. It was preferable for Israelis, who are by their nature activists, not to have to face the implications of a passive submitting to the enemy suggested by the Holocaust. One other observation may throw additional light on this subject. The observation concerns what has been termed the "Massada complex," formulated by extremists such as Rabbi Kahane in their "Never Again" slogan. While the defenders of the Massada fortress against the Roman legions in the year 73 C.E. decided not to surrender but rather to kill each other until the last person, Israeli ideology demanded an active defense. In the Israel Defense Forces, this same principle led later to the decision to carry any war to the enemy's territory. Thus, the modern "Massada complex" requires Israelis to set up an active defense, one which will "never again" lead to a situation where they—we—can be besieged, surrounded, and ultimately vanquished. The imperative, then, is not to allow a repetition of what happened two thousand years ago, or thirty-eight years ago.

Interestingly enough, the term "Holocaust syndrome" is also used by psychologically oriented political scientists (Brecher and Geist 1980); in analyzing decisions made by the Israeli government in 1967 and 1973, they define this syndrome as "the fear that Israel's survival was threatened." Mostly, though not always, this fear of annihilation and extinction was openly related to the events of the Holocaust, which thus served to underline the perceived dangers. However, if we look at the Israeli's way of dealing with his own emotional reactions to his external situation, we must consider a variety of psychological defense mechanisms which appeared in response to the Arab-Israeli conflict (Moses 1982). One of these consists of a denial of external dangers as they are encountered in everyday life. Israel is a country where terrorist attacks are not infrequent, where before 1967 occasional snipings from across the border were not an unusual civilian occurrence; a country where major wars had been erupting at intervals of about eight years or less. In any violent and dangerous environment some denial of daily dangers is a necessary ingredient of adaptation. It would be impossible to continue one's life while expecting at each step and at every hour to be faced by an enemy attack which endangers one's life and limb. In Israel, denial thus serves an important intrapsychic and social function closely related to the use of denial in relation to the Holocaust. Some observers (Moses 1983 a, c) have described in addition a denial of aggression by Israelis, while at the same time noting that aggression is unusually high-pitched in daily encounters—e.g., while standing in line or while driving (Landau 1982). Expectedly, this aggressivity is more noticeable to people coming from the outside than to Israelis, for whom it is like daily furniture which goes unnoticed. Aggression in Israel can also be seen to be dealt with by a number of other psychological defense mechanisms, such as projection and scapegoating (Moses 1983 a, c). Reactions to the Holocaust by individuals and by groups similarly raise the question of how aggression is dealt with. Swamped with enormous quantities of unbridled aggression, how do individuals or groups react? Though we know something about some such reactions—e.g., the intense constriction and the passivity of survivors on the one hand, and the occasional explosions on the other (Danieli 1981)—there seems to be much more to discover in this area. The mechanism of projection, for instance, has been observed frequently in Holocaust survivors; it may both bind and discharge agression, and thus may have an important function.

There is one final area in the response of Israeli society to the Holocaust which deserves special mention. It is the sometimes widespread usage made by some of Israel's leaders of Holocaust terminology as applied to the present-day political situation. I am referring to the perception of the political conflict between Israelis and Arabs in terms of Holocaust events and particularly to the perception of enemies of Israel as Nazis. From a psychodynamic point of view it is important to distinguish two levels of this mechanism. One is seen in the viewing of, for example, Palestine Liberation Organization terrorists as representative of the Nazi mentality. Here we see an application of concepts and emotions toward present-day enemies in terms of the past. There is, however, a use of this imagery taken one step further, when present-day enemies are viewed as the *personification* of the Nazis of the Holocaust. Such perceptions have, among others, been used to explain and justify the 1982 war in Lebanon, euphemistically termed Operation Peace for Galilee. To rout the PLO in Lebanon was seen as the need to destroy the most dangerous enemies of Israel. One Israeli minister has even been reported to have used the term "final solution" as applied to the PLO. The use of this term has been deeply resented by Israelis when adopted by foreign mass media while reporting the Lebanon War. Thus, Prime Minister Begin responded to criticism of Israeli policies in the German mass media during the Lebanon War, especially reacting, apparently, to their use of such Holocaust-derived terms as "final solution," "Warsaw ghetto," and "Holocaust," by stating that "exterminators and the sons of exterminators" are in no position to pass judgment on Israel or on him. Similarly, such a personification has been specifically applied to the siege of Beirut, where the PLO leader in the bunker in Beirut was to Prime Minister Begin as Hitler was in the bunker in Berlin at the end of the Nazi Holocaust.

It is obviously of interest—though at this time we can speak only of impressions—that such use of Holocaust imagery has in recent years become much more prevalent in Israel. Thus, while fifteen or twenty years ago the epithet "Nazi" still seemed to carry with it such an intense emotional charge that it was almost never used by one child against another, this seems now to have changed. A brute or bully is called a "Nazi" not so rarely nowadays. Similarly, the daubing of swastikas on the part of Sephardic Jews against Ashkenazic ones in Israel and calling the latter "Ashke*nazis*" are newly acquired ways of behaving. On the face of it, it would seem that this indicates some watering down of the once highly charged terms, yet at the same time they are epithets which one knows will hurt deeply and elicit rage.

We cannot but raise the question whether such a usage of Holocaust imagery and such a view of the past (publicly by some of Israel's leaders), when transposed into the current political situation, does not carry with it the danger of reviving the specific relationship of victim-persecutor which existed at the time of the Holocaust. Perhaps it is already an indication of such a carryover. This perpetuation of a role relationship from the past can be understood in two opposing but by no means mutually exclusive ways, passive or active. In either case we are viewing a repetition compulsion of a relationship which has been experienced in the past, and which, through this as well as other mechanisms, is reexperienced and reenacted time and again (Moses 1983 *c*). We know this mechanism only too well from our clinical work. Much of our analytic energy goes into working-through our seeming need to repeat over and over again experiences and relationships which caused more pain than pleasure. These are the strange occasions where we cannot help seeing that man does not, at times, learn from experience.

When we inquire whether such a repetition compulsion also occurs in groups, we are entering new territory and must be cautious in our extrapolations. Some may argue that there is a historical repetition by the Jewish people—or by Israel—of past relationships where Jews have been persecuted and victimized. The danger of such a mechanism, of course, is that of a self-fulfilling prophecy: that the victim may contribute to his further persecution. While I believe that we must thoroughly examine the role of this unconsciously motivated group behavior in the history of the Jewish people, I also believe that we must give special consideration to the existing external reality (cf., by contrast, Stein 1978 and Diner 1983).

Clearly, at this point in time, Holocaust imagery is not used in political discussions only as a result of deep unconscious processes. It is also being used, presumably more or less deliberately, in order to attain political advantage. Phrased differently, the Holocaust is at times being wielded by politicians as a political club. That is one form of reality; quite another form is that Israel is actually threatened with objective dangers (e.g., terrorist acts and a hostile Arab world) which, indeed, plausibly threaten her very existence. Yet, clearly, there are different ways of responding to a dangerous or hostile environment. Some responses will lead more toward armed confrontation, others more toward peaceful reconciliation. Dangers need to be assessed and risks taken. But always there is an interweaving of psychological reality—of unconscious and conscious attitudes—with the external reality in which one lives. In one way, then, it is probably more dangerous to impute unconscious psychological motives to the behavior of groups than to that of individuals. And yet there exists at least an equal danger in *not* taking into account unconscious motives for the behavior of the group.

To return, then, to the possibility of unconscious repetition compulsion leading to the reenactment of the past relationship of persecutor-victim for the Jewish people in Israel, we must keep in mind two possibilities. First, there is behavior which might lead to the re-creation of being persecuted, with the secondary gains of righteous anger and all the advantages and disadvantages accruing from one's status as a victim. Secondly, and no less important, is the other form of perpetuating the persecutor-victim relationship, which forms what Freud called "turning passive into active" (S. Freud 1920), and which has also been described as identification with the aggressor (A. Freud 1936).

When Israel carries out certain military acts which appear aggressive from the outside, e.g., recent oppressive acts against the population of the occupied territories; the siege of Beirut, with its implacable bombardments, both aerial and artillery—acts which to many observers did not seem necessary to attain the intended goals—then we must carefully consider the possibility that the persecuted has now turned persecutor.

Again I feel it is essential to present both sides of the coin. It is all too easy to go overboard in needlessly criticizing aggressive behavior, especially for enemies of Israel, but equally out of what some Israeli politicians (out of their self-interest?) call "self-hatred." This is even more necessary when such behavior is supposed to be psychologically and even unconsciously determined. There can also be little question that a complex political situation, which for years has led to cruel bloodbaths, as took place in Lebanon prior to the 1982 massacre of Palestinians by Phalangist soldiers, lends itself only too easily to the acting out of aggressive wishes and fantasies, especially "by proxy." But to find convincing evidence may well require as painstaking work psychologically as was done by the Israeli Judicial Committee of Inquiry in 1982–83.

A WORD ON METHODOLOGICAL PROBLEMS OF STUDYING THE LARGE GROUP

I have approached the problem of how psychological mechanisms, which we know well in the individual from our psychoanalytic observations, can be ascertained to exist in a group. There are, however, considerable methodological problems that need to be addressed. We have amassed a great deal of knowledge of group processes from a variety of settings beyond what happens intrapsychically within the individual. However, we have not yet systematized our knowledge, nor have we dealt adequately with the methodological problem of how to make valid inferences about psychological processes in groups that have not enlisted our therapeutic or investigative help. To my mind, those skeptics or overly careful methodologists who think that we should not deal with the psychological problems of large groups until we have made some major methodological breakthroughs err on the side of caution. If we clinicians are cautious enough in approaching the problem, our contribution should not and will not, I think, be dismissed out of hand. Rather it will contribute to a broader understanding and to a sharpening of our research tools (Moses 1982, and 1983*a*).

CONCLUDING REMARKS

I have offered some personal psychoanalytic observations regarding the Holocaust and its survivors as they have affected Israeli society and on the responses they have elicited. I would like to end this essay with two comments related to the understanding and rehabilitation of Holocaust survivors. First, it is important for us to realize the limitations of our psychopathology-oriented model and to consider ways in which this view, valuable as we deem it, can be complemented. There are a variety of ways in which hard-won knowledge of unconscious and preconscious psychic processes in the individual has been and can be extended. To name only a few from a broad spectrum: T-groups and Leicester conferences on authority and leadership, the study of social systems pioneered by the Tavistock Institute of Human Relations and applied to industrial enterprises and to labor negotiations, to general hospitals and to prisons (Menzies 1960). Similarly, there are many different projects in political psychology which make more and more use of depth psychology (see, for example, Davidson and Montville 1981–82; Mitscherlich and Mitscherlich 1967; Rangell 1980; Volkan 1979).

With regard to the Holocaust, we might consider programs such as the Group Project for Holocaust Survivors and their Children in New York, which has preventive as well as reparative goals, and uses individual, family, group, and community methods. The unique World Gathering of Jewish Holocaust Survivors (in Jerusalem, June 1981) was an innovative project and had a Mental Health Aid Service for participants. There is room for a tactful community outreach approach to Holocaust survivors, irrespective of whether they have sought professional help. This would be useful for providing help and for research purposes. There is also a need to examine national responses to the Holocaust and its influence on the shaping of current political and social policies (cf., for another context, Mitscherlich and Mitscherlich 1967; and the Conference on Mutual Perceptions of Germans and Israelis One Generation after the Holocaust, held in Jerusalem in November 1982).

Finally, the imprint of the Holocaust is perhaps most indelible in Israel, because it is a Jewish state and because it was set up so soon after the Holocaust and has so many survivor-citizens. Perhaps there is hope that in Israel the more open, sometimes acrimonious debates held on many subjects will *not* respect the sanctity of the Holocaust. Perhaps it may not be too much to expect that remembrance of the Holocaust in Israel, which is so necessary to the survivors, but also to Jews and non-Jews everywhere, will not remain a decreed institutionalized event; that visits to the Yad Vashem Martyrs and Heroes Remembrance Authority will not always be regimented, demanded, or even expected. Perhaps then the remembering, the mourning, and the bearing witness will become a freer dialogue in which the individual chooses the time, the place, and the manner of commemorating in his own way the terrible tragedy that befell the Jewish people. Such freedom, I believe, would also further the study of the aftereffects of the Holocaust—a field of study for which we have little time left.

REFERENCES

Arendt, Hannah. 1963. *Eichmann in Jerusalem: A Report on the Banality of Evil.* New York: Viking Press.

Brecher, M., and Geist, B. 1980. *Decisions in Crisis: Israel 1967 and 1973.* Los Angeles: University of California Press.

Council of Jews from Germany. 1962. *After the Eichmann Trial.* Tel Aviv: Bitaon.

Danieli, Y. 1981. "The Aging Survivor of the Holocaust." *Geriatric Psychiatry* 14:191–210.

Davidson, W. D., and Montville, D. V. 1981–82. "Foreign Policy According to Freud." *Foreign Policy* 45:145–152.

Dayan, Y. 1960. *Envy the Frightened,* London: Weidenfeld & Nicholson.

Diner, Dan. 1983. *Israel und das Trauma der Massenvernichtung*. Germany. In press.

Eisenstadt, S. 1967. *Israeli Society*. Jerusalem: Magnes Press.

Freud, A. 1936. *The Ego and the Mechanisms of Defense*. New York: International Universities Press.

Freud, S. 1920. *Beyond the Pleasure Principle*. Standard Edition, 18:5–64. London: Hogarth Press.

Higgin, G. W., and Bridger, H. 1964. "The Psychodynamics of an Intergroup Experience." *Human Relations* 17:391–446.

Hilberg, Raul. 1961. *The Destruction of the European Jews*. Chicago: Quadrangle.

Jaques, E. 1971. "Social Systems as a Defense Against Persecutory and Depressive Anxiety." In *New Directions in Psychoanalysis,* ed. M. Klein, P. Heinman, and R. Money-Kryle, pp. 478–498. London: Tavistock.

Landau, S. 1982. "Trends in Violence and Aggression." Unpublished.

Menzies, I. E. P. 1960. "A Case Study in the Functioning of Social Systems as a Defense Against Anxiety." *Human Relations* 13 (2).

Mitscherlich, A., and Mitscherlich, M. 1967. *The Inability to Mourn,* Munich: Piper.

Moses, R., and Kligler, D. 1966. "The Institutionalization of Mental Health Values: A Comparison Between the United States and Israel." *Israel Annual of Psychiatry* 4:148–161.

——— et al. 1976. "A Rear Unit for the Treatment of Combat Reactions in the Wake of the Yom Kippur War." *Psychiatry* 39:153–163.

———. 1983*a*. "Emotional Response to Stress in Israel: A Psychoanalytic Perspective." In *Stress in Israel,* ed. S. Bresnitz. New York: Van Nostrand Reinhold.

———. 1983*b*. "Guilt Feelings on the Israeli Side of the Arab-Israeli Conflict." To be published.

———. 1983*c*. "The Perpetuation of the Victim-Victimizer Relationship: A Psychoanalytic View of the Israeli Side of the Arab-Israeli Conflict." In press, third volume on psychological stress and adjustment in time of war and peace. Hemisphere (McGraw-Hill).

———. The Group Self and the Arab-Israeli Conflict, *International Review of Psychoanalysis,* 9:55-65, 1982).

———; Hrushovski, R.; Rosenfeld, J.; and Beumel, R. 1983. "Forced Evacuation: A Psychological View." To be published.

Niederland, W. G., 1961. "The Problem of the Survivor." *Journal of Hillside Hospital* 10:233–247.

———. 1964. Psychiatric Disorder among Persecution Victims." *Journal of Nervous and Mental Disorders* 139:458–474.

Rangell, L. 1980. *The Mind of Watergate: An Exploration of the Compromise of Integrity,* New York: Norton.

Stein, H. 1978. "Judaism and the Group Fantasy of Martyrdom: The Psychodynamic Paradox of Survival Through Persecution." *The Journal of Psychohistory* 6 (2):151–210.

Volkan, V. D. 1979. *Cyprus—War and Adaptation: A Psychoanalytic History of Two Ethnic Groups in Conflict*. Charlottesville: University Press of Virginia.

Von Baeyer, W. R.; Haefner, H.; and Kisher, K. P. 1964. *Psychiatrie der Verfolgten*. Berlin: Springer.

Zborowski, M., and Herzog, E. 1962. *Life Is with People: The Culture of the Shtetl*. New York: Schocken.

INTRODUCTION

Dr. Pattison begins his essay by observing that psychoanalytic theorists often state that the Holocaust was an evil process, that it is an immoral affront to our collective human conscience, and that genocide could well be considered a monstrous example of the sinfulness of man's inhumanity to man. The terms *evil, immoral,* and *sin* are introduced into such discussions because they reflect the personal tenor of how members of the psychoanalytic profession have responded to the events of the Holocaust. Yet curiously, the theoretical structure of psychoanalysis and of psychodynamics lacks a coherent integration of the concepts of evil, morality, and sin. Pattison's paper directly addresses the historical background and development of psychoanalytic concepts about the nature of evil, the psychodynamics of morality, and the appropriate placement of the concept of sin into current theory. He shows that the concepts of evil, morality, and sin are not anachronistic or antiscientific, but are critical elements in our construction of the human enterprise. These concepts are not antithetical to current psychoanalytic theory, but are shown to enrich such theory. The author proposes that there can be no coherent psychoanalytic approach to the Holocaust without these concepts. This is demonstrated in three major conclusions. One, if psychoanalysis is to be a moral science, it must affirm the presence of objectively evil acts of man. Only then can psychoanalysis affirm the evil of the Holocaust. Second, psychoanalysis cannot reduce the evil acts of the Holocaust to simple psychopathology. It must account for the capacity to choose good or evil, the capacity of man to sin. Third, psychoanalysis cannot dismiss the Holocaust as an isolated aberration of human behavior. It must reckon with the fact that all mankind are flawed creatures who cannot transcend their human natures, and that man will act with inhumanity to man unless checked by the context of moral force—flawed man is the concept of original sin. In turn, Pattison concludes, the Holocaust is a sinful saga.

The Holocaust as Sin: Requirements in Psychoanalytic Theory for Human Evil and Mature Morality

E. MANSELL PATTISON

Most clinicians and theorists in the psychoanalytic tradition would no doubt agree with the assertion that the Holocaust was an evil process, was an immoral affront to the collective human conscience, and that genocide is a monstrous sin of man's inhumanity to man.

I deliberately introduce the words *evil, immoral,* and *sin* into our consideration. How else do we confront the Holocaust in human terms? Should I select technical scientific terms to describe the process? I might talk about neurotic acting out of infantile conflict, or immature character development, or sadomasochistic psychosexual fixation, but we all realize that we cannot reduce the Holocaust events to merely individual clinical psychopathology.

Shall we stop there—content to describe psychopathology? In fact we have not. As persons we express repugnance, dismay, anger, hurt, sorrow, indignation. We return again and again to describe, discuss, dissect, and analyze the meanings, causes, and consequences. Is this concern, in turn, merely the reflection of our individual psychodynamic perseveration? Our perturbed ego-ideals and superegos that have been stimulated by unfamiliar events? Our reality testing tilted askew by a new set of unfamiliar realities that we are just now learning to adapt to, so that we can appropriately process the reality of the Holocaust without flutters of anxiety within our ego operations? Of course not. We claim the right and do express our moral indignation in denouncing the evilness of the Holocaust.

Yet here is the curious paradox. As persons within the psychoanalytic tradition, we take seriously the issues of morals, sin, and evil when confronted with the Holocaust. We do not treat the Holocaust epoch as merely a set of intriguing and unusual human events. We are not detached, neutral, dispassionate scientific observers and analyzers of these human affairs. No, we make moral protest.

The paradox is that in our lives and actions, indeed in our professional papers, we assume a moral stance, denounce evil, claim the sinfulness of the Holocaust—is it not? But in our psychoanalytic theories we find little of reference to sin, evil, and immorality. In this chapter I address this dysjunction between personal moral outcry and the lack of a theoretical appreciation of the moral dimensions of human behavior.

Science is not a moral arbiter—it is merely a methodology to describe natural processes. Psychoanalysis, as a science of human behavior, cannot and does not speak to moral issues. From this vantage point, psychoanalysis cannot speak to the Holocaust except in descriptive terms of cause and effect. There is no morality in such discourse. The Holocaust is just another concatenation of perhaps predictable consequences of human nature. The Holocaust is neither good nor bad, desirable nor undesirable, neither to be prevented nor to be promoted. The Holocaust is just another event in human history to be analyzed.

But let us not confuse science with life. Science informs our lives but does not guide our lives. Science, per se, is an inadequate basis for human existence because science is a method of inquiry, not a moral code. Science is concerned with means, not goals. Scientists may be moral, but science is not. Science produces facts, not truth. Psychoanalysis as science has nothing to say about the morality of the Holocaust.

But if we assert that psychoanalysis seeks to apprehend and comprehend human behavior and the human condition, then we move beyond science to the larger realm of philosophy and religion, of belief and ideology, to the affirmation of morals and values, to righteousness and evil, to truth and falsehood.

I do not suggest that psychoanalysis, as a science of human behavior, can or should establish moral norms. On the other hand, I do assert that psychoanalytic theory must include recognition of *mature moral process* and *normative moral content* as critical elements of individual and communal existence. If those of us in the psychoanalytic tradition find the Holocaust to be morally offensive, then our theoretical framework must recognize the moral sense of man.

In this chapter, then, I shall provide an overview of psychoanalytic thinking pertinent to the topics of morality, evil, and sin. I shall illustrate some critical deficits in current psychoanalytic theory from both a conceptual and an empirical point of view. And I shall argue for three major conclusions in relation to the Holocaust:

1. The Holocaust demands our definition and recognition of objective evil acts.
2. The Holocaust demands a reformulation of the psychodynamics of moral process that recognizes the capacity of man to choose evil action.
3. The Holocaust emphasizes in dramatic fashion that man is born into the world with a flawed nature, which if unchecked will ineluctably lead to evil actions—the concept of original sin.

I. THE MORAL SENSE OF MAN

A moral sense is traditionally considered a unique attribute of the human personality. The transformation from a solely biological organism to a socially responsible individual is the hallmark of the development of mature personhood, and at the same time is a shared social development necessary for a viable human society. According to the historian J. H. Breasted, individual character and society coalesced in the discovery of morality: "a world of inner values transcending matter—a world for the first time aware of such values, for the first time conscious of character and striving to attain it."[1] The same sense of the individual and society is reflected in the etymological roots of the term "conscience." C. S. Lewis traces this to the Latin root *socio* ("I know") and the Latin prefix *con* ("with") to literally become *conscio* ("I know together with, I share the knowledge with").[2] Thus conscience, or the moral sense of man, is to be of like mind or shared concern. Lewis elaborates the concept "conscience" to refer both to a general set of moral principles and to the application of those principles to our own actions. The moral attributes of man are thus at once personal and social.

But the essence of morality is disputed. A modern philosopher, B. Wand, has summarized these conceptual debates nicely.

> It has been said of conscience that it is fallible, that it is infallible, that its ultimate base is emotional, that its ultimate source is rational, that it is the voice of God, or the voice of custom; that it is merely advisory, that it is command internally imposed; that it is conscious, that it is unconscious; that it is a faculty, that it is not; that it is a

> disposition to have certain beliefs, emotions, and connotations, which when operative, issue in conscientious action, and that it *is* conscientious action.[3]

In the past four decades, morals, values, and ethics have become a legitimate domain of behavioral science study. However, the essence of morality and the nature of conscience remain elusive.[4] In part, confusion stems from semantic ambiguity, in that the term *morality* is issued to refer to strikingly different aspects of human behavior; and in part, disparate research methods produce divergent empirical data, which have not been articulately integrated. In the history of psychoanalytic theory, much of this inquiry into moral process has been ignored.

II. THE PSYCHOANALYTIC IMAGE OF MAN

Every psychological theory of human behavior carries with it a set of implicit assumptions about the nature of man. So too, psychoanalytic theory has developed in accord with implicit assumptions about the basic nature of man derived directly from the process of Western thought forms.

Classic Western thought up through the medieval period envisioned a static universe, with man partaking of both good and evil, caught betwixt the tensions. The onset of the Enlightenment period did not forsake the tension between good and evil, but foresaw the power of the rational man to overcome evil and pursue good. Thus each man possessed the potential for moral action, with internal and social balances against evil, as God had endowed each man with unique personality characteristics.[5]

The critical transition in Western thought occurred in the nineteenth century with the ascension of empirical science wedded to a philosophy of materialistic naturalism. The human enterprise was naturalized and secularized. Psychology became a "natural science." Good and evil, right and wrong, were expelled from psychological discourse. There was no longer any "ought," only "is."

Man was a natural animal, a biologic organism. Psychology in the end is a biology. Society became an epiphenomenon of biological "herd instincts." Coupled with this image of man were both a biological evolution of man and a social evolution of man. The evil man or bad man was the primitive man. Man was evolving into a good man; *pari passu,* society was evolving into a good society. Empirical science was the handmaiden to rational man, to hasten and refine this natural progression to "higher forms." It is noteworthy that the concept of "original sin" was jettisoned, for man is not a flawed creation, but merely an organism moving along a natural line of development. There is no sin or evil in the world—only more or less adaptive behavior. Maladaptive behavior is primitive, adaptive behavior is mature. Health is homeostatic adaptation that promotes survival.[6]

Psychoanalysis in general has been a major legatee as well as promoter of this naturalistic image of man. It is no wonder then that we do not find evil and sin as concepts in psychoanalytic thought. This does not mean that psychoanalysis discarded value judgments. Rather psychoanalysis participated in a subtle but radical *redefinition* of evil and sin. Evil, if there be evil, was the distortion of the natural nature of man by oppressive forces of society.

It is beyond our scope to fully elucidate the antinomies of thought reflected in the entire corpus of Freud. Certainly he was more complex than his subsequent redactors. Yet the basic thrust of his thought, which has influenced psychoanalysis as an intellectual movement, is clear, as shown in the exegesis by Roazen.[7] For Freud the attributes of human existence to be highly valued were *rationality* and *independence*. Freud was a child of the Enlightenment. Yet at the same time, he was a precursor of modern existential man—man the individualist—modern man existing in ennui and anomie.

The ideal image of man which Freud portrays is man who can reckon with his own impulses, who can overcome himself. Where id was there shall ego be, indeed. But Freud was also an elitist, who saw few who could achieve the Stoic ideal of toleration and control of the self. For the average man on the street, "the opiate of society" would be necessary to assuage anxiety and control aggression.

In this view, man is not evil but merely inadequate, immature, unsophisticated, irrational, or neurotic. Perhaps victimized by his own natural impulses, but not evil. We must acknowledge that Freud was both an idealist and a realist pessimist, whereas subsequent psychoanalytic theorists have been more wont to stress the idealist nature of man, and to ignore the seeming ineluctable expressions of human destructiveness. This latter trend reached its apogee in the humanistic thinking of Abraham Maslow and Carl Rogers, for whom man has the natural ability to become good—obstructed only by the vicissitudes of constriction enforced by society.[8]

If there is no evil in man, it cannot be said that there is no evil in society. But rather than to define evil social action, it is society or *culture* *itself which is evil*—in the sense that culture constricts, distorts, or enmeshes the individual, and thereby *reduces individual freedom*. If maximization of individual choice and individual action is a value axiom of psychoanalytic thought, then evil is any social force interfering with individual freedom. As Roazen has demonstrated, Freud came perilously close to *social anarchy* in his social and political perspectives.[9] Society did not contribute anything positive to the human enterprise, except as a second-best assist to inadequate souls who could not cope effectively with just their own individualistic resources. As Pattison has shown in a recent social analysis,[10] Freud and his followers saw only the negative coercive aspects of society, and failed to appreciate either the social nature of individual development and function or the constructive and critically necessary components of social coercion.*

Finally, without explicit values to be found in the individual or the society, Freud completed the naturalistic and materialistic transition by finding value and defining good and evil in terms of the abstract notion of *health*. Mental or psychological health became the summum bonum. Roazen comments: "The notion of health inherent in Freud's concept of psychoanalytic treatment is of crucial importance. . . . his concept of psychological normality is one possible answer to the liberal quest for an elucidation of the value of self-fulfillment. . . . he was demonstrating in practice the importance of health as a goal."[11] Note that we have shifted subtly, but profoundly, from social goals to personal goals, from moral goals to biologic goals. Health is good, ill-health is bad. The mature genital character is good, the neurotic character is evil. Good health is the goal of existence, and good actions are those which promote individual good health. With health as the fulcrum of good and evil, it is easy to see how such a conceptual framework fitted the Western drift toward narcissistic culture, individualistic culture, and culture preoccupied with individual self-satisfaction and self-gratification regardless of the cost. It is no accident that in Western culture health services consume increasing portions of the national budget, with escalating personal and social costs. Goodness is healthiness. To be sick is evil.

---

*The reader should be aware of an alternative position on this matter. Bettelheim argues that "Freud was convinced that the creation of civilized society, despite all its shortcomings, was still man's noblest achievement" (*Freud and Man's Soul* [New York: Knopf, 1983], p. 16). Moreover, Freud wrote in a letter to Einstein, "For incalculable ages mankind has been passing through a process of evolution of culture. We owe to that process the best of what we have become, as well as a good part of what we suffer from" (Standard Edition, vol. 22, p. 214) (eds.).

In sum, a broad sketch of psychoanalytic thought presents us with a naturalistic and materialistic image of man, in which the values of existence are rationality, individuality, and freedom. As a natural organism there are not good or evil attributes of man, but merely degrees of effective survival or adaptation. Social action is a necessary evil, to be tolerated and minimized until such time in social evolution when natural man is no longer dependent upon culture, while the values of existence have been transformed into health values. Good health promotes individual survival and social evolution. Bad health is evil, in that it interferes with individualization and promotes dependency.

III. PSYCHOANALYTIC THEORIES OF EVIL

Against the backdrop of the naturalistic and materialistic image of man described above, it is not surprising that we find almost no topical entries for the words *evil* or *sin* in psychiatric and psychoanalytic literature. Does this mean that psychoanalysis is only concerned with issues of health and is unconcerned about evil? Or are issues of evil really only issues of health? Or are issues of health and issues of evil both of concern to psychoanalysis? Let us review the answers posed by a variety of psychoanalytic commentators.

Freud and Evil

As Wallace has noted, Freud's thinking was both vacillating and ambiguous about the exact nature of evil, but in all, evil were those natural human instincts that needed to be channeled and controlled by the good instincts.[12] The exact good or bad instincts varied in Freud's analysis. In 1915 the ego instincts were good and sexual instincts were bad. In 1920 and 1921 the aggressive drive was bad and libidinal drive was good. In 1930 uninhibited sensuality was bad and aim-inhibited libido was good.

Now the valuation of human instincts as either neutral or intrinsically good and evil is a conceptual problem. Freud opted to assume that instincts were naturalistically neutral in the formal sense, yet he never altogether abandoned the sense of intrinsic evil drives or instincts. On the other hand, we can with equal logic assume good and evil drives (the assumption of Plato and Western thought up through medievalism). Or we can assume the value-neutrality of instincts and drives, and still assume an original sin, implacable evil aspects of man: that is, the flawed incapacity of man to transcend his own nature. In sum, the description of drive and instinct psychodynamics does not imply any particular conceptual assumptions about the nature of evil. However, it was the *naturalistic assumption* of Freud and the psychoanalytic movement that arbitrarily removed the concept of evil from our consideration of human nature.

It is striking that Freud himself avoided a direct confrontation with the conceptual, philosophical, or theological implications of his own assumptive position. On occasion he sought refuge in a reductionistic avoidance of the issue, as when, in his letters, he branded any asking of big questions as pathological: "The moment a man questions the meaning and value of life, he is sick, since objectively, neither has any existence; by asking this question one is merely admitting to a store of unsatisfied libido to which something else must have happened, a kind of fermentation leading to sadness and depression."[13] Or he appealed directly to his naturalistic assumption, as in his monograph on *Civilization and Its Discontents,* where he asserts that one has "a right to dismiss the question of the meaning of life, for it seems to derive from human presumptuousness. . . . Nobody talks about the purpose of life of animals."[14]

Yet despite such overt aversions to the "big questions," Freud persisted after morality as a central issue of his thought, as Rieff has shown.[15] Freud lived and practiced a scrupulous conventional life, despite a libertarian, anarchic, intellectual stance. This paradox, says Kung, reflects the fact that Freud knew evil and eschewed it, but did not know why.[16] It is illuminating of Freud's own personal paradox to compare the reductionistic dismissal of evil and morality in his official publications with his personal statements, as in the following letter to Oskar Pfister:

> . . . moral demands may be the correct expression of the valid order of things analogous to the hygienic order. . . . Immoralism cannot possibly be the last word, otherwise hypocrisy and lies would be as good and valuable as honesty and integrity, and battling with the drawn sword for truth would be folly. . . . Your morality, my dear professors, has made a deep impact on me. . . . I am oppressed by the lack of seriousness . . . regarding confrontation with the highest ethical values. . . . I prefer to deal analytically with the moral imperative, which I regard as an inadequate expression of a system of imperatives intended for the good of mankind. If this highest biological and ethical principle is deprived of its moral impulse, the effect is oppressive and alarming, while the reestablishment of the higher meaning leads to release and healing. . . . I prefer complete moralisation.[17]

If the preceding quotation seems like a complete reversal of the more familiar Freudian statements, it should be recalled that the personal words above are actually more consonant with his obdurate personal life and implicit admonitions about the goals of psychoanalysis. It should not be surprising, in fact, that there is such a wide divergence between Freud's theory and life. In fact, Karl Menninger has commented that Freud's moral and theological operations were the major unanalyzed segment of his own life.[18]

In sum, Freud left an ambiguous and conflicted legacy of thought and action in regard to evil. As I read the record, Freud persisted in grappling with the problem of evil throughout his work and life. But he was inconsistent. His formal and official positions were modified by his many asides. He never integrated what he knew of evil into his formal psychoanalytic concepts. Yet his awareness of evil remained.

Traditional Psychoanalytic Concepts of Evil

A major classical contribution to moral thought was Flugel's *Man, Morals, and Society*. Here Flugel concentrates on the vicissitudes of superego development as the main moral agency of man. Like Freud, he locates the concept of evil in the instinctual drive of man: "In dealing with immorality and criminality . . . we are all of us born criminals in the sense that we are extensively endowed with impulses which, if unchecked, lead to antisocial conduct. This is no doubt the element of truth in the doctrine of original sin."[19]

Consistent with the naturalistic assumption, Flugel analyzes individual problems of superego malfunction. But Flugel does not look at the issue of social evil, nor question his limitation of moral function to solely superego operations.

As for the nature of evil, that issue is virtually ignored or dismissed by most of the major psychoanalytic theoreticians. The assumption that scientific man will rationally achieve health is the pervading theme. For example, H. S. Sullivan says: "I found myself defining evil as the unwarranted interference with life."[20] In a similar vein. Franz Alexander defines social life as lived by biologically independent organisms, in which social problems are due to ignorance. Alexander questions and answers: "Can psychoanalysis contribute to the social problem by increasing the social conscience in the individual? Obviously sound education is the only possible course."[21]

The traditional psychoanalytic view has pursued the theme of good and evil beyond just instincts, to include good and evil object relations. Thus Fairburn observes:

> It is [to] the realm of these bad objects . . . that the ultimate origin of all psychopathological developments is to be traced, for it may be said of all psychoneurosis and psychotic patients that, if a True Mass is being celebrated in the chancel, a Black Mass is being celebrated in the crypt. It becomes evident accordingly, that the psychotherapist is the true successor to the exorcist, and that he is concerned, not only with the "forgiveness of sins," but also with the "casting out of devils."[22]

Note how consistently he has *subjectivized evil* here. The problem of evil is a therapeutic problem, not a moral issue. Human values are persistently defined as health values.

In sum, we may conclude that traditional psychoanalytic thought treats evil not only in purely secular terms but in personal and individual terms. There is no objective evil, there are only evil psychological processes. Sin has been thoroughly transformed into sickness. There is no justice for evil, nor forgiveness of sins; rather there is therapy for neurosis. Moral inquiry has been reduced to the analysis of psychopathology.

Contemporary Psychoanalytic Views of Evil

Heinz Hartmann addressed the moral dimensions of psychoanalysis in remarkably perceptive manner.[23] He notes that psychoanalysis as a therapy may provide integration and unity of psychological processes, and thereby increase the *capacity* for moral thought and action. Yet Hartmann is careful to conclude that psychological healthiness by no means guarantees moral action or a moral person. Thus Hartmann does separate healthiness from goodness. Yet Hartmann limits his discourse to the psychological processes of self-knowledge, and does not explore the larger normative issues of good and evil. To him these are "beyond scientific discourse."

Normative aspects of good and evil are explicated within an *adaptive* frame of reference, hence relativistic and not normative. This is clearly seen in the work of Erik Erikson, who staunchly sets forth the Golden Rule and proclaims social virtues in the name of human dignity and social survival.[24] Adaptation is the key concept, which rests on a latter-day humanism—pessimistic about the human condition and pleading for mankind to save itself. In this case we have moved from naturalism (traditional psychoanalysis) to humanism (contemporary psychoanalysis).

But if contemporary psychoanalysis in its humanistic form acknowledges evil, it is sanguine, but philosophically naive in its underpinnings. For where is the ground of certainty for such a humanism or its rationalistic enterprise? Some perceptive psychoanalytic voices have begun to ask normative questions about evil. To mind come the assertions of Robert Coles about social inequity, or the existential anxieties of the atomic age and our moral turpitude about war examined by Robert Lifton. The soft underbelly of rationalism in the modern age is exposed by Allen Wheelis, who finds that psychoanalysis as science has no answer for the problem of evil.

> Science and faith do not now contend for the same domain, and faith is undiminished by the growth of science. . . . life proceeds on something dark and deep, and, however clothed in the garb of reason, ultimately arbitrary. . . .
> Certainty is the basis for attacking evil. Knowing absolutely what is right authorizes the assault on what is wrong. But certainty is hard to find. . . . We have lived a delusion, we cannot know the world.[25]

So we have come a far distance in psychoanalytic thought, from a passionate attack by the rational materialists in the time of Freud, through the comfortable assurance of traditional scientific psychoanalysis, to a disquieted contemporary psychoanalytic humanism, and finally to existential angst in which psychoanalysts proclaim normative evil and see no answer to that evil in the therapeusis of the individual.

Critiques of the Psychoanalytic View of Evil

First, let us consider the assumption of man as a natural organism and particularly the reduction of man to a homeostatic biologic organism.

Chein argues that the key issue is the choice between two images of man: either as helpless, powerless reagent or an active, responsible agent.[26] If we choose the latter, then evil is a viable option of man in action, and man is a conscious moral agent. Easterbrook trenchantly recasts the human free will as the key element to moral choice and moral responsibility, which is always set within the social context.[27] The biologic and naturalistic image of man is not humanness, asserts Eisenberg; rather, the unique human trait is moral choice against the evil action of mankind.[28] In sum, the image of man as simply a natural organism who *is,* is challenged by the notion of man who *ought*. This latter position conceives of man as capable of evil choice and action—of man who possesses moral responsibility—of man who chooses to sin.

The second line of criticism is voiced against the notion of society as simply an oppressive agent: the failure to grasp the *reality* of the social construction of evil. We must come to grips with the objective reality of evil intent, evil action, and evil social organization, asserts Doob.[29] Man is capable of immense evil, from which we try to escape, says Becker.[30] Elsewhere, Becker argues that it is the failure to confront his own evil and need for salvation that is the dilemma of modern man: "Thus the plight of modern man: a sinner with no word for it, or worse, who looks for the word for it in a dictionary of psychology and thus only aggravates the problem of his separateness and hyperconsciousness."[31] If man has the potential for evil, then certainly society can be constructed to evil ends. But in contrast to traditional Freudian thought, where society is the evil, the critique asserts the moral responsibility of man to create good or evil forces of society. The most trenchant critic of the classic psychoanalytic view of society has been Phillip Rieff, who argues that psychoanalysis exposed the moralistic vagaries of society in its attack on social conventions, which led, however, only to "negative" concepts of community, requiring no commitment and offering no salvation. To Rieff, therefore, psychoanalysis contributed to the symbolic impoverishment of culture. More importantly, classic psychoanalysis saw only the immorality of culture and its destructive elements. Whereas to Rieff, morality is the essence of culture:

> To speak of a moral culture would be reduntant. Every culture has two main functions: (1) to organize the moral demands men make upon themselves . . . (2) to organize the expressive remissions by which men release themselves. . . . The process by which a culture changes at its profoundest levels may be traced to the shifting balances of controls and releases which constitute a system of moral demands.[32]

To conclude, Rieff notes that it is not enough that psychoanalysis be a science of morals, but that to address the human condition, it must become a *moral science*.

The final step of the critique is to question the transformation of all issues of evil and sin into health issues. Hiltner puts the critical questions succinctly:

> Do you believe that virtually all of man's troubles and sufferings are of the nature of sickness or illness? . . .Do you imply that he, as a subject, has no kind of responsibility for confronting and dealing with his condition? . . . If man's actual condition involves more than deviation from health, however, what else do you include?[33]

Existential Psychoanalytic Views of Evil

The common "existential" thread which unties this frame of reference is an emphasis upon an image of man as a unique organism with the capacity for moral choice and moral responsibility, a general view of society as an organic part of life which is essentially unchanging in its moral dilemmas, and a clear distinction between health values and moral values.

Weisman notes the general religious humanism of existential thought (as in Boss, Binswanger, Minkowski, May, and Frankl), in which there is a terminological translation: "divine being" becomes "being," "nature" is "existence," "love" is "care," and "sin" is "nonbeing."[34] Weisman suggests that existentialism is a "theology of man." The existential focus is upon the development of a "reality sense" of a real world of good and evil, and upon assuming personal moral responsibility.

In *Whatever Became of Sin?* Karl Menninger emphasizes the objective reality of evil in the world and the evil potential of man as a fallen creation: "Sin is the transgression of the law of God; disobdience of the divine will; moral failure. Sin is failure to realize in conduct and character the moral ideal, at least as fully as possible under existing circumstance; failure to do as one ought toward one's fellow man."[35]

Binswanger offers the following critique of classic Freudian metapsychology, in which "psychology must take the place of theology, health of redemption, symptom of suffering, the physician of priest, and that instead of the meaning and substance of life, pleasure and unpleasure have become the major problems of life."[36]

In summary, the whole stream of existential thought takes the reality of evil constructed in society as a central issue of life that flows out of an image of man as a moral organism who chooses good and evil courses of action.

IV. THE MORAL PROCESS IN MAN

Part of the problem in constructing a place for evil and sin in psychoanalytic theory has been the inadequate conceptual base for an analysis of moral process. Therefore, I shall briefly review four basic areas of research on moral process: an affective-psychodynamic approach, a developmental-structural approach, a content-values approach, and a social-behavioral approach.

The Affective-Psychodynamic Approach

Psychoanalytic theory has addressed morality in terms of the superego, the ego ideal, moral aspects of ego, and moral aspects of self.

In his 1914 paper "On Narcissism," Freud anticipated a conceptual framework for morality.

> It would not surprise us if we were to find a special psychical agency which performs the task of seeing that narcissistic satisfactions from the ego ideal is ensured and which, with this end in view, constantly watches the actual ego and measures it by the ideal. . . . what we call our conscience has the required characteristics.[37]

Here Freud intimates both superego and an *evaluative moral function of the ego*. Later, in "The Ego and the Id," Freud combines the unconscious superego functions and the conscious ego functions into a joint moral function: "unconscious moral demands . . . together with the conscious moral exigencies of man . . . have since then been called the superego."[38] Loewenstein observes that the ego is therefore involved in coping with conscious moral issues as well as the unconscious superego morality.[39] The inherent ambiguity of Freud's formulation is noted by Chassell, for the superego is used to refer to both unconscious and conscious elements of morality: "The concept is most ambiguous, referring on the one hand to a narrowly delineated, specifically derived, separate agency of the mind determined by the earliest parental images, and on the other to complex process and structure implied in socialization."[40]

A second psychic agency of morality is the ego ideal, which is an image of what one aspires to be developing out of identifications with significant others. It is closely related to the superego in moral function, as well as in origin, structure, and function.

Still a third psychic dimension concerns the recent formulations of self-object theory, and in particular the degree of self-other differentiation and good-bad object ambivalence resolution. Here again unconscious determinants of behavior must be separated from the conscious ego attributes of self and self-other operations.

It is clinical truism that the moral behavior of a person may stem primarily from unconscious determinants of supergo guilt, ego-ideal shame, and pursuit of narcissistic symbiosis with other objects, or to resolve good-bad object splitting. To the observer, such behavior may indeed be moral in its consequences, although not necessarily reflecting a moral person. Similarly, unconscious determinants may easily result in immoral behavior pursued in the name of morality, such as the zealot or moral masochist. What we have, in fact, is not morality, but a *private* moral code of the unconscious, which is at best quasi-morality or moralism.

Three different views have been taken of such unconscious determinants of morality. The first asserts that all such unconscious determinants should be minimized—we would all be better off without experiencing much, if any, guilt or shame. This view at best seems a misapprehension of the important functions of unconscious psychic structure. A second view asserts that we should deliberately reinforce the strength and activity of such unconscious psychic elements. This would seem to promote greater victimization of the conscious self. The third view, represented by current ego psychology, focuses upon morality in terms of ego functions, and I have termed this "ego morality."[41]

In his formulation of autonomous ego functions, Hartmann suggested that unconscious moral forces should become *signals* to the ego, rather than obdurate moral forces that overwhelm the ego.[42] Conscious ego activities of the person are involved in the choice of moral values and the choice of moral actions. What are the ego functions associated with morality? Jacobson has elaborated: "The mature self-critical ego, though participating in this moral self-evaluation, also judges our ego functions and our practical relations to reality . . . evaluates behavior not only in terms of correct or incorrect, true or false, appropriate or inappropriate, reasonable or unreasonable . . . [and] ego goals."[43]

To summarize the affective-psychodynamic approach to morality, it has emphasized the unconscious intrapsychic aspects of *emotional moral force*. In itself, this is an inadequate approach to morality. However, the unconscious determinants are significant, and do serve important functions for effective moral operations of the ego.

The Development-Structural Approach

Is a moral capacity an inherent attribute of the human? If so, is such a capacity epigenetic, a potential to be evoked, or is it a capacity for learning? These are questions addressed by the developmentalists. Jean

Piaget asserted that all morality consists in a system of rules. Morality is the acquisition of ability to use these rules. Piaget proposed an epigenetic unfolding of the child's inherent capacity to formulate and use such rules. Based on his child-development observations, Piaget postulated eleven epigenetic stages of moral development.

Lawrence Kohlberg empirically refined these epigenetic stages into six stages of moral development.[44] His moral stages bear a rough correspondence to the psychodynamic stages of ego development. And indeed, Kohlberg reported that ego-strength and "good moral character" were closely associated with his stages of moral capacity. He found that the ego variables associated with moral capacity include the ability:

1. to withstand temptation and behave honestly
2. to act in conformance with social norms that require impulse control
3. to defer immediate gratification in favor of more distant rewards
4. to maintain focused attention on one task
5. to control unsocialized fantasies

Similarly, in a recent review of child-rearing practices, Hoffman reports that training in specific moral acts (i.e., inculcation of unconscious morality) does not produce moral capacity, whereas the nurturance of development of self and discriminatory ego functions does produce moral capacity.[45]

The contributions of the developmental-structural approach include its emphasis on the demonstrated innate capacity to engage in moral cognition, the significance of different levels of moral reflection, and the important linkage between character development and moral capacity.

The problems with this approach are that moral capacity is strongly linked to intellectual facility, moral education, and cultural variables. Furthermore, moral thought is not necessarily moral action. Finally, this analysis of cognitive levels of moral reflection does not account for the *content* of moral thought. It deals only with moral thought *process*.

The Content-Values Approach

The content approach to morality focuses upon the *what* of morality rather than the *how*. Are some moral principles or values of a higher order than others? The issues of moral content are perhaps more forcibly addressed in *Moral Development and Behavior,* by Thomas Lickona.

> A psychology of moral development must be able to hierarchically order the morality of a martyr for justice and the morality of his assassin. To be able to construct a moral hierarchy is required for any kind of social intervention, which is ethically justifiable only on the grounds that the resulting social change moves people toward a rationally higher level of moral functioning. To delimit explicitly moral criteria is also necessary to both conceive and to study moral development, since development, whether psychological or biological, is by definition movement toward something, toward some endpoint which represents a demonstrably higher, more integrated form of functioning.[46]

The most salient experimental work in this approach has been done by Feather and by Rokeach, who have both argued that the content of higher-order moral principles must be used to deduce particular concrete decisions and actions appropriately within a given culture.[47]

The Social-Behavioral Approach

The social-behavioral approach explores the effect of the social environment on the acquisition of moral awareness, moral capacity, and moral behavior. This approach emphasizes that the child must learn to translate moral reasoning into moral behavior. The problems posed here are stated by Wright:

> We need to know how people's theoretical moralities relate to the rest of their moral lives. There are two aspects to this problem. The first is the link between theoretical morality and the way an individual thinks of the situations in which he is actually being called upon to make moral decisions. . . . The second aspect is the relationship between an individual's theoretical morality and the way he actually behaves in morally challenging situations.[48]

Several lines of research suggest that formal moral capacities and actual moral behavior are indeed not necessarily congruent. First, longitudinal observations of children reveal that levels of actual moral behavior lag as much as two years or more behind the levels of moral reasoning achieved by the child. Second, moral behavior is not directly related to either moral reasoning or moral content. The learning of actual moral behavior is mediated by observation of older children and adults, leading to role imitation, role practice, and role learning. Third, moral performance is not necessarily consistent with moral sentiments, but often is more consistent with the social and situational context that either reinforces or undermines one's actual moral performance.

In sum, moral or "prosocial" behavior is based upon social learning and social reinforcement that catalyzes the translation of principle into action. Is moral character, then, a general attribute of the person or a situational social response? It is both. Prosocial behavior requires affective and cognitive developmental integration of the self along with socially learned and reinforced role behaviors.

Finally, we may ask why there is social evil in the world. Here is the age-old problem of man's inhumanity to man. In their recent analysis of the roots of evil, Sanford and Comstock find the social tree of evil rooted in personal maldevelopment, in family dysfunction, in community dysfunction, and in social sanction of dehumanization.[49]

In turn, we might ask, how do we promote moral development, prosocial behavior, and the reduction of destructive social process? Our analysis suggests attention to child-rearing that promotes affective and cognitive growth and integration of effective ego functions; attention to education and training in moral reasoning and to values education; attention to the social definitions and expectations of moral social-role behavior; and the explication of social moral commitments in our society.

In summary, moral process is a complex combination of individual development, an appropriate set of moral precepts, and a social context that monitors human behavior in accord with universal transcendent moral principles. We see that the concept of moral process in human psychodynamics is much larger than merely the unconscious elements of ego ideal or superego. A mature conscience goes beyond the unconscious to a unique set of conscious ego operations. As Loevinger has elegantly stated, man in his operations of consciousness can choose for good or for evil.[50]

CONCLUSIONS

I return now to apply our observations to the theoretical implications for psychoanalysis as we consider the Holocaust.

First, psychoanalytic theory cannot maintain a naturalistic, individualistic, and solely health-oriented frame of reference if it is to consider the Holocaust an evil epoch. If psychoanalysis is to be a moral science, it must affirm the presence of objectively evil acts of man. Only then, can psychoanalysis affirm the evil of the Holocaust.

Second, psychoanalysis cannot proffer reductionistic explanations of human behavior, based solely on instincts, drives, and unconscious determinants of human behavior. To do so reduces the evil acts of the Holocaust to mere psychopathology. A psychodynamic description of the moral process in man must account for the capacity to choose good or evil. Our study demonstrates that man has the capacity, if you will, to sin.

Third, the Holocaust is no isolated aberration of human behavior. Genocide has occurred before and will occur again if we do not maintain vigilance. History teaches us that normal persons commit atrocities. We dare not assume that good family upbringing and the best education will somehow avert the evil propensities of all of us. As Marmor has documented, even becoming a training analyst does not preclude immoral behavior.[51] No, we must reckon with the fact that all of us are flawed creatures—we cannot transcend our human natures. The concept of original sin does not, then, seem preposterous—if we understand it to mean that all of us are born with limited capacities to pursue the good, and that left to our own devices all of us will betray ourselves and our fellow man.[52] Man's inhumanity to man is a reflection of the natural course of human affairs when unchecked by a context of moral force.

Finally, I suggest that we might well consider restoring the concepts of sin, evil, and moral process to our psychoanalytic lexicon as major components of human behavior that are uniquely human attributes. I believe that the psychoanalytic tradition is not violated in these propositions, but in fact is enriched. More importantly, I believe that from this perspective psychoanalytic theory can address the Holocaust as the sinful saga that it is.

REFERENCES

1. J. H. Breasted, *The Dawn of Conscience* (New York: Scribners, 1933).
2. C. S. Lewis, *Studies in Words* (London: Cambridge University Press, 1960).
3. B. Wand, "The Content and Function of Conscience," *Journal of Philosophy* 58, (1961): 771.
4. W. C. Bier, ed., *Conscience: Its Freedom and Limitations* (New York: Fordham University Press, 1971); C. E. Nelson, ed., *Conscience: Theological and Psychological Perspectives* (New York: Newman Press, 1973); S. C. Post,

ed., *Moral Values and the Super Ego Concept in Psychoanalysis* (New York: International Universities Press, 1972).

5. M. Curti, *Human Nature in American Thought: A History* (Madison: University of Wisconsin Press, 1980).

6. R. Nisbet, *History of the Idea of Progress* (New York: Basic Books, 1980).

7. P. Roazen, *Freud: Social and Political Thought* (New York: Knopf, 1968).

8. E. M. Pattison, "Contemporary Views of Man in Psychology," *Pastoral Psychology* 16 (1965): 21–26.

9. Roazen, *Freud: Social and Political Thought.*

10. E. M. Pattison, "Religion and Compliance," in *Compliance,* ed. M. Rosenbaum (New York: Human Sciences Press, 1982).

11. Roazen, *Freud,* p. 283.

12. E. R. Wallace, *Freud and Anthropology: A History and Re-Appraisal* (New York: International Universities Press, 1982).

13. E. Freud, ed., *The Letters of Sigmund Freud* (New York: Basic Books, 1975), p. 436.

14. S. Freud, *Civilization and Its Discontents* (London: Hogarth Press, 1930), p. 64. Standard Edition, 21:164–145.

15. P. Rieff, *The Triumph of the Therapeutic: Uses of Faith after Freud* (New York: Harper & Row, 1966).

16. H. Kung, *Freud and the Problem of God* (New Haven: Yale University Press, 1979).

17. H. Meng, and E. Freud, eds., *Psychoanalysis and Faith* (New York: Basic Books, 1963), pp. 136–137.

18. K. Menninger, *Whatever Became of Sin?* (New York: Hawthorn, 1972).

19. J. C. Flugel, *Man, Morals, and Society* (New York: Viking, 1961), p. 187.

20. H. S. Sullivan, "The Fusion of Psychiatry and Social Sciences," in *The Collected Works of H. S. Sullivan* (New York: Basic Books, 1956), p. 329.

21. F. Alexander, *The Scope of Psychoanalysis* (New York: Basic Books, 1961), p. 406.

22. W. D. R. Fairburn, *An Object-Relations Theory of Personality* (New York: Basic Books, 1954), p. 70.

23. H. Hartmann, *Psychoanalysis and Moral Values* (New York: International Universities Press, 1960).

24. E. Erikson, *Insight and Responsibility* (New York: Norton, 1964).

25. A. Wheelis, *The End of the Modern Age* (New York: Basic Books, 1971), pp. 108–114.

26. I. Chein, "The Image of Man," *Journal of Social Issues* 18 (1962): 1–35.

27. J. A. Easterbrook, *The Determinants of Free Will* (New York: Academic Press, 1978).

28. L. Eisenberg, "The Human Nature of Human Nature," *Science* 176 (1972): 125–128.

29. J. E. Doob, *Panorama of Evil* (Westport, Conn.: Greenwood Press, 1978).

30. E. Becker, *The Denial of Death* (New York: Free Press, 1973).

31. E. Becker, *Escape from Evil* (New York: Free Press, 1975), p. 198.
32. Rieff, *Triumph of the Therapeutic*, p. 233.
33. S. Hiltner, "Man's Problems and Potentialities," in *The Nature of Man*, ed. S. Doniger (New York: Harper, 1962), p. 260.
34. A. D. Weisman, *The Existential Core of Psychoanalysis* (Boston: Little, Brown, 1965).
35. Menninger, *Whatever Became of Sin?*, pp. 18–19.
36. L. Binswanger, *Being-in-the-World* (New York: Basic Books, 1963), p. 179.
37. S. Freud, "On Narcissism" (1914) *Standard Edition*, vol. 14 (London: Hogarth).
38. S. Freud, "The Ego and the Id" (1923), in *Standard Edition*, vol. 19 (London: Hogarth).
39. R. M. Loewenstein, "On the Theory of the Superego: A Discussion," in *Psychoanalysis—A General Psychology*, ed. R. M. Loewenstein (New York: International Universities Press, 1966).
40. J. O. Chassel, "Old Wine in New Bottles: Superego as a Structuring of Roles," in *Cross-Currents in Psychiatry and Psychoanalysis*, ed. R. W. Gibson (Philadelphia: Lippincott, 1967), p. 241.
41. E. M. Pattison, "Ego Morality: An emerging Psychotherapeutic Concept," *Psychoanalytic Review* 55 (1968): 187–222.
42. H. Hartmann, *Essays on Ego Psychology* (New York: International Universities Press, 1964).
43. E. Jacobson, *Self and Object World* (New York: International Universities Press, 1964), p. 153.
44. L. Kohlberg, "Development of Moral Character and Moral Ideology," *Review of Child Development Research*, vol. 1, ed. M. L. Hoffman, and L. W. Hoffman (New York: Russell Sage Foundation, 1964).
45. M. L. Hoffman, "Development of Internal Moral Standards in Children," *Research and Religious Development*, ed M. P. Strommen (New York: Hawthorn Books, 1971).
46. T. Lickona, ed. *Moral Development and Behavior: Theory, Research, and Social Issues* (New York: Holt, Rinehart & Winston, 1976), p. 374.
47. N. T. Feather, *Values in Education and Society* (New York: Free Press, 1975); M. Rokeach, *Beliefs, Attitudes, and Values* (San Francisco: Jossey-Bass, 1968).
48. D. Wright, *The Psychology of Moral Behavior* (Baltimore: Penguin, 1971).
49. N. Sanford and C. Comstock, *Sanctions for Evil* (San Francisco: Jossey-Bass, 1971).
50. J. Loevinger, *Ego Development* (San Francisco: Jossey-Bass, 1976).
51. J. Marmor, "Psychoanalytic Training," *Archives of General Psychiatry* 36 (1979): 486–489.
52. H. S. Smith, *Changing Concepts of Original Sin* (New York: Scribners, 1955).

II

DIFFERING VIEWS of SURVIVORSHIP

INTRODUCTION

Dr. Hoppe was ten years old and living in Berlin when Hitler came to power. He writes, "During the next twelve years, my development was ambivalently influenced by the Nazi power; on the one hand, I was a member of the Hitler Youth and later on of the German army. On the other, I wrote a drama about persecution of Jews in 1939 and was the son of a man who was put in solitary confinement by the Nazis, only liberated from execution in May 1945." Hoppe concludes, "These experiences of my childhood and youth influenced me deeply."

Dr. Hoppe has been a committed advocate of survivors for the last twenty-five years both as a psychotherapist and as a psychiatric expert in the postwar German medical-compensation process. In his essay he tries to illuminate the dynamics of Holocaust survivors, their arbitrators, and their enemies.

Hoppe first summarizes his central clinical findings regarding diagnosis, psychodynamics, and therapeutic issues concerning survivors. The concepts of chronic reactive aggression (or hate addiction) and the "master-slave-seesaw relationship" reveal the destructive impact of enforced regression on the survivor's superego and self-representation. The important role of anger and anxiety in psychosomatic disorders is also discussed. Hoppe points out that Holocaust survivors are frequently suffering from alexithymic features (i.e., no words for feelings) which can be viewed as a sequel to the emotional stupor that developed during their persecution. The paucity of expressed feelings and fantasies might be related to a functional cerebral lateralization (strong interhemispheric blocking leading to the interruption of the preconscious stream and resulting in a marked paucity of dreams, fantasies, and symbolization).

Hoppe then examines the various attitudes of psychiatric experts and psychotherapists toward Holocaust survivors. If the therapist's process of critical self-observation grows weak, and the working-through of his biases and prejudices stops, then the expert/therapist becomes in reality the enemy of the survivor.

The author concludes his essay by pointing out not only that apathy in the face of the Holocaust leads to denial and rationalizations of past and present persecutions, but also that it continues to truncate our ties to humanity and to empathy. Hoppe concludes on a note of affirmation, but not before pointing out that, indeed, the image of man has been disfigured by Auschwitz.

Severed Ties

KLAUS D. HOPPE

The other day, I observed some birds on the grass in my garden, picking seeds, ruffling their feathers, bathing splendidly in the sunshine, toward which they would soar with widened, beating wings. What a peaceful, idyllic scene! So peaceful, idyllic, a suspended image, that joined with my memory of one Auschwitz survivor who had told me his yearning envy for the birds beyond the barbed wire. They are free, he had thought, animals, much more blessed than we numbered humans designated for extermination.

This and similar associations influenced me, guided further by personal experiences, to help survivors of persecution. In the first part of this essay, findings based on multitudinous evaluations and psychotherapies of survivors of Nazi persecution will be summarized. The second part will consider the attitudes of psychiatric experts. Concluding this study will be a scrutiny of societal response to victims of persecution.

There is a common denominator to these otherwise different groups noted above; not only survivors still suffering from the aftereffects of gruesome persecution, but also, often, those who served them, arbitrators and then enemies, reveal the same tragic phenomenon of uprootedness. There are severed ties in modern man, who gassed his soul in the ovens of Auschwitz.

I. SEVERED TIES IN SURVIVORS

A survey of the enormous literature concerning the psychic aftereffects of Nazi persecution reveals that the most common findings are:[1]

1. Anxiety, combined with phobic and hypochondriacal fears, nightmares, and insomnia
2. Disturbances of cognition and memory

3. Chronic reactive depression accompanied by survivor guilt, psychic numbness, and regression
4. Psychotic-like manifestations
5. A persistent sense of heightened vulnerability
6. Disturbances in the sense of identity, of body image, and of self-image
7. Permanent personality changes
8. Psychosomatic symptoms and disorders

Because of the wide range of symptoms, many different diagnoses—for instance, "concentration camp syndrome," "survivor syndrome," "change of personality due to traumatic life experiences," "chronic stress syndrome," "psycho-traumatic syndrome," "neurosis of extermination," etc.—were developed.

For purposes of evaluation, the term *chronic reactive depression,* or depression due to uprooting, coined by Strauss in 1958,[2] seemed to be the most acceptable, albeit Strauss later held that the "uprooting" was mainly due to conditions encountered after the liberation.[3] The term "chronic reactive depression" focuses not only on the main symptoms of survivors but also refutes Kraepelin's previous assumptions that chronic depression cannot be reactive and reactive depression cannot be chronic.

I found the degree of lack of self-esteem to be proportional to the degree of chronic reactive depression. Based upon the initial findings of Cohen[4] and Bettelheim,[5] this writer postulated that the depth of depression depended on the extent of narcissistic regression and defusion of libidinal and aggressive drives.[6]

In a small group of survivors, a lasting hate was detected and described as a *chronic reactive aggression.*[7] By contrast to depressed survivors, victims who developed chronic reactive aggression and hate addiction were protected from relating unconsciously to their torturers as parental figures by a firm ego ideal, by shame, pride, and by the idea of having a mission. The aggressive survivor has externalized part of his superego and is still fighting against the representative of the externalized punitive conscience. This aggression creates new guilt feelings, especially if the survivor's hate addiction is directed against his own family.[8]

The psychodynamics of children and adolescents after persecution were studied by Anna Freud and Sophie Dann.[9] Based on Erikson's concept, the writer found disturbed identity formation in adolescents, following concentration camp experiences. Due to enforced regression and loss of basic trust, serious problems with identity consolidation were observed.[6]

Many authors in the United States and Europe have described *psychosomatic symptoms* in survivors.[1] In 1971 Eitinger published his findings regarding 227 concentration camp survivors in Norway and Israel.[10] Premature aging and frequent illness were pervasive symptoms. Apart from neurological and mental diseases, illnesses involved digestive organs, entailing diarrhea, peptic ulcer, cardiovascular illness, and diseases of the respiratory system, affecting 80 percent of ex-prisoners.

I found that out of a sample of 145 survivors, 144 individuals suffered from psychosomatic reactions, such as tension headaches, insomnia, and gastrointestinal disturbances, regardless of age, sex, sociocultural background, degree of persecution, and diagnosis.[11] In 28 survivors, these conditions were accompanied by psychosomatic disorders, i.e., asthma, ulcer, hypertension, etc. The single exception was a patient who had developed schizophrenia following persecution.

A study of the affects, anger, depression, withdrawal, anxiety, led to the following hypothetical conclusions:

1. Moderate or strong anger, combined with regression and inability to sublimate, favored the occurrence of psychosomatic disorders.
2. Moderate and strong anxiety stimulated somatization and was bound by psychosomatic disorders.

The impression arose that a pronounced occurrence of resomatization of affect in survivors was due to enforced regression to pre-Oedipal stages during persecution, resulting in a revival of primitive anxiety concerning the integrity of one's body. Niederland stated that in victims whose survival depended for years on the appearance and the functioning of their bodies, the cathexis of body image changed completely.[12]

Recently, new concepts of *pensée opératoire,* alexithymia, and functional commissurotomy, or isolated cerebral lateralization, offered deeper understanding concerning the plight of persecuted survivors. *Alexithymia,* a term first used by Sifneos,[13] further developed by Nemiah,[14] describes the inability to express and to define feelings and fantasies. *Pensée opératoire* (concrete or operational thinking) was discerned in psychosomatic patients by Marty and de M'Uzan in Paris.[15] Operational thinking is linked to reality, reflecting the cognitive style of left-hemisphere functioning.

This writer found a high degree of alexithymia and operational thinking in twelve patients who, suffering from intractable epilepsy, had surgery to sever the connections between the two hemispheres of the brain (commissurotomy—"split brain").[16] I speculated that this might also take place *functionally* in persons who, like survivors, show a paucity of fantasies, have difficulties in expressing feelings, and dream constantly about their gruesome concentration camp experiences (functional commissurotomy or isolated cerebral lateralization).

To verify these impressions, I reviewed forty-three comprehensive opinions I wrote for survivors and found the following:

1. Thirty survivors had unimaginative, utilitarian night dreams tied to experiences of persecution and murdered family members. Only three showed condensation, displacement, and symbolization in their dreams and associations.
2. Thirty-one survivors had daydreams very seldom; only four displayed imaginative fantasies which expanded the recollections of experiences of persecution and murdered family members.
3. With regard to symbolization, in thirty-seven survivors, the capacity was concretistic; in thirty-eight the structure was discursive; and in thirty-five the quality was rigid.
4. With regard to preference of inanimate objects versus people, twenty survivors preferred things over people; ten were indecisive.
5. Forty-one out of forty-three survivors felt a lack of inner sense of life; only two showed active commitment to life orientation.
6. Forty-one survivors had a low self-esteem; thirty-eight a low body-image; and thirty-one felt socially alienated.
7. Out of the same group of forty-three survivors, forty suffered headaches; thirty-nine insomnia; twenty-one gastrointestinal complaints; fifteen showed a decreased vita sexualis; fourteen suffered dizziness; thirteen, back and leg pain; and seven, palpitations and breathing difficulties. In addition, there were thirty-six organic or psychophysiological disorders like pulmonary tuberculosis, diabetes, rheumatoid arthritis, essential hypertension, peptic ulcer, liver disease, hyperthyroidism, and psoriasis.
8. During the examinations, thirty out of forty-three survivors showed emotional block; twenty-two lacked spontaneity; and twenty-one were in social and inner isolation; sixteen were outstandingly apathetic. While thirty survivors showed diminished concentration and attention, eleven were without disturbances in cognitive functions.
9. During interviews, seven survivors experienced sweating and tremor, fifteen survivors, only sweating.

Thus, it can be stated that a high frequency of psychosomatic reactions as well as features of alexithymia or isolated cerebral lateralization are noticeable in survivors of persecution.[17] These findings are solely based on clinical observations and not verified by a control group.

With regard to *psychotherapy,* I would like to present a vignette of an Auschwitz survivor that will sum up the main features of diagnostic, psychodynamic, and psychosomatic aspects regarding victims in addition to the specific nature of the therapeutic situation.[18]

Mrs. Ruth C had over one hundred hours of psychotherapy. She terminated because she felt too guilty that the German authorities had not paid for the treatment, despite the fact that she was assured that the treatment would continue without payment. She had been born in Warsaw in 1906. Since suffering her ordeal, she complained about daily, frequently unbearable headaches, insomnia, recurrent dreams of persecution, and utter dejection. Her hatred and anger were at times so strong that she felt like tearing herself to pieces. This woman could not tolerate having anyone around and soon became impatient when her sons and grandchildren visited. Frequently, she insulted neighbors, accusing them of being Nazis. Her husband, who had escaped to England during the war, was hated and not permitted to touch her anymore.

In the beginning of psychotherapy, Mrs. C talked in detail about her experiences at Auschwitz, where she had to work in an ammunition factory. One day, a female kapo, a former prostitute, threw Ruth to the floor, laid bricks all over her, and then walked on them. On another occasion, she was given twenty-five lashes, which left her unable to stand or work. The following day some SS officials examined her body. She had to say she felt well, lest the female kapo kill her. She hated her torturers and wished they would die. After liberation, when she was called as a witness in the trial of another female kapo, Mrs. C broke through the courtroom guards and hit the face of the defendant.

During treatment, Ruth admitted that she had at times been very angry at God for permitting such cruelties. Often, she told God: "Stop treating me like this. You have punished me enough!" She was so angry that she kept dropping things; she hurt and burned herself. Sometimes she would shout: "I do not believe in You anymore." Nevertheless, Ruth kept her faith in God and remained convinced that He would punish her torturers as He punished Eichmann. After such outbursts, she asked forgiveness for her accusations.

Mrs. C was convinced that it was only because of God's protection that she was still alive. Thus, she survived the death march from Auschwitz to Ravensbrueck in January 1945. An elderly German soldier helped her when she collapsed and even gave her a piece of bread. She felt as if heaven had sent him. During the selection in Auschwitz-Birkenau, she ran after friends who were being loaded on a truck. Dr. Mengele, the "Black Angel of Auschwitz," sent her back to the other side, thus saving her life.

Summing up, one might say that her concentration camp experiences shook the pillars of her inner life structure. Forced regression to infantile levels led to apathy, lack of basic trust, estrangement, disturbance of experiences of the past and future, and a marked defusion of aggressive and libidinal drives. For a brief period after liberation, narcissistic and exhibitionistic traits appeared, but they were soon repressed by reinforced defense mechanisms. Deneutralized aggressive drives, however, broke through time and again. Ruth C hated not only the SS and Germans but the whole world and even God, who had permitted such cruelties. In turn, these accusations against God produced guilt feelings which led to self-punishment and increased dejection.

It seems, therefore, that Mrs. C was suffering not only from chronic reactive depression but also from chronic reactive aggression. Persistent anger and hate addiction, identification with the aggressor, frequently combined with hysterical and paranoid traits, feelings of being chosen to survive, a marked process of resomatization of affect, i.e., psychosomatic symptoms, as well as the constant externalization of a harsh and punitive conscience represent the main features of chronic reactive aggression.

From the beginning of treatment, I made a connection between recollections of suffering in the concentration camps, childhood experiences, and her present condition, using some aspects of working alliance,[19] and expressing interest in her concentration camp experiences.

During later sessions, she was asked several times whether she rejected me as a German or whether she considered me a Nazi. The patient denied both with a smile. On other occasions, she blamed me for forcing her to recall painful experiences. She emphasized that she had suffered enough and preferred to be insensitive, dead.

Mrs. C's dreams reflected her condition, responses to treatment and changes in resistance. During the first months, she was flooded with dreams of persecution. Later, she stated angrily that she couldn't remember any dreams but only woke up tense and frightened. A month later, she reported a happy dream—the first one in over twenty years—but she couldn't recall the content. Simultaneously with this change, she experienced the therapeutic situation as more real, not as dreamlike, as formerly.

A remarkable transference reaction was produced by a gift at Christmas time. Ruth reported that at first, for a minute, she rejoiced at the new sweater because she had wanted one like it for a long time but had never been able to buy one. Right afterwards, she felt deeply unhappy and depressed. It shocked her that a person could really care about her. This thought hurt like a beating on the head. Since Auschwitz, she had been convinced that people are more or less beasts and that she could not really trust anybody. From then on, Ruth wore her sweater to every session. Not the gift itself, but acceptance of her ambivalent feelings about it and the interpretation which followed, seemed responsible for the increase of positive transference feelings. This development helped overcome her distrust.

Besides the importance of introduction and the acceptance of a secondary transitional object, the sweater, in the sense of Winnicott,[20] the concept of master-slave-seesaw relationship, helped clarify the patient's inner and outer condition and the role of the therapist. It seemed especially important for the therapist to work-through his own guilt feelings, possibly resulting from his life in Nazi Germany or lack of open resistance inside or outside Germany. The therapist should be prepared constantly to be identified with the aggressor. Further, he needs to scrutinize his own tendencies to give in to the patient's demands. I found that it is possible to overcome the survivor's lack of trust, unfortunately so deeply rooted in reality, but also widely inflated by generalizations and projections.[21]

As mentioned above, further help in the treatment of Holocaust survivors is by applcation of the concept *master-slave-seesaw* relationship.[22] The inner master consists of a harsh, punitive conscience* and a demanding, too-high, ego-ideal which forces the self into a slave position. The Holocaust survivor has lasting depression, mainly from that oppression. The enslaved self feels doomed, condemned, haunted by survivor guilt, and the shame of not being able to fulfill ego-ideal expectations. Any attempt of the enslaved self to rebel against the inner master failed because that power was reinforced cruelly by the outside master, the SS, and it continues to be strengthened by any outside authority on which the inner master was projected. This externalized negative conscience and the too-high ego-ideal enhanced the oppression and sustained the position of the enslaved self.

In contrast to the depressed victim of persecution, the Holocaust survivor, suffering from a chronic aggressive reaction or hate addiction, rebels continuously against the inner and outer master. He permanently

*The severity of which is maintained by the availability of an everpresent supply of aggressive energy (eds.).

externalizes the punitive conscience-part of the inner master onto any close person, especially an authoritarian one, and fights against this outside master. By this process, the survivor gains the position of master for himself, close to his ego-ideal, but he enslaves the other, who becomes a scapegoat. The negative reaction of the other, who feels unjustly treated, and the personal guilt feelings of the survivor lead to the enslavement of the self again. The process of first enslaving the self, then externalizing the master, and the seesaw relationship between internal slave and external master, internal master and external slave, is self-serving, and keeps the Holocaust survivor chained to his gruesome past.

It is, therefore, understandable that aggressive survivors suffer particularly from lack of empathy and callousness in their environment. Fantasies of revenge are harbored. There is a clinging to idealized expectations of justice and humanity, constantly threatened by the ambient world.

II. SEVERED TIES IN EXPERTS

Such repetitive callousness and lack of empathy were often encountered by survivors of Nazi persecution in the course of being evaluated for compensation purposes. In agreement with the literature and on the basis of my own experience, I distinguished four main categories of experts and showed the reactions of survivors to them.[23]*

1. Experts: complete denial
   Survivors: increase of symptoms and defense mechanisms
2. Experts: reaction formation, rationalization, and isolation
   Survivors: conformity, followed by confusion and distrust
3. Experts: overidentification
   Survivors: dependence, followed by identity-resistance
4. Experts: controlled identification
   Survivors: decrease of defense mechanisms and distrust

1. *Complete denial on the part of experts.* This category is the one most often mentioned in the literature. It is easily recognizable by the expert making use of antiquated psychiatric concepts, by equating the survivor with a malingerer or a neurotic seeking litigation, and by neglecting the history of the survivor's life and suffering. This attitude is often combined

*This is, of course, only a working model; in reality the listed traits are not so clearcut, sometimes they overlap.

with a vicious attack on psychoanalysis. These experts quite openly identified with the aggressor, showed an unabashed contempt for the previous psychiatrist's claim of restitution, and were inclined to distort historical facts about the Third Reich, possibly owing to their own screen memories.

For example, the psychiatrist of a German indemnification office used two notations from the Buchenwald infirmary records of 1944–45 to "prove" that an adolescent inmate who had undergone a multiplicity of life-shattering experiences, including the loss of several family members, and who was still suffering from a chronic reactive depression, was able to work at that time and ever since.

Another illustration is a professor of the psychiatry department of a respected German university who attacked me and psychoanalysis in several of his opinions. When confronted with his assertions, which a third party attested as untrue, he could not recall them but directed his attack to an American colleague, a psychiatrist, himself a concentration camp survivor. The professor replied: "I am not interested in these facts at all. His psychoanalytic statements are utter nonsense and unscientific."

The primary gain of denial in this context is the binding of anxiety, of shame and guilt feelings, of doubt about oneself and one's role as expert. The "scapegoat addiction"[24] of such individuals is directed toward the survivor and his defender; both serve as representatives of an externalized negative conscience.

The dichotomy "idealization-vilification"[25] and the use of defense mechanisms, such as denial, displacement, and projection, may be due to the experts' own past, stamped by submission to terror and prejudice. In general, prejudiced individuals are alloplastically oriented[26] and are inclined to relieve their tension through sadistic action.

It is a shameful but psychodynamically explainable fact that some Jewish psychiatrists, emigrés from Germany, are part of this group. Their defense mechanisms and rebuff of psychoanalysis are no less primitive and cynical than those of the German experts.

The effect of this on the survivor is disastrous: he experiences a repetition of torture and persecution, which deepens his disorder. Psychic and somatic symptoms, already severe, become reinforced. Anxiety, withdrawal, depression, and distrust, as well as regression, often tinged with paranoid ideas, are strengthened.

Several survivors, confronted with this type of expert, showed submissiveness during initial examination but voiced bitterness and open hostility when asked about it later. Their attempt to compensate for a renewed and enforced regression fails, especially since they are punished additionally by being refused compensatory recognition of their suffering.

2. *Reaction formation, rationalization, and isolation.* This group of experts appears more sophisticated and overtly suited to their task. Their opinions are interspersed with ornamental epithets and sentences, such as "Even under the utmost consideration of the deplorable fate, we sincerely regret that we are unable to," etc.

They present a facade of open-minded, well-intentioned psychiatrists, reluctant, but unfortunately compelled, to arrive at such an unfavorable conclusion despite allegedly intensive research and painstaking soul-searching. According to their view, the survivor's psychic damage is, of course, not zero percent, but too low to justify compensation.

The rejections by these experts are veiled and burdened with rationalizations, reaction formation, and, sometimes, isolation. These responses are uniformly repeated and finally uncovered by their verdict, regardless of the symptomatology and life history of the survivor.

What are the motivations for this "No doubt, but" attitude?

First, there is the benefit of avoiding total denial. Lip service or minimizing the facts of persecution alleviates the psychiatrist's own feelings of shame and guilt and helps to build his self-image as a putative helper to the victim. Second, a reward of approbation is granted by the German officials for his "remarkably reasonable, humane, and scientific manner." Third, survivors themselves often react to this attitude with conformity and appreciation, believing fully in the expert. Later, even before the double game is uncovered, they sometimes associate and dream about "the nice examiner" as an SS officer who offered them cigarettes or tried to bribe them.

While the survivor immediately recognizes as his enemy the expert who uses complete denial, he feels ambivalent about and confused by the "No doubt, but" attitude of this second group. It seems to me that the final damage they inflict is more severe. The survivor's deepened and lasting distrust, often projected and generalized toward family members, friends, and the whole world, is the end result of the unscrupulous manipulation of this type of expert.

3. *Overidentification.** Experts who are overwhelmed by pity constitute a small and rather self-limited group. Only for a brief period can reality permit overidentification with the survivor and his suffering which

---

*See Jack Terry's essay in this volume for elaboration of this concept (below, pp. 135-148).

partially gratifies the therapist's omnipotent and narcissistic needs. A secondary gain is achieved through the admiration, gratitude, and utter dependence of the survivor. The revival of omnipotent-hero fantasies restricts self-critical and discriminatory functions of the ego and interferes with superego functioning.[27] For example, some experts of this group went so far as to base their "qualified" evaluation on a list of damages and complaints fabricated by a lawyer who lacked all knowledge of the survivor.

In the long run, the overly pitiful expert must fail: not only will the German officials reject him, but survivors who requested his counteropinion will find out that he discarded their cases.

Beneath the surface attitude of pity and overwhelming sympathy of these experts† lies an unsolved conflict between hatred for the Nazis, who betrayed their idealistic hopes, and self-accusations because of their crimes.[28] This conflict leads the expert to vituperatively and unjustly attack other experts and to rebut everyone who does not completely agree with his opinion.

Such attitudes may serve as a defense against deep guilt feelings regarding the expert's own past behavior which could not be worked-through. Rebellion against authority, the conviction that the present German government is as untrustworthy as the former Nazi government, and the generalization that "the Germans are to blame for everything" may also be an outgrowth of this attitude.

Sometimes the expert may use a combination of projection upon and identification with the survivor, i.e., "altruistic surrender."[29] He thus gratifies his own libidinal needs and simultaneously liberates inhibited aggressive drives.

In addition, he puts himself into the role of an alter ego of the survivor: he attacks the German officials, giving in to the manipulative wishes of the survivor, who is still afraid of the authorities. In this way, he permits the survivor to mobilize the expert as a substitute.[30]

Dependency in the survivor may be followed by a greatly belated "identity resistance"[31] which develops out of fear that the expert's strong incursions might destroy the weak core of the survivor's identity.

Although still deeply depressed and withdrawn, a former inmate of concentration camps may regain his ability to differentiate between facsimiles of kapos, foremen or opportunists, as distinct from his genuine friends and comrades-in-suffering. Ultimately he will place the expert in

†Hoppe is referring to German psychiatrists involved in the medical restitution process (eds.).

the former group and resist his intrusion into the terror of his private experiences and will defend that core of identity. The disorder, however, is profound and may last for life.

4. *Controlled identification.* This category of experts can deal with the problem of the survivor with identification: with empathy instead of sympathy; self-awareness and self-criticism instead of defense mechanisms.

This is a difficult goal to achieve: while the Scylla of overidentification lures as an anchorage, the Charybdis of defense mechanisms constantly threatens.

The interferences due to countertransference, listed by Menninger,[32] also apply to the relationship of expert and survivor—for example, the inability to understand certain kinds of material which touch on the interviewer's own personal problems, or the feeling that the patient must get compensation for the sake of the doctor's reputation and prestige. I confess to having used many, if not all, of them at different times.

The extremely difficult task of evaluation offers many such opportunities. At first, judgment has to be suspended; the survivor's experiences—often unbelievable—must be believed, and the terror—unacceptable—must be accepted. Then, judgment must be used concerning the psychopathology and the degree of damage.

Having followed these two rather contradictory steps, the expert often feels some frustration because he may not have done justice to the survivor. On the other hand, the Holocaust survivor himself may feel misjudged and say so. My experiences have led me to the conclusion that a complete denial presents a rather rare pitfall for an alert and self-critical expert. Rationalization, reaction formation, and isolation can be avoided through full attention to, and open acceptance of, the survivor's life history.

One should be particularly aware of the danger of insinuating hysteria or malingering through belittling and degrading the survivor and the cruelties he has experienced. Very few survivors show hysterical features in addition to the aftereffects of persecution. The opposite is frequently true: the survivor is inclined to minimize his experiences and sufferings in order to avoid the pain of recollection.

Overidentification seems to be a greater danger. The demarcation between this defense mechanism and controlled identification may appear rather indistinct. There seems to be a parallel between sublimation and controlled identification: the expert, who has overcome archaic patterns of reaction, seems well equipped to differentiate ideationally and to judge in a relatively "conflict-free sphere." As I have emphasized above, working-through one's own guilt feelings and the willingness to serve as a stand-in for the persecutor, without retaliation of the survivor's accusations, are crucial prerequisites for controlled identification.

In the long run, the survivor's reactions will indicate whether the desired goal has been attained; if the patient shows a decrease of futile defense mechanisms and an increase in trust, notwithstanding the short duration of communication, then controlled identification has been achieved. Finally, we must always keep in mind that it is not the expert's task to measure, but to understand human suffering empathically.

III. SEVERED TIES IN MODERN MAN

How often, however, did the psychiatric expert empathically understand? How often did we fail to comprehend the world after Auschwitz, to see the world through Auschwitz? Tadeusz Borowski, the young Polish poet and prisoner at Auschwitz, begins his recall of "a voyage to the limit of a particular experience" with the sentence: "All of us walk around naked."[33]

Only in Auschwitz? Only they whose inner horizon is still contaminated by the cloud of the crematorium? Or is the whole world really like a concentration camp? Borowski wrote to his fiancée, incarcerated in Birkenau: "We are as insensitive as trees, as stones. And we remain as numb as trees when they are being cut down, or stones when they are being crushed."[34] Robert Lifton observed psychic numbing not only in the suvivors of Hiroshima[35] but also in the SS physicians at Auschwitz.[36] In them he noticed a doubling process, a primal self of being a healing doctor and a secondary self of an indoctrinated killer.

In a paper entitled "Persecution and Conscience," I formulated a similar concept by showing that the ideological mass murderer developed a total externalization of superego functions.[8] In following his beloved leader without any shame or guilt, he reached a magic eternalization of the present. The thousand-year empire had begun, and the fanatic follower of the Third Reich could identify with the status quo. For the Holocaust survivor, too, time was standing still, but for other reasons. For him, present and future were closed off, since hope and confidence were completely destroyed. It seems to me remarkable that in both the persecutor and the survivor there is a disturbance of inner time experience.

Psychic numbing and "blanketing of emotive themes" exist not only in

SS physicians and mass murderers.[37] Recently Stierlin explored the Nazi past of German parents and the dialogue between the generations.[38] He found that the majority of German parents blurred or manipulated their pasts, using Nazi-tainted ideology and subterfuges which distort or limit their perceptions, continue to immunize them against guilt, and cause them to belittle the crimes. Their children, i.e., most of the present young generation of Germany, have learned to live with their parents' Nazi past, or perhaps more correctly, have learned to keep it buried.

The phenomenon of severed ties in us and around us is not restricted to Holocaust survivors or to German people. Lifton speaks of "death equivalents": image-feelings of separation, stasis, and disintegration, leading to despair in modern man, who no longer experiences a sense of immortality and human involvements.[39]* Lifton shows that Auschwitz is connected with Hiroshima—the nuclear Holocaust causes "nuclear numbing" and a "double life," especially between knowledge and feelings.

This intrapsychic dissociation seems similar to "isolated cerebral lateralization," in which the left hemisphere is busy with logical-abstract details and sequential thinking, functionally severed from the right hemisphere, which predominantly expresses dreams, fantasies, symbols, and the whole gestalt. If one feels nothing, then death is not taking place, and so Auschwitz and Hiroshima did not and do not exist.

During World War I, Freud wrote: "To sum up: our unconscious is just as inaccessible to the idea of our own death, just as murderously inclined towards strangers, just as divided (that is, ambivalent) towards those we love, as was primeval man. . . . It is easy to see how war impinges on this dichotomy. It strips off the later acquisitions of civilization, and lays bare the primal man in each of us."[40] Freud ended his famous paper "Thoughts on War and Death" with the words: "We recall the old saying: si vis pacem, para bellum. If you want to preserve peace, arm for war. It would be in keeping with the times to alter it: si vis vitam, para mortem. If you want to endure life, prepare yourself for death."

How many are willing and able to follow Freud's advice? Has modern man not continued to be involved in mass murder and genocide under the umbrella of a nuclear holocaust? The voice of poets, philosophers, psychologists, clergymen, of women, old and young people, even of some politicians may answer loudly: "Yes!" And they could point to the narcissism of modern man,[41] his ruthless selfishness, his callous lack of empathy.

---

*See Robert Jay Lifton's essay in this volume for further elaboration (above, pps. 11-33).

Alas, my sophisticated reader, the total condemnation of our present situation and civilization, the romantic expectation of a paradise on earth, is the polar opposite to which the inner pendulum likes to swing from the hell of persecution and destruction. Three hundred years ago, Blaise Pascal observed: "Man is neither an angel nor an animal. The more he tries to become an angel, the more is he in danger to be like an animal."[42]

Indeed, there are severed ties in us; too much psychic numbing, too much isolated cerebral lateralization, and too many death equivalents cripple thought and mind. Rationality and intellect alone cannot counteract the formidable power of evil. We must not give up hope that the emotional realization of apathy in the face of human suffering may arouse the possibility of an interpersonal and cosmic empathy into which narcissism could be transformed.*

Thus, between the shores of Holocaust and atomic bomb, on the bridge of cosmic empathy, we may learn the art of living, loving and dying.

REFERENCES

1. K. Hoppe, "The Aftermath of Nazi Persecution Reflected in Recent Psychiatric Literature," in *Psychic Traumatization: International Psychiatric Clinics,* ed. H. Krystal and W. G. Niederland (Boston: Little, Brown, 1971).

2. H. Strauss, "Besonderheiten der nichtpsychotischen Stoerungen bei Opfern der nationalsozialistischen Verfolgung und ihre Bedeutung bei der Begutachtung," *Nervenarzt* 23 (1957): 344.

3. H. Strauss, "Psychiatric Disturbances in Victims of Racial Persecution," *Proceedings of the Third World Congress of Psychiatry* (Montreal, 1961).

4. E. Cohen, *Human Behavior in the Concentration Camps* (New York: Universal Library, 1953).

5. B. Bettelheim, *The Informed Heart* (Glencoe, I11.: Free Press, 1960).

6. K. Hoppe, "Persecution, Depression and Aggression," *Bulletin of the Menninger Clinic* 26 (1962): 195; "Verfolgung, Aggression und Depression," *Psyche* (Stuttgart) 16 (1962): 521.

7. K. Hoppe, "Chronic Reactive Aggression in Survivors of Severe Persecution," *Comprehensive Psychiatry* 12 (1971): 230.

8. K. Hoppe, "Persecution and Conscience," *Psychoanaltic Review* 52 (1965): 106; "Verfolgung und Gewissen," *Psyche* (Stuttgart) 13 (1964–65): 305.

*The author's hopefulness is echoed in the work of the late H. Kohut, who has well described a transformation of narcissism as seen in the mature capacity for empathy, humor, wisdom, and creativity. See his "Forms and Transformations of Narcissism," *Journal of the American Psychoanalytic Association* 14 (1966): 243–272 (eds.).

9. A. Freud and S. Dann, "An Experiment in Group-Upbringing," in *Psychoanalytic Study of the Child,* ed. R. Eissler vol. 6 (New York: International Universities Press, 1951).

10. L. Eitinger, *Concentration Camp Survivors in Norway and Israel* (Oslo: Universitetsforlaget; London: Allen & Unwin, 1964).

11. K. Hoppe, "Resomatization of Affect in Survivors of Persecution," *International Journal of Psychoanalysis* 49 (1968): 324; "Psychosomatische Reaktionen und Erkrankungen bei Ueberlebenden schwerer Verfolgung," *Psyche* (Stuttgart) 22 (1968): 464.

12. W. Niederland, "Psychiatric Disorders Among Persecution Victims," *Journal of Nervous Mental Diseases* 139 (1964): 458.

13. P. Sifneos, "The Prevalence of Alexithymia (Characteristics in Psychosomatic Patients)"; *Psychotherapy—Psychosomatics* 22 (1973): 255.

14. J. Nemiah, "Denial Revisited: Reflections on Psychosomatic Theories," *Psychother.-Psychosom.* 26 (1975): 140.

15. P. Marty and M. de M'Uzan, "La pensée opératoire," *Revue Francaise de Psychanalyse,* 27 (1963): 345.

16. K. Hoppe, "Split Brains and Psychoanalysis," *Psychoanalytic Quarterly* 66 (1977): 220; "Split Brains—Psychoanalytic Findings and Hypothesis," *Journal of the American Academy of Psychoanalysis* 6 (1978): 193.

17. K. Hoppe, "Alexithymia or Functional Commissurotomy of Survivors of Nazi Persecution" (Paper presented at the Fifth World Congress of the International College of Psychosomatic Medicine, Jerusalem, 1979), in *Psicosomatica da stress,* ed. F. Atonelli and J. Shanon (Rome: Borla, 1981).

18. K. Hoppe, "Psychotherapy with Survivors of Nazi Persecution," in *Massive Psychic Trauma,* ed. H. Krystal (New York: International Universities Press, 1968); "Psychotherapie bei Konzentrationslageropfern," *Psyche* (Stuttgart) 19 (1965): 390.

19. R. Greenson, *The Technique and Practice of Psychoanalysis,* vol. 1 (New York: International Universities Press, 1967).

20. D. Winnicott, "Transitional Objects and Transitional Phenomena," *International Journal of Psychoanalysis* 34 (1953): 89.

21. K. Hoppe, "The Psychodynamics of Concentration Camp Victims," *Psychoanalytic Forum* 1 (1966): 76.

22. K. Hoppe, "The Master-Slave-Seesaw-Relationship in Psychotherapy," *Bulletin of the Reiss Davis Clinic* 8 (1971): 2:117.

23. K. Hoppe, "Emotional Reactions of Psychiatrists in Confronting Survivors of Persecution," in *Psychoanalytic Forum,* ed. J. Lindon vol. 3 (New York: Science House, 1969).

24. E. Kris, quoted by Frenkel-Brunswick and Sanford in "The Anti-Semitic Personality: A Research Report," in *Anti-Semitism; A Social Disease,* ed E. Simmel (New York: International Universities Press, 1946).

25. M. Wangh, "National Socialism and the Genocide of the Jews," *International Journal of Psychoanalysis* 45 (1964).

26. T. W. Adorno, et al., *The Authoritarian Personality* (New York: Harper, 1950).

27. H. Hartmann and R. M. Loewenstein, "Notes on the Superego," *Psychoanalytic Study of the Child,* 17 (1962).

28. P. Fuerstenau, "Zur Psychologie der Nachwirkung des Nationalsozialismus," in *Antisemitismus,* ed. H. Huss and A. Schroeder (Frankfurt, 1965).

29. A. Freud, *The Ego and the Mechanisms of Defense* (New York: International Universities Press, 1946).

30. M. Wangh, "Die Mobilisierung eines Stellvertreters," *Psyche* 17 (1963–64).

31. E. Erikson, "Identity and Life Cycle," *Psychiatric Issues* 1 (1958).

32. K. Menninger, *Theory of Psychoanalytic Technique* (New York: Basic Books, 1958).

33. T. Borowski, *This Way for the Gas, Ladies and Gentlemen* (New York, Penguin Books, 1967).

34. Ibid., p. 138.

35. R. Lifton, *Death and Life: Suvivors of Hiroshima* (New York: Random House, 1967).

36. R. Lifton, "Healing and Killing in Auschwitz" (Paper presented at Meeting of American Academy of Psychoanalysis, San Francisco, Calif., 1980); "Nazi Doctors and the Psychology of Therapeutic Murder" (Paper presented at Franz Alexander Memorial Lecture, Beverly Hills, Calif. 1982).

37. H. Dicks, *Licensed Mass Murder* (New York: Basic Books, 1972).

38. H. Stierlin, "The Parent's Nazi Past and the Dialogue between the Generations," *Family Process* 10 (1981): 4:379.

39. R. Lifton, *The Broken Connection* (New York: Simon & Schuster, 1979).

40. S. Freud, "Thoughts on War and Death." Standard Edition, vol. 13 (London: Hogart Press, 1957).

41. C. Lasch, *The Culture of Narcissism* (New York: Norton, 1979).

42. B. Pascal, *Pensées* (New York: Penguin, 1966).

INTRODUCTION

Dr. Krystal, himself a survivor, has written a clinical essay based on several decades of work with concentration camp survivors who were seen as part of the German restitution process and in psychotherapy. He is concerned with the awful degradation experienced by survivors that makes it difficult for them to integrate facets of their lives as they enter senescence. Krystal observes that due to their Holocaust-related experiences, many aging survivors suffer from anhedonia (inability to experience pleasurable sensations) as well as alexithymia.

Krystal suggests that the central task of old age—accepting one's painful past—is the same for the person in psychoanalysis. For the survivor, accepting the past implies an acceptance of Nazi brutality as "justified by its causes," and this acceptance calls to mind the submission to Nazi persecution with all its helplessness, shame, and pain. Self-healing, contributing to personality integration, thus becomes equated with giving Hitler a "posthumous victory," and some survivors therefore, angrily reject it. Their current survival is dependent on remaining enraged at the injustice of the Holocaust. This rage, however seemingly justified, impedes the self-healing process and contributes to the chronic discomfort experienced by many survivors.

Krystal is honest in admitting the limitations of psychotherapy with survivors, primarily because their ability to effectively grieve has been impaired by the enormity of their suffering and losses.

Integration and Self-Healing in Posttraumatic States

HENRY KRYSTAL

> *I can now report that my own advanced aging is the choicest product of my hygienic development. In my life's sunset it is wonderful to be able to feel sure that I, as everyone else in the world, can concentrate upon calling my soul my own, and my all my soul!*
>
> —Dorsey 1976, p. 451

The difficulties of the Holocaust survivors that Niederland (1961) described twenty years ago are still being studied (Eitinger and Strøm 1973; Eitinger 1980; Chodoff 1980). Many of these patients have continued to suffer depression, sleep disturbances, repetitive dreams, various chronic pain syndromes, and chronic anxiety (Eitinger 1980) as well as characterological difficulties.

Eitinger's (1980) follow-up of the entire Norwegian population of former concentration camp inmates leads him to the conclusion that

> the greater morbidity among survivors is not restricted to any special diagnosis. The differences between ex-prisoners and the controls vary somewhat from diagnostic group to diagnostic group, but there are more ex-prisoners than controls suffering from the various illnesses. . . .
>
> The ex-prisoner's sick periods and hospitalization periods were about three times as long as those of the controls, and the average number of sick leaves per person, sick days per person and sick days per sick-leave was greater for the ex-prisoners than for the controls" [p. 155].

Chodoff's (1980) review of his experiences in treating survivors shows their continuing unhappiness with "ill-advised marriages," and he describes them as living in "withdrawn depression, uninfluenced by any available measures" (p. 208). Among the aftereffects of the Holocaust that he found made psychotherapy inapplicable to the survivors were the following: the destruction of their "basic trust," their inability to reexperience and describe some of their harmful experiences, the retroactive idealization of their childhood, guilt feelings over surviving (which Chodoff describes as "intractable to psychotherapy"), the continuation of regressive disturbances in body image induced by the traumatic experiences, continuing aggression of an intensity that cannot be handled in psychotherapy, and the tendency to deal with the aggression by means of a rigid, religiously oriented superego.

Danieli (1981*b*) notes that the characteristic patterns and disturbances in families of survivors are different when, for example, the parents experienced the persecution in a passive way ("victim"-type families) than when the survivors were able to remain active and carry on some kind of resistance ("fighter"-type families). These observations are consistent with those regarding the key role of surrender to inevitable danger in initiating the catastrophic trauma state and the survivors' aftereffects (Krystal 1978*b*). Danieli (1981*c*) stresses the wide spectrum of family patterns of adaptation, from manifest success in many areas (those who "made it") to survival only on the basis of severe constriction ("numb" families), leading to affective problems. Danieli also reviews the difficult countertransference problems encountered in psychotherapy and even in less intensive contacts with these patients (1981*a*).

My own contacts with concentration camp survivors have consisted of about a thousand people who were requested to come in for a follow-up by the German restitution authorities or who sought consultation because of difficulties in their lives. About a dozen of these patients, who were as old as seventy-eight, have been in psychoanalytic psychotherapy with me. My findings basically coincide with those reported by others. These survivors continue to experience problems of chronic depression, masochistic life patterns, chronic anxiety, and psychosomatic disease. At the time of these survivors' retirement, the reexamination of their life reactivates some dormant problems and produces intense pain. For instance, individuals who lost a child or mate during the Holocaust develop severe "survivor guilt," and some assume a depressive or penitent life-style. Other specific acts or wishes that originated during the persecution may, in similar fashion, become the focus of a depressive preoccupation.

Rather than reviewing the problems of technique, I want to focus on the relationship of certain posttraumatic constellations to survivors' revision in old age of their evaluation of their life. Old age normally poses a problem of diminishing gratification, and with serious to severe anhedonia commonly found in this population (Krystal 1971), we might expect special difficulty. Progressive loss of gratification, support, and distractions limits one's choices to *integrating* one's life or living in despair. I shall try to show that the major task of senescence is identical with that of psychoanalysis or psychoanalytic psychotherapy. In old age, as in treatment, we come to a point where our past lies unfolded before us, and the question is, What should be done with it? The answer is, it must be accepted or we must keep waging an internal war against the ghosts of our past. The influences in this task consist of the elements of one's life story, which continue to generate painful affects, and the nature of the affective processes and the hedonic level that has been maintained by the individual. For this reason, I will be forced to take a long digression in order to provide the background by reviewing the nature of the problems of anhedonia and alexithymia.

AFFECTIVE AND HEDONIC SEQUELAE OF TRAUMA

Follow-up of a large group of concentration camp survivors for thirty-five years after their liberation has given me a chance to observe certain aftereffects of massive psychic traumatization. In the process of working with these patients, I have found that the economic conception of psychic trauma was inadequate to explain the problem and unsuited to dealing with it. In previous publications I have described some of the aftereffects of the concentration camp experience, which were separate from such consequences of surviving the Holocaust as survivor guilt (Krystal 1978*b*). Among these aftereffects were certain disturbances of affective and cognitive patterns, which are now known as "alexithymia" (Krystal 1971). Immersed in my attempts to understand the problems of survivorship and trauma, I was surprised to find that these patterns of emotional responses were also common and conspicuous among substance-dependent individuals (Krystal 1962; Krystal and Raskin 1970). About the same time, a group of Paris psychoanalytic researchers described the same pattern in psychosomatic patients (Marty and de M'Uzan 1963). Sifneos and Nemiah in Boston have also been working on this phenomenon since 1967, when Sifneos coined the term "alexithymia."

Reconciling these diverse observations turned out to be both simple and productive. I had earlier reported a very high rate of psychosomatic disease among concentration camp survivors—as high as 30 to 70 percent

(Krystal 1971). As I worked with these data, it became clear that I was dealing with a pattern of regression in expression of affect. This realization, in turn, made it possible to reconstruct the genetic development of affects and their basic developmental lines, consisting of verbalization, desomatization, and differentiation (Krystal 1974). The regression in affect form produced the main aspects of alexithymia. At the same time, "operative thinking" was commonly found among the survivors—an exaggerated emphasis on the mundane details of the "things" in their life, and a severe impairment in the capacity for wish-fulfillment fantasy. Although the etiology and meaning of these difficulties is still being studied, I believe I have demonstrated that when alexithymia is posttraumatic, it is accompanied by some anhedonia, often of a severe degree (Krystal 1978*a, b*).

INFANTILE TRAUMA

To consider the connection between the diminution in the capacity for pleasure, joy, and happiness, and psychic trauma, I must step back again and retrace my work on psychic trauma. The recognition that affects themselves undergo a developmental change made it possible to separate the pattern of infantile psychic trauma from the adult catastrophic type (Krystal 1978*b*). Because of the primitive nature of the infantile forerunners of affect—in that they are mostly somatic and undifferentiated—they can become overwhelming and cause a response that I term the "infantile trauma pattern."

The infantile gross stress or "alarm" pattern is behavior in all animals basically designed to prevent separation of the young from the mother. Since separation is a matter of life and death, the whole affective apparatus of the young is mobilized, and they become as frantic and noisy as possible. They instantly assume a search pattern as permitted by their motor skill development—at its highest development, searching for the mother in concentric circles in increasing radius and vocalizing in a way that provokes pity and caring responses. Periodically the young give in to exhaustion and apathy and become stationary, whimpering in the most piteous way possible. This "freezing" represents another basic response pattern. In contrast to the adult state of catastrophic trauma, which may lead directly to psychogenic death, the young have a safety valve: they will go to sleep for a while, only to awaken with a start and resume the frantic search. At the same time, the young in this traumatic state are in a frenzy of "total excitement." The whole organism is in a state of alarm and mobilization.

The emotional responses of the child represent an activation of affect precursors or ur-affects and with it the entire emotional brain and centers for pleasure, distress, and the hedonic regulators. The affect forerunners are general—there is only one pattern for all states of distress and one for well-being and contentment. In the course of normal development, this global response pattern gradually becomes differentiated and, through verbilization and desomatization, assumes the affective patterns known to adults. The affect precursors that constitute the infantile pattern also include the as-yet-undifferentiated pain responses, since there is neither the neurological nor psychological development to localize and identify the experience of pain. That is why the infantile mass response can be imagined to mobilize the entire limbic system as well as a number of specialized areas involved with pain, pleasure, distress, and even orgasm regulation.

If this infantile emergency pattern goes on for an appreciable period of time, the child's pleasure and pain regulatory centers, including those for vital functions, are modified. For if this state continues too long, or is repeated too often, it leads to a failure to thrive, marasmus, hospitalism, anaclitic depression, and eventually death. This pattern has been found in all mammals. It must be noted that the question is not one of nutrition but of the necessary affective support of mothering. If adequate mothering is not resumed promptly, but enough care is available to make survival possible, anhedonia sets in.

I would like to present a case of infantile psychic trauma resulting in anhedonia and depression in old age. This patient, a man in his late sixties, consulted me because of a problem of depression. He had been the youngest child of a large family, an unwanted burden to an already exhausted and depressed mother. Having many siblings, he somehow obtained enough care from them to "make it." Although he seemed stunted physically, his intellectual development was precocious. He assumed a "provider" role early on, starting to work at about nine years of age. Eventually he became successful and known for his "good deeds." During his forties he underwent a lengthy analysis, mainly because of obsessive-compulsive problems and difficulties with sexuality involving a feeling of deprivation and resentment of what he experienced as his wife's "monopolistic" controlling. Despite many opportunities, he was not unfaithful, but he always felt deprived and profoundly unhappy.

His analysis, which lasted for many years, produced satisfactory results in regard to the neurosis, and he "absorbed" his unhappiness by redoubling his work and good deeds. In his mid-sixties he managed to retire. Although he was able to keep meaningfully busy, the retirement turned out quite badly.

In the following year he developed a severe depression, which led him to withdraw from most social contacts. He retreated to a brooding self-preoccupation in which he seemed to be unable to carry out the simplest task because of severe obsessions and self-doubts. Every thought or impulse became blocked by a simultaneous counterthought.

In psychotherapy we gradually reconstructed the onset of his depression following his retirement and its relationship to his sensing of his lifelong anhedonia. When he finally became able to deal with this issue consciously, he would go over his life and enumerate his many and varied successes, lamenting, "What did I get out of it all? I never could *enjoy* anything, and I was always preoccupied with the worries and troubles!" He experienced much self-directed rage, but behind it was a feeling of having been cheated since birth—not only by the original deprivation of affection, security, and well-being, but also by becoming permanently unable to experience any degree of pleasure, happiness, or joy.

We found, in retrospect, that he was motivated all his life by a dread of deprivation and by a search for something that would give him a state of well-being—the "nirvana" of a contented child going blissfully off to sleep. Unfortunately, every one of his successes and every occasion that others might have enjoyed were just additional stresses to him that he grew to resent. He enjoyed none of his achievements and continued to feel tense, insecure, deprived, and increasingly angry and depressed.

As already mentioned, he had never quite realized that his capacity for pleasure, joy, and happiness had been nil. He had been driven by his insecurity and the enormous "hypertrophy" of his sense of duty and responsibility. In looking back, we found that the awareness of his anhedonia had "flickered" on and off in his mind. He had learned to dismiss it by denying it and promising himself that with one more achievement, his work would be done, and then he would devote his life to travel and pleasure. In the meantime, however, it was his own well-kept secret that he enjoyed none of the recreational activities in which he participated.

His reaction to sex was similar. After years of resenting his busy wife's perfunctory and preoccupied responses to him, he was relieved when he lost his potency and no longer had to be "bothered" with it. His wife soon became quite vocal about her deprivation. He not only secretly enjoyed her suffering, but also betrayed his vengeful attitude by using the excuse of his impotence to terminate *all* physical contact, so that they no longer shared any affection or tenderness. When confronted with his use of impotence as an alibi, he realized that he always resented having to be bothered with sex, for it was "more trouble than it was worth."

The treatment, which extended over a period of several years, was first devoted to his acceptance of his lifelong anhedonia. We also tried to highlight and cultivate his capacity for pleasure, with limited success. Our efforts served to mitigate the severity of his rage and depression, however.

This case represents a common story, often called "involutional depression." Most individuals with this condition have a compulsive character structure and/or some degree of anhedonia residual from severe psychic trauma in the first two years of life. These individuals tend to have a "doomsday" orientation to life, based on a dread that their infantile traumatic state will return. Regardless of how they rationalize their fears as fear of death and, secondarily, fear of their own affects, the dreaded "fate worse than death" is the return of the infantile psychic traumatic state.

ADULT CATASTROPHIC PSYCHIC TRAUMA

In contrast to the infantile traumatic state, which is caused by the nature of the affect pattern, the adult catastrophic trauma state is determined by the presence of *unavoidable danger*. Adults are capable of experiencing "affect storms" without being overwhelmed by them. In fact, intense stimulation is frequently sought out as a source of thrills or trances. Adult psychic trauma is *not* caused by the intensity of stimuli (Krystal 1970). The adult traumatic state is initiated by the recognition of inevitable danger and surrendering to it. Thereupon the affective state changes from anxiety—the signal of avoidable danger—to a pattern of surrender—the common pattern of "freezing," "playing possum," or "panic inaction" found throughout the animal kingdom (for reviews, see Cannon 1942; Tyhurst 1951; Seligman 1975).

Since these patterns have been reviewed elsewhere (Krystal 1978*b*), I will just mention that with surrender to what is perceived as inevitable, inescapable, immediate danger, an affective process is initiated that Stern (1951) has called "catatonoid reaction." Briefly, it consists of a paralysis of initiative, followed by *varying degrees of immobilization, leading to* *automatic obedience. At the same time, the process of "numbing" blocks all affective and pain responses,* leading to what Minkowski (1946) called "affective anesthesia." Lifton extended the idea to "psychic closing off" (1967). The broader conception is useful, because the next aspect of the traumatic process is *progressive constriction of cognitive processes, including memory and problem-solving, until a mere vestige of self-observing ego is preserved.** This process may culminate in psychogenic death (Krystal 1978*b*).

On the other hand, it is possible for this process to stop at the point at which a degree of "psychic closing off" has taken place that permits the automatonlike behavior necessary for survival in situations of subjugation, such as prison and concentration camps (Krystal 1968; Krystal and Niederland 1968). Greenson (1949), in his study of prisoners of war, seems to have sensed, with his usual keenness, that apathy represented an aspect of the traumatic state, although he did not appreciate the full impact and future consequences of his observations.

At present, I wish to focus on just some of the aftereffects of such experiences. As might be expected, some people show such severe changes that no semblance of normal function can be restored. These types are best referred to, using the term coined by Murray (1967), as "dead to the world." Murray believed such people were exemplified by Herman Melville himself and portrayed by that author in his characters of Captain Ahab and Bartelby the Scrivener. Contemporary examples of such posttraumatic personalities are portrayed by Wallant (1962) in his pawnbroker and Camus (1946) in his "stranger." In addition to such totally devastated individuals, who achieve a deadening of their intrapsychic life or experience their world as irreparably deadened, there is an entire spectrum of numbing and withdrawal responses. Lifton (1976) has studied this spectrum of self-deadening, calling them "death imprint" patterns.

I am especially interested in emphasizing the *specific* aftereffects of catastrophic adult psychic trauma, i.e., aftereffects that represent a continuation of the traumatic process. These disturbances consist of the following: (1) a continuation of cognitive constriction in various forms of dullness, obtuseness, or inability to function as parents; (2) episodic "freezing" when under stress, which may result in an inability to act assertively and/or aggressively, producing a general picture of either passivity or blundering (as caricatured by the Inspector Clousseau char-

*T. A. Petty 1975: personal communication.

acter in the "Pink Panther" movies) or a variety of "surrender" patterns manifested in "defeated" or "slave" personalities; (3) pseudophobia, usually related to some memory or affect representing a traumatic screen, and consequently, dreaded and avoided. In posttraumatic states, the repetitive anxiety dream represents the trauma screens. They illustrate the "doomsday orientation" in which the return of the traumatic state is both dreaded and expected. Individuals who have experienced catastrophic psychic trauma in adult life also show such signs of continuing the trauma patterns as hypervigilance and anxiety dreams. Some experience a driven need to talk about the events of the traumatic period and others to avoid doing so. By contrast, survivors of infantile trauma often have no recollection or even a suspicion of their traumatic history and have no pattern of behavior directly traceable to the traumatic process.

This brings us to the two sequelae *shared* by both infantile and adult types of psychic trauma. They are, as mentioned already, anhedonia and alexithymia. Anhedonia is a characteristic and reliable indication of posttraumatic states, whether the trauma took place in infancy or later life. Alexithymia, however, represents a broader range of problems, and can be found in certain hereditary (Heiberg and Heiberg 1977), psychosomatic, and addictive states as well as in reactions to acute, life-endangering illness (Freyberger 1977). Next I would like to consider the impact of alexithymia and anhedonia on the problems of aging and on psychotherapy with the aged.

ALEXITHYMIA, ANHEDONIA, AND INTEGRITY IN OLD AGE

> *I see clearly that I owe happiness to myself and I am certain that a reliable way to it is through unhappiness.*
>
> —*Dorsey* 1976, p. 456

One need not belabor the many reasons why aging involves a gradual diminution in the potential for pleasure and gratification. If the process runs its full course, the individual is left to enjoy nothing but the vegetative functions. As the attrition proceeds, it is easy to observe that people vary in their hedonic potential, and that some individuals enter old age with an already diminished hedonic capacity (Meehl 1975). Among the factors at the opposite poles of this hedonic capacity are the ability to play (Krystal 1981) and problems of masochism and guilt. The population of Holocaust survivors is, of course, quite high in masochism and quite low in their potential to become "playboys" and "playgirls" when they are forced to retire. The hedonic potential of every aged person needs to be carefully evaluated, as there is a marked difference among similar populations. Individuals with a good hedonic capacity can enjoy practically anything—even if it is just inhaling and exhaling—and have been known for their "sunny dispositions" since childhood. Hedonic capacity has been identified as a personality factor (Meehl et al. 1971) and has been called "surgency," a term coined by Catell (1935). But regardless of where on this spectrum of capacity for pleasure, joy, and happiness the individual falls, he or she cannot avoid the progressive ravages of age to the hedonic span. Particularly severe losses are sustained in the things one *does*—in all spheres of activity, from sexual, occupational, avocational, and recreational. These losses force a shift from doing to thinking, from planning to reminiscing, from preoccupation with everyday events and long-range planning to reviewing and rethinking one's life.

Being forced to recall and remember is in itself frightening and stressful to survivors of the Holocaust, who have spent most of their time "fighting off" their memories. Many go to great lengths to avoid any historical material. When I asked such patients to associate to TAT cards 1, 3, and 5, their responses were usually limited to one or two sentences predicting a dismal future for everyone in the picture. Some patients even volunteered the observation that they are so afraid of "make-believe" that they do not want to view or read any fictional stories. One patient who had had some psychotherapy realized that she kept describing TAT cards in terms of her own life. She commented: "The past is always catching up to the present in my mind." The reasons for "running away from one's history" have been described by Klein (1976) as resulting from the "sensitivity to cleavage and dissonance," which "reaches its crest . . . in the twilight years when irreversible finitude is finally to be faced and the effort to bring together past, present and the shrinking future into a self-justifying meaning is especially poignant and difficult" (p. 231).

Old age, with its losses, imposes the inescapable necessity of facing one's past. One then either accepts oneself and one's past or continues to reject it angrily. As Erikson (1959) puts it, the choice is integration or despair. But integration means that one has to acquiesce to the "accidental coincidence of but one life cycle with but one segment of history" (Erikson 1959, p. 98). Erikson explains that to achieve integrity, one must achieve acceptance of "one's own and only life cycle and of the people who have become significant to it as something that had to be and that, by necessity permitted no substitutions" (p. 98). This task, as I mentioned earlier, can also be said to represent the very goal and essence of all psychoanalytic psychotherapy.

The heart of the work of psychoanalysis can be reviewed in two parts: (1) the expansion of the *consciously* acknowledged self and object representations, and (2) the acceptance of the inevitability and necessity of every event of one's life as having been *justified by its causes*. It may be said that the challenge in the acceptance of one's old age and in the completion of psychoanalytic work is the same—to accept and embrace what has happened and renounce continuing anger about it. But psychotherapy with individuals in posttraumatic states encounters special difficulties with this task.

Acceptance on the part of survivors of the Holocaust that what happened to them was *justified by its causes* implies an acceptance that Hitler, Nazism, and the bizarre events they experienced were also justified by their causes. Such an acceptance is too closely reminiscent of the *submission* to persecution. The process of making peace with oneself becomes impossible when it brings back the helplessness and shame of the past. Many survivors would experience this self-healing as "granting Hitler a posthumous victory," and they therefore angrily reject it. To them, self-integration appears antithetical to the only justification for their survival: to be angry witnesses against the outrage of the Holocaust.

Moreover, to give up the infantile wishes—including omnipotence, the quest for perfection, and entitlement to ideal parents—to accept the negative aspects of oneself, including these angry and vengeful feelings, requires a capacity for effective grieving. However, to be able to mourn, one has to have available the adult-type affects that are precisely what (by definition) the alexithymic patients are lacking. In addition, the "operative thinking" characteristic of alexithymia interferes further with the capacity for symbolization, transference elaboration, and achievement of changes and sublimations. Finally, one must have good affect tolerance (Krystal 1975*a*) to be able to carry out the process of mourning without it snowballing into a maladaptive state of depression. In fact, the chronic depressive state in which these survivors live can be defined by the mourning that needs to be accomplished but is precluded. These patients keep berating and accusing themselves and revealing a low opinion of themselves, yet they never lower their high self-expectations. The belated discovery of their anhedonia is the last blow, one that causes bitter rejection of their lifelong self-reparative efforts because they have failed to produce the yearned-for pleasure and well-being. The feeling of depression results from the failure to produce gratification. These patients also face the tragic choice of continuing the "hate addiction" (Hoppe 1962) or of turning against themselves in contempt for having missed the point of life.*

A common finding in working with survivors of the Holocaust was that even when alexithymia and impairment in affect tolerance were relatively absent, there was a limit to how much the survivors could absorb through grieving and the degree to which they could achieve integrity and good-natured acceptance of the past. There seems to be an absolute limit to how much an individual is able to give up through grieving. The limitation is twofold. First, a person can grieve over only so much *at one time*. For instance, in the Coconut Grove disaster (Lindemann 1944), individuals who were severely burned and who lost a spouse at the same time were not able to deal with the object loss for quite some time while they were attending to their corporeal losses. Second, there is an absolute or lifetime limit to what individuals can absorb either in terms of loss or of accepting negative qualities in themselves.

There are both qualitative and quantitative limitations on what can be dealt with through mourning. The quantity or quality of losses may be beyond the individual's capacity to integrate, as in the case of the Holocaust when one's entire people and civilization perished. Danieli (1981*a*) points out the difference it makes that the survivors of the Holocaust are reacting to the *murder* rather than the natural demise of their relatives. Their reaction is further compounded by feelings about being abandoned by their nation and fellow citizens and about the world's tacit compliance with Hitler's program, some of which may be unbearable in and of themselves. During the Holocaust, the "final solution" was preceded by years of perfidious abuse and degradation, mass robbery, isolation, and deprivation of the minimal essential of dignity and even of cleanliness. The survivors of defeat and humiliation have a multitude of unbearably painful emotions to face before the question of mastery or integration of their past can ever be possible.

But even if we were to discount these difficulties, whose enumeration

---

*The recent discovery of a whole system of neurotransmitters related to hedonic regulation opens some hope for future relief of the problems of anhedonia of old age. Already there are indications that cannabinoids selectively and directly stimulate the pleasure centers of the brain (Heath 1977). This suggests that anhedonia in old age should be a direct indication for the medical prescribing of cannabis—constituting a third exception to the proscription of this substance by the Federal Controlled Substances Act (in addition to glaucoma and cancer chemotherapy).

could fill volumes, we still come back to the simple, basic fact that there are limitations to the kinds of losses an individual may be able to deal with through mourning. Parents' loss of a child is an example in which the parents may not be capable of completing the process of mourning, and various forms of denial, idealization, and introject "walling off" may become necessary. As example of a negative quality within an individual that cannot be accepted but must be compensated for is found in Conrad's (1900) story of *Lord Jim:* The hero has to sacrifice his life to show that he is not, after all, a coward.

In addition, the survivor of a genocidal Holocaust stands the risk of polarizing the object and self-representations into victim and perpetrators. The anhedonia and alexithymia propel the survivor to continue to experience him- or herself as the victim, and with this comes the longing to change places with the oppressor. But the identification with the aggressor must remain unconscious or else it will flood the self-representation with psychotic rage. This unsolvable dilemma was well portrayed by Robert Shaw (1967) in his novel *The Man in the Glass Booth*. The story, which was subsequently turned into a play and movie, involves a spectacularly successful but very unhappy and unstable survivor. His identity remains in question: Is this Goldman, the former prisoner, or his cousin SS Colonel Dorff of the *Einsatz* (mass-murder) commandos and death camps? The Jewish community in Montreal became sharply divided over staging the play. Two survivors consulted during rehearsals felt that the play was anti-Semitic and seemed to say that "there is no blame, no culpability and no guilt for the Nazis and their murderous action" (Rudin 1975). These survivors and Rabbi Rudin, who described the incident (1974), missed the opportunity for self-integration that the play offers. In commenting on the theme of the play (Krystal 1975*b*), I pointed out that the failure to own up to our own memories, regardless of how painful they are, leaves us in the state of "hate addiction." Recently, the *Detroit Jewish News* (November 21, 1980) carried an article about a forthcoming talk by a Holocaust survivor to a women's group; its theme was "never forgive and never forget" (p. 42).

In Dr. Danieli's discussion of this paper (see pp. 191–210), she explains that it may be just too painful for the individuals who were immersed in the horrors of the Holocaust to accomplish integration. She points out that the world at large has as yet shown no capacity for integrating Auschwitz. Indeed, her observation is nicely confirmed by the public reaction to the plays of Arthur Miller in which he poses this challenge. Since *After the Fall* (1964), Miller has written two other plays—*Incident in Vichy* (1965) and *Creation of the World and Other Matters* (1973)—and each time the theme of aggression in each person's life has been ignored. His latest effort to get beyond the polarization into images of "monster" and "victim" was the screenplay for the CBS production *Playing for Time* (presented October 1, 1980). To the extent that anyone noticed that Miller made Dr. Mengele and an SS woman somewhat "human" and a character representing a Zionist somewhat ridiculous, the observations were received incredulously with pain and indignation by the survivors. But most people missed the issue of self-insight and the need to overcome splitting, with its concomitant idealization and vilification. Hardly anyone sensed the opportunity to recognize the humanity of all involved.

Paradoxically, although it may be painful and difficult for an individual who has endured serious psychic traumatization to achieve intrapsychic integration, this is what the survivor needs most of all. One of the most devastating aftereffects of trauma is the widespread use of repression, denial, and psychic splitting. Much of the psychic representation of the "enemy" or "oppressor" or even of impersonal elements such as "fate" and of clearly personal attributes like one's own emotions come to be experienced as outside the self-representation. *Thus the posttraumatic state is characterized by an impoverishment of the areas of the mind to which the "I" feeling of self-sameness is extended, and a hypertrophy of the "not-I" alienated areas*. The symptoms of "pseudophobia," fear of one's dreams and of one's own emotions, are all the result of this posttraumatic depletion of the consciously recognized spheres of selfhood.

The issue of moral and ethical judgment is often substituted for self-healing. It seems virtuous to "feed" righteous indignation and treasonous to stop the rage. In this respect, it is useful to consider that hate, anger, guilt, and depression are forms of pain. It is a masochistic perversion for survivors to promote the continuation of these pains within themselves. Rather, to the extent possible, they should soothe themselves and gain peace through self-acceptance.

Lifton (1979) has addressed himself to the issue of posttraumatic integration, but has focused on the confrontation with death rather than on the reaction to the loss of love objects. As he sees it, "Death tests everyone's integrity; the dying person's immediate survivors, and the attending healers contribute to a collective psychic constellation within which issues of continuity, discontinuity, self-completion and disintegration are addressed" (p. 109). Emphasizing the confrontation with "absurd" death—mass destruction—leads Lifton to understand that the survivors' "life review" is derailed by "psychic numbing, desymbolization, deformation" or "decentralization" (p. 69), and an inability to restore a feeling of intimacy because of a suspicion of "counterfeit nurturance." In effect, then, Lifton's observations coincide with the view expressed in this paper that the difficulties which become conspicuous in the survivors' old age may be considered a paradigm of many of the major difficulties found in the attempt at posttraumatic self-healing and mastery of intrapsychic injuries. The main point is that since mourning and grieving work requires the availability of adult-type affects, alexithymia becomes a specific obstacle, but by no means the only one found under these circumstances.

Survivors of the Holocaust age early and have higher than average rates of early death from all causes (Eitinger and Strøm 1973). This early loss of vitality should not be viewed as separate from the alexithymia or anhedonia. Rado (1969) had long stressed the importance of the "pleasure economy." He believed that a "deficiency in welfare emotions (joy, pleasure, happiness, love, affection, etc.) alters every operation of the integrative apparatus. No phase of life, no area of behavior remains unaffected" (p. 24). My observations and the findings of Eitinger (1980) prove the validity of Rado's ideas. Survivors manifest a combination of anhedonia, special guilt, quite possibly an attachment to pain (Valenstein 1973), and a fear of joy and happiness. Psychotherapeutic work with survivors has been ineffective because, in addition, they fear their emotions—they have a posttraumatic impairment of affect tolerance because they experience their own emotions as heralds of trauma (Krystal 1975*a*, 1979). Past that, one encounters the problems of alexithymia. These patients do not *recognize* their emotions because they experience them in an undifferentiated way, poorly verbalized, and because they have poor reflective self-awareness. As a result, they tend to complain of symptoms, such as pain, palpitations, or insomnia, rather than being able to form complete emotions and to recognize them as "feelings." Their tendency is to try to block the distress by the use of medication and to keep "proposing a physical illness" (Balint 1964) instead of utilizing their emotions as signals.

But the underlying problem of depression and guilt still requires integration through mourning, lowering of narcissistic expectations of oneself, and acceptance of the necessity of what happened. For instance, survivors of the Holocaust still suffer from a feeling of shame over the idea that they did not fight back enough. An effort is being made by certain groups on behalf of the Jewish people to create a mythology about the heroic resistance, which is intended to stop the shame. The futility of this effort illustrates the task and challenge of integration in the life of every aging person. Whatever one is ashamed of has to be lovingly accepted as a part of one's life that was unavoidable. Every pain aroused in the process of reviewing one's life as an individual or the history of a group merely marks an area that as yet is deprived of the self-healing application of the feeling of identity, self-sameness, or selfhood. One feels anger, guilt, or shame whenever one is unable (refuses) to accept the necessity and unavoidability of what happened. The trouble is that in this process of reviewing one's life, as the memories are restored to the self-representation and are owned up to (in other words, in the process of the return of the repressed) the individual experiences pain. In fact, Freud was puzzled by just this pain in mourning. Freud (1917) said that he could not explain why mourning was so "extraordinarily painful" *"in terms of economics"* (p. 245, emphasis mine). But in terms of the task that is carried out during senescence, one can see many reasons why mourning must be so painful. For the purposes of our discussion, however, I will only stress one.

The successful completion of mourning and/or the successful integration of the individual's life bring the individual to the position of being able to own up to all of his or her living as his or her own, including the object representations. This state gives the individual a chance to discover that in ordinary living we maintain our object representations in a type of *repression through externalization* (Krystal, 1974, 1978*a*). That is, we maintain our mental representation of them in a "nonself" status. Thus, if we mourn to the point of owning up to the self-sameness of our object representations, there is a type of return of the repressed. The illusion of externality that was maintained toward our object representations achieved a kind of analgesia, and when self-integration is achieved, this analgesia wears off. The motivation for the externalization lies in dealing with infantile aggression. I believe that infantile trauma and the resulting ambivalence lead to a distortion of the self-representation so that vital and affective aspects of oneself are attributed to the object representation, which is rigidly "walled-off"—thus rendering one's capabilities for self-care functionally inaccessible (Krystal 1978*a*).

Because mourning and integration must include affective components (a situation that parallels Freud's discovery [Freud and Breuer 1893] that recollection did not do anything for hysteria if it was devoid of emotions), affect tolerance is a major issue. That is also the reason why normal, adult-type, mostly cognitive and signallike affects are necessary for the completion of the process of mourning. Otherwise, in the presence of alexithymia, the undifferentiated, mostly somatic, unverbalized affect responses are so intense, threatening, and painful that one must ward them off by deadening oneself or abort the process by escaping into denial.

Another, clearly related subject is religiousness. The French have a proverb that when the Devil gets old, he becomes pious. Desperate attempts are made by many survivors to restore and maintain their faith in God. However, since problems of aggression and the destruction of basic trust that resulted from the events of the Holocaust (Krystal 1978*b*) make true faith and trust in the benevolence of an omnipotent God impossible, the yearning for the comfort of religion only results in a piling up of rituals. People who are unable to complete the process of mourning and people troubled with their religious ambivalence have another tendency in common—the building of monumental and ecclesiastic edifices—which can be observed in the survivor group.

In addition, the survivor has to maintain intrapsychic barriers against the ambivalence, doubts, guilt, and rage. A widespread constriction of fantasy results, in both actual imagination and transference reactions (Krystal 1979).

As I have followed a large number of survivors of the Holocaust who are *not* in psychotherapy, I have been impressed with the point that in old age one is confronted with certain choices and tasks identical to those offered in analytic treatment. As preoccupation with work and gratification of the senses diminishes, the mind's activities turn inward and toward the past. "Your old men shall dream dreams, your young men shall see visions," said the prophet (Joel 3:1). These dreams may be a renewal of childhood fantasizing—we see this in the current tendency to create a mythology among survivors of the Holocaust. The choices are integration or denial, self-acceptance or repression and depletion.

The survivors do not necessarily consciously recognize or complain of their depression. More commonly, they handle their problems by constriction of interest, by avoidance of both pleasure and excitement. This psychic depletion state is often preceded by a lifelong avoidance of all excitement. The dread of their own affects extends from anxiety to any sense of aliveness. At last the diminution in the tonic aspect of affect produces a retardation. The retardation may affect the psychomotor sphere primarily, but more commonly results in an alteration in life-preserving functions, such as immune responses or other health-maintaining processes. A rapidly accumulating body of evidence indicates that despair represents a most important predisposition for illness (see Achterberg, Simonton, and Simonton-Matthews 1976; Holden 1978; Giovacchini and Muslin 1965; Reiser 1975).

In conclusion, I have to admit that my attempts to engage aging survivors of the Holocaust in psychoanalytic psychotherapy have been for the most part unsuccessful. I have been able to take a variety of supportive measures that make their life more bearable. Among these, improving the "management," that is, acceptance, of their distressing affective states has been most often necessary. But in regard to the survivors' capacity to work-through their losses and problems of guilt and shame in order to accomplish integrity in aging, I have always run into the problem of the necessity for effective grieving (Wetmore 1963). Effective grieving requires total emotional responses, which are felt and recognized as such.

Beyond being unable to complete mourning and achieve integration, alexithymic individuals become early prey to that devastating preoccupation of old age: "Who loves me? Who *cares* if I live?" The problem is particularly difficult for these individuals because of their regression in affect—they do not experience love, nor do they have the kind of empathy that would permit them to sense their object's affection for them. One has to feel love to be able to believe in its existence. Most of all, one has to feel love to be able to accept one's own self and one's own past. Thus, the ideal for the Holocaust survivor, as for any other aging person, is summed up by Dorsey (1976):

> I must discipline my self to be able to love difficulty in order to achieve every access of my life appreciation. There can be nothing for me to resist (be unwilling to live lovingly) except difficult self-consciousness. . . . Psychoanalytic psychotherapy is the process of working up the accessible self love required to observe "It is I" of whatever before I could observe only "It is not I" [p. 457].

REFERENCES

Achterberg, J.; Simonton, C.; and Simonton-Matthews, S. 1976. *Stress, Psychological Factors and Cancer*. Fort Worth, Tex.: New Medicine Press.

Balint, M. 1964. *The Doctor, His Patient and the Illness*. New York: International Universities Press.

Camus, A. 1946. *The Stranger*. New York: Knopf.

Cannon, W. B. 1942. "Voodoo Deaths." *American Anthropologist*. 44:169–181.
Catell, R. B. 1935. "Perseveration and Personality: Some Experiments and a Hypothesis." *Journal of Mental Science* 81:115–167.
Chodoff, P. 1980. "Psychotherapy with the Survivor." In *Survivors, Victims and Perpetrators*, ed. J. Dimsdale, pp. 205–218. Washington, D.C.: Hemisphere.
Conrad, J. 1900. *Lord Jim*. New York: Dell (1961).
Danieli, Y. 1981a. "Countertransference in the Treatment and Study of Nazi Holocaust Survivors and Their Children." *Victimology: An Int. J.* 5:45–53.
———. 1981b. "Differing Adaptational Styles in Families of Survivors of the Nazi Holocaust: Some Implications for Treatment." *Children Today* 10:34–35.
———. 1981c. "Families of Survivors of the Nazi Holocaust: Some Short- and Long-Term Effects. In *Stress and Anxiety*, vol. 8. *Psychological Stress and Adjustment in Time of War and Peace*, ed. C. D. Spielberger. I. G. Sarason, N. Milgram, pp. 405–421, New York: McGraw-Hill.
Dorsey, J. M. 1976. "The Science of the Senescent Process." In *Selected Essays*, pp. 450–486. Detroit: Center for Health Education.
Eitinger, L. 1980. "The Concentration Camp Syndrome and Its Late Sequelae." In *Survivors, Victims and Perpetrators*, ed. J. Dimsdale, pp. 127–162. Washington, D.C.: Hemisphere.
——— and Strøm, A. 1973. *Mortality and Morbidity of Excessive Stress*. New York: Humanities Press.
Erikson, E. H. 1959. "Identity and the Life Cycle." *Psychological Issues* 1. New York: International Universities Press.
Freud, S. 1917. "Mourning and Melancholia." *Standard Edition*, 14:237–258. London: Hogarth Press, 1957.
——— and Breuer, J. 1893. "On the Psychical Mechanism of Hysterical Phenomena: Preliminary Communication." *Standard Edition*, 2:1–18. London: Hogarth Press, 1955.
Freyberger, H. 1977. "Supportive Psychotherapeutic Technique in Primary and Secondary Alexithymia." *Psychother. Psychosom.*, 28:337–342.
Giovacchini, P. L., and Muslin, H. 1965. "Ego Equilibrium and Cancer of the Breast." *Psychomatic Medicine* 27:524–532.
Greenson, R. R. 1949. "The Psychology of Apathy." *Psychoanalytic Quarterly* 18:290–302.
Health, R. G. 1977. "Modulation of Emotion with a Brain Pacemaker. *Journal of Nervous and Mental Disease* 165:300–317.
Heiberg, A., and Heiberg, A. 1977. "Alexithymia an Inherited Trait? *Psychother. Psychosom*. 28:221–225.
Holden, C. 1978. "Cancer and the Mind: How Are They Connected?" *Science* 200:1363–1369.
Hoppe, K. 1962. "Persecution, Depression and Aggression." *Bulletin of the Menninger Clinic* 26:195–203.
Klein, G. S. 1976. *Theory of Psychoanalysis*. New York: International Universities Press.

Krystal, H. 1962. "The Opiate-Withdrawal Syndrome as a State of Stress." *Psychiatric Quarterly* 36 (suppl.) 53–65.

———. 1968. *Massive Psychic Trauma.* New York: International Universities Press.

———. 1970. "Trauma and the Stimulus Barrier." Paper presented at the annual meeting of the Psychoanalytic Association, San Francisco.

———. 1971. "Trauma: Consideration of Severity and Chronicity." In *Psychic Traumatization,* ed. H. Krystal and W. Niederland, pp. 11–28. Boston: Little, Brown.

———. 1974. "The Genetic Development of Affects and Affect Regression." *Annual of Psychoanalysis* 2:98–126. New York: International Universities Press.

———. 1975*a*. "Affect Tolerance." *Annual of Psychoanalysis* 3:179–219. New York: International Universities Press.

———. 1975*b*. Letter to the editor, *Midstream,* 29:3–4.

———. 1978*a*. "Self-Representation and the Capacity for Self-Care." *Annual of Psychoanalysis* 6:209–246. New York: International Universities Press.

———. 1978*b*. "Trauma and Affects." *Psychoanalytic Study of the Child* 33:81–116. New Haven, Conn.: Yale University Press.

———. 1979. "Alexithymia and Psychotherapy." *American Journal of Psychotherapy,* 33:17–31.

———. 1981. "The Hedonic Element in Affectivity." *Annual of Psychoanalysis* 9:93–113. New York: International Universities Press.

——— and Niederland, W. 1968. "Clinical Observations on the Survivor Syndrome." In *Massive Psychic Trauma,* ed. H. Krystal, pp. 327–348. New York: International Universities Press.

——— and Raskin, H. A. 1970. *Drug Dependence: Aspects of Ego Function.* Detroit: Wayne State University Press.

Lifton, R. J. 1967. *Death in Life: Survivors of Hiroshima.* New York: Random House.

———. 1976. *The Life of the Self.* New York: Touchstone Books.

———. 1979. *The Broken Connection: On Death and the Continuity of Life.* New York: Simon & Schuster.

Lindemann, E. 1944. "Symptomatology and Management of Acute Grief." *American Journal of Psychiatry* 101:141–149.

Marty, P., and de M'Uzan, M. 1963. "La 'pensée opératoire.' " *Revue Française de Psychanalyse* 527:1345–1356.

Meehl, P. E. 1975. "Hedonic Capacity: Some Conjectures." *Bulletin of the Menninger Clinic* 30:295–307.

———. Likken, D.; Schafield, W.; and Pellegen, L. 1971. "Recaptured Item Technique (RIT): A Method for Reducing Somewhat the Subjective Element in Factor Naming." *J. Exp. Res. Pers.* 5:171–190.

Miller, A. 1964. *After the Fall.* New York: Viking Press.

———. 1965. *Incident in Vichy*. New York: Viking Press.

———. 1973. *The Creation of the World and Other Matters*. New York: Viking Press.

Minkowski, E. 1946. "L'anastesie affective." *Ann. Medico-psychol.* 104:8–13.

Murray, H. A. 1967. *Dead to the World*. In *Essays in Self-Destruction*, ed. E. S. Schneidman, New York: Science House.

Niederland, W. 1961. "The Problem of the Survivor." *Journal of the Hillside Hospital* 10:233–247.

Rado, S. 1969. *Adaptational Psychodynamics: Motivation and Control*, ed. J. Jameson and H. Klein. New York: Science House.

Reiser, M. F. 1975. "Changing Theoretical Concepts in Psychosomatic Medicine." In *American Handbook of Psychiatry*, vol. 4, ed. S. Arieti, pp. 477–499. 2d ed.; New York: Basic Books.

Rudin, A. J. 1974. "Crisis at the Bronfman Center. 'The Man in the Glass Booth' Controversy." *Midstream*, no. 10, 48–58.

———. 1975. Letter to the editor, *Midstream*, 29:4–5.

Seligman, M. E. P. 1975. *Helplessness*. San Francisco: W. H. Freeman.

Shaw, R. 1967. *The Man in the Glass Booth*. London: Chatto & Windus.

Sifneos, P. E. 1967. "Clinical Observations on Some Patients Suffering from a Variety of Psychosomatic Diseases." *Proceedings of the Seventh Conference on Psychosomatic Research*, pp. 1–10. Basel: Karger.

Stern, M. M. 1951. "Pavor nocturnus." *International Journal of Psycho-Analysis* 32:302–309.

Tyhurst, J. S. 1951. "Individual Reactions to Community Disasters." *American Journal of Psychiatry* 107:764–769.

Valenstein, A. 1973. "On Attachment to Painful Feelings and the Negative Therapeutic Reaction." *Psychoanalytic Study of the Child* 28:365–392. New Haven: Yale University Press.

Wallant, E. L. 1962. *The Pawnbroker*. New York: Macfadden.

Wetmore, R. J. 1963. "The Role of Grief in Psychoanalysis." *International Journal of Psychoanalysis*, 44:97–103.

INTRODUCTION

Dr. Terry has worked clinically with survivors for many years. He has written a critical paper arguing against the reflexive usage of the diagnostic entity that has come to be known as the "survivor syndrome." He argues that psychotherapists and others stereotype and label survivors, thereby robbing them of their individuality and dignity. Terry states that the survivor syndrome originated with the first psychiatric "experts," who briefly examined candidates for German restitution. Their lack of objectivity, he argues, suggests that they, more than the survivors, were suffering from "survivor guilt." Terry also emphasizes the unconscious contempt for the victim present in all of us, and the effect this has had on our view of the survivor.

The author further points out that the concentration camp trauma per se does not inevitably lead to psychopathology in the survivor. The more potentially destructive trauma is the loss of loved ones and the inability to fully mourn them. Terry also makes an interesting point on the medical compensation process as a distortion of the therapeutic process.

Finally, an important implication of Terry's paper is his tacit call for a major attitudinal shift on the part of mental health professionals. This would be reflected in a greater willingness to avoid making premature clinical judgments and to remain empathic and self-critical as they enter the survivor's world.

The Damaging Effects of the "Survivor Syndrome"

JACK TERRY

The literature of the Holocaust has become extensive in the past few years, in contrast to the first two decades after the war. The Holocaust has become an increasingly popular and exploited subject: often politicized, commercialized, and trivialized by some, its existence has even been denied by others. Because of its enormity and uniqueness, both its impact and its exploitation have been far-reaching. Even those whose avowed purpose it has been to aid survivors may have been unwitting agents of this exploitation.

In the psychiatric literature on the Holocaust, one is struck by a general lack of objectivity. Perhaps objectivity on the subject is not possible. In general we are accustomed to drawing conclusions from reliable clinical data that usually are obtained from patients in traditional psychoanalysis. Before accepting the conclusions, we tend to assess the material based on the analyzability of the patient and the competence of the analyst. In the case of the Holocaust, however, even usually reputable psychoanalysts who have distinguished themselves in other areas of psychoanalysis have failed to be even minimally objective or "scientific." To be more specific, when a survivor comes for treatment, the "syndrome" is presumed and often insisted upon. For example, on several occasions colleagues have referred survivor patients to me whom they had diagnosed as suffering from the "survivor syndrome" although they had not examined them. Some have even extended this designation to referrals of children of survivors. Patients have also, on initial visits, told me that they had been told that they suffer from "survivor guilt."

Those who have written on the Holocaust extensively, and relatively early, are often referred to as "pioneers" or "experts." Along with these designations comes a certain authority—their statements on the subject are not questioned and are frequently quoted as fact even when their original views were tentative. Their writings are based on a large number of brief interviews of those survivors who came to be examined for restitution compensation from the German government. None of these survivors was in psychoanalysis (they were prejudged to be too damaged), and few were in psychotherapy before the "survivor syndrome" was established as an entity in the literature. In order to receive restitution compensation, a survivor had to convince the Germans that his symptoms were directly related to the suffering sustained in, or aggravated by, the Holocaust. It is unfortunate that a person's having spent time in concentration camps was not considered to be sufficient reason for him to "deserve" compensation and that proof of impairment of physical or mental efficiency was and still remains a requirement.

The American psychiatrists who interviewed these survivors were usually German-speakers who had themselves escaped (in the nick of time) from being incarcerated in concentration camps, and who had left members of their families, relatives, or friends behind. It therefore stands to reason that it would be these individuals who were most likely to suffer from so-called survivor guilt and not the ones who had paid so dearly for their survival during their years in concentration camps. For the psychiatrists, not to recommend restitution money would be an open expression of hostility toward the survivor and would have left the psychiatrist open to being identified with the Nazi aggressor. The thrust, therefore, was more toward helping the victims of persecution obtain compensation than toward learning about *ourselves;* i.e., the lessons of the Holocaust.

In any psychiatric-forensic evaluation there are "experts" on both sides, and, of course, the German government had its share. Frequently these experts did not acknowledge a causal relationship of any symptoms with the atrocities that had been suffered, and compensation was denied. They adhered to the theory of constitutional etiology.* In contrast, the view of those who supported compensation for the survivors was expressed by Niederland (1968, pp. 11–12):

> In view of such negative attitudes on the part of the so-called experts (who, it must be added, are not always German physicians) it appears essential to familiarize ourselves at least phenomenologically with those psychiatric disorders which can be found with some regularity

*The belief that mental disturbances are caused by hereditary factors (eds.).

in a number of surviving victims. An attempt at clarification is the more indicated since much psychiatric testimony is wasted, or sometimes used against the legitimate compensation claims of the victim, because it trails off in abstract discussion of forensically irrelevant comments such as *anlage,* constitutional components, infantile sexuality or the like, instead of on the severely traumatizing experiences suffered by the claimant during the years of persecution. As important as early developmental factors for the pathogenetic manifestations of neurotic and psychotic conditions are, they can never be the sole consideration in the psychiatric evaluation of mental disorders in concentration-camp survivors. Even reports from competent specialists or reputable psychiatric institutions sometimes contain only a sentence or two on the persecution experiences of such patients, but they hardly ever fail to describe in detail certain features of their sexual behavior, family difficulties and other problems.

Dr. Niederland points out the skewed and prejudiced views on the part of the so-called experts appointed by the German government. This frequently resulted in denial of reparations for the victims. However, great damage to the victims has also resulted from the skewed data presented by the experts sympathetic to the victims. An example is in Monograph V of the Kris Study Group of the New York Psychoanalytic Institute (Waldhorn and Fine, 1974, p. 7):

> Dr. William G. Niederland, together with Dr. Martin Wangh, discussed some of the findings derived from their work with survivors of Nazi concentration camps. Niederland had seen hundreds of such patients over a 15 year period, *although never in analysis,* and had found a symptom picture displayed with such great regularity that the term "survivor syndrome" was coined to refer to it. *It is important to note that this syndrome was present regardless of the premorbid personality of the patient, and did not seem to be significantly influenced by his previous background and individual history. Without exception, all people exposed to the concentration camp experiences showed marked after-effects of the traumatic experiences, the intensity of which was so great that none escaped without serious personality damage* [emphasis added]. . . .

The above, written by well-respected analysts writing in a highly regarded publication, is obviously the opposite view of that taken by the German government's physicians. The Kris Study Group presented analytic case material followed by discussions. Notably, however, they concluded that "no external event could be clearly independent of prior experience in the process of producing a psychic illness." Therefore, the important central point emerging from the study was that "a traumatic experience could only be understood in terms of the whole context of the individual's previous history and his ego and libidinal development at the time of the experience." Thus, it appears that the findings presented by Drs. Niederland and Wangh stand apart from the rest of the study and seem to have been greatly influenced by the desire to help the victims receive compensation.

Compensation for survivors of Nazi concentration camps is also the subject of a paper by Eissler (1967). He criticizes the generalizations, and cites vignettes of physicians appointed by the German Consulate who repeatedly gave their "expert" opinion that the victims' pathology was unconnected to the trauma of their persecution. Eissler writes of the injustice and asks:

> . . . what [motives do] these physicians have for continuing to act as experts in spite of their knowing that, if they refused and let others write opinions instead, the claimants would have a far better chance of obtaining compensation. What can be the reason for their open or concealed hostility against those who have had to bear great suffering?

He answers his own question:

> One major reason has to do with the contempt that man still tends to feel for the humiliated, for those who have had to submit to physical punishment, suffering, and torture. . . .
>
> The archaic contempt, scorn, or spite for the sufferer is rather complex. It is connected with the whole problem of sadomasochism and the reaction to various shades of narcissism. . . . The persecuted has been utterly depleted of any narcissistic cathexes. During his persecution, nothing belonged to him any longer—not even his own body. No decision was left to him; he was reduced to sheer nothingness. . . . The narcissism of the persecuted was, therefore, reduced to zero. . . . As impressive as the tragic hero who is punished for a

> narcissistic misdeed, *just as contemptible does the survivor seem to appear to the unconscious* [emphasis added]. He does not even have a narcissistic crime to his credit, one that would account for his suffering.

Eissler writes that he is

> compelled to draw the conclusion that among the many causes for hostility towards victims of persecution, regression to the pagan feeling of contempt for those who are suffering physically must be included. And it may well be the most insidious and most potent cause of all. Why some act out this contempt, while others are capable of repressing it, I do not know; but my belief is that *with few exceptions the feeling of contempt for suffering is something of a universal reaction very much alive in most all of us* [emphasis added].

Is this contempt present even in those who are seemingly sympathetic toward the victims of persecution? In my judgment the answer is yes. The survivor has been avoided, blamed, "syndromized," exploited, and rarely understood, even by those who profess to support his best interests. I suggest that the unconscious contempt for the survivor plays a role in generalizations and classifications such as the "survivor syndrome."

The Nazis did not distinguish among individuals who were Jews. Similarly, the "syndrome" does not distinguish among individuals who are survivors. In the ghettos and in the concentration camps, the survivor was classified by having to wear a yellow star, an arm band, and a tattooed number.

Generalizations (made by Dr. Niederland in the previously mentioned Kris Study Group monograph, Waldhorn and Fine 1974, p. 9) such as "the nature of the pretraumatic personality had no influence on the symptomatic outcome" and "None were able to escape the traumatic impact" are not only incorrect, but also deprive the individual of his individuality. One meets people out of those hells who survived and who have a dignity and serenity and even a hope far beyond the average. They carried something inside them that remained undamaged. That is not to say that they were not affected by what they endured and witnessed. The effect has given many a unique knowledge and a keen appreciation for freedom and for life that few others possess. In short, not everything in everyone was damaged.* The pretraumatic personality had a great influence on the individual's reaction to the trauma; the degree of libidinal and ego and superego development played a great ròle. An external experience cannot be independent of one's personal history if it is to have an effect.

Must external trauma be pathogenic? The traumatic and the pathogenic are frequently confused by observers. Only through analysis is it possible to trace which event or aspect of an event is responsible for the pathogenic process. What is frequently seen by the observer of an event or events as traumatic often turns out not to be so. Bergen (1958) reports the analysis of a girl, Ellen, whose mother was murdered by her father in Ellen's presence. As her father inflicted four serious and fatal chest wounds, her mother yelled out to Ellen: "Get out of here." In the course of the analysis it was established that the outstanding traumatic effect was not the murder but rather her mother's yelling "Get out of here," which was experienced by the child as being excluded and rejected.

Gyomroi (1963) reports on the analysis of Elizabeth, a young concentration camp victim. In her case, too, the pathogenic factor seemed to have been not the horror of the camp but rather the object losses before object constancy was achieved.

According to A. Freud (1958, p. 114):

> . . .we do not know which aspect or element of a given experience will be selected for cathexis and emotional involvement.
>
> The latter statement is borne out by our analysis of children who have been subjected to war and concentration-camp experiences. Where we expected to unearth buried memories of death, destruction, violence, hatred, etc., we found usually the traces of separations, motor restrictions, deprivation (of toys, pleasures), together with all the usual emotional upsets which are inseparable from any child's life. I was impressed in this respect by the story of a boy who, at four and a half years, had escaped with his family from enemy-

*Recent research supports these observations. See, for example, S. Moskowitz's study, *Love Despite Hate: Child Survivors of the Holocaust and Their Adult Lives,* (New York: Schocken, 1983), in which she interviewed twenty-four child survivors, including the six who were treated by Anna Freud and Sophie Dann—the Bulldogs Bank Children. Moskowitz concluded: "For, despite the persistance of problems and the ashes of the past, what we note . . . are endurance, resilience and great individual adaptability." Furthermore, "contrary to previously accepted notions, we learn powerfully from their lives that life long emotional disability does not automatically follow early trauma, even such devastating pervasive trauma as experienced here" (p. 237) (eds.).

occupied territory. A subsequent analysis showed which element of the experience had been singled out for traumatic value: he had suffered a severe shock from the fact that the invaders had deprived his father of his car. This, to him, meant that the father had been robbed of his potency. Besides this all-important oedipal experience, everything else (loss of home, security, friends) paled into insignificance.

Similarly, two examples from my analytic practice illustrate the same point. The patients had survived Auschwitz and Stutthof concentration camps, respectively, and both had endured the worst those camps stand for. They both were the sole survivors in their families, and both spoke freely of the objective realities of the camps. However, the central organizing factors in their pathology were not the horrors they had witnessed and endured but rather their intense repressed conflicts with their fathers. For example, one patient recovered a memory from the winter of 1940 when, as a young boy of ten in Poland, he accompanied his father on a very cold day to help unload and receive for resettlement a transport of Jews from Germany. At the dinner table that Friday night he saw his father with tears in his eyes saying with resignation in his voice: "I will now [at age forty-four] consider myself seventy years old and that my life is at its end." It was not until his analysis that the patient realized the full impact this statement had had on him. He said, "I was only ten years old, and had not yet started to live." His intense repressed fury toward his father for not considering him and his resultant feeling of abandonment at a time like this was a more significant traumatic experience than were the objective realities of the camps.

The other patient until his analysis could not talk about his father or forgive him, since although he had had the means and opportunities to take his family out of Poland, he had failed to do so. When the war broke out, the patient's father tried to save his business; he chose to stay with his mother in another town, leaving his wife, the patient, and his sister alone. He never made an effort to reunite the family. "It was like a commanding officer abandoning his troops on the front line." The patient's rage toward his father because of this abandonment ultimately led to his hostile identification with him and his subsequent acting this out by ignoring his own little son. In working through the various experiences, nothing was as painful, he stated, as being so treated by his own father.

Why aren't such sources of individual pathology usually considered? Why is it assumed that the pathology was inevitably caused solely by the concentration camp experience? Many important questions are never asked. We should ask such pertinent questions as: What is an individual's capacity to adapt to a totally irrational environment? How do individuals' reactions vary under extreme and prolonged stress? On what is the individual's capacity to overcome trauma based?

I believe that these questions have not been considered because of the preoccupation with restitution, the need to prove that the survivor's symptomatology was not caused by constitutional factors (*anlagebedingt*), and above all, the unconscious problem(s) of the psychiatrist. Sterba (1968, p. 88) summarized this when he said:

> I'm very deeply impressed, in a two-fold way: first, by the immense human misery which has been demonstrated; and secondly by *the difficulties in trying to look at it objectively. Such studies are so difficult, that they must require a long period of self-training in order not to become involved emotionally in one countertransference or another* [emphasis added], and in outcries of indignation of such mistreatment of human beings. I would like to express my admiration for the people who can do this work, and am afraid that their number will always be very small.

I suggest that most, if not all, psychiatrists were not able to overcome the difficulties of emotional involvement, lack of objectivity, and countertransference. More than a long period of self-training is needed. Even a personal analysis is in most cases not sufficient. To be objective with such patients requires an unusual individual, an individual who, above all else, does not suffer from guilt for either having escaped and survived or for not having done anything but remain silent. It is also impossible not to become emotionally involved, especially if the therapist is to play a role in the question of restitution.

It has been my experience in treating survivors who receive compensation that they frequently have unconscious needs as well as a conscious need to remain "damaged," so that their compensation will not be terminated. The treating physician is often asked to write to the German government in such a way as not to jeopardize the patient's 25 or 40 percent disability. Such a collaboration in maintaining the survivor's pathology is an additional obstacle to his possible recovery. I question why the survivor is asked to prove that he is "damaged" in order to receive compensation. It is another way of designating him as an *untermensch* even now.

The restitution compensation should originally have been entirely a legal matter between victim and victimizer and should have been handled entirely by the legal and not the psychiatric profession.

Why such preoccupation with compensation? What effect has the process of trying to get compensation had on the survivor? What effect has it had on the physician? The answers would require a separate essay. However, one major effect is that it diverts attention from the by now almost chronic despair experienced by many victims, a despair that has resulted in a number of suicides and in many persons who regretted having survived. Many experts formulated the reasons for this despair as "survivor's guilt." Had the physicians listened carefully, they would have heard that this despair stemmed from the survivors' disappointment with the way they were received and not from guilt for having survived. After the liberation they were faced with the realization that so few people cared about their plight or understood them.

Kitty Hart, a survivor, expressed this when she said:

> The most traumatic time was after the war. My fellow Jews did not want to know about our experience in the concentration camps because it made them uncomfortable. My English relatives forbade me to speak of it. One has more anger towards one's own people because one expects them to understand. I've tried to forgive, but it's hard not to feel betrayal. ("Kitty—Return to Auschwitz," Public Broadcasting System documentary, Feb. 4, 1981.)

The survivor's feeling of betrayal stems from the other person's lack of understanding and empathy for his need to tell of his experience. He was discouraged from talking about it in various ways, but was also blamed for not talking. The discomfort of the listener can be partly explained by the activation of guilt for having remained passive and silent. On an unconscious level the survivor perceives the therapist's uneasiness as betrayal.

This sentiment has been expressed in a variety of ways by nearly all of my patients in psychoanalysis or in intensive psychotherapy. They have complained that those they talked to would frequently show their discomfort with tears or a variety of facial expressions. Some would tell them: "Forget the past, don't think or speak of it any more." One patient in analysis recalled that his mother had written letters to her sister in South America; the patient wanted them, as he was actively mourning her death after thirty years and wanted something tangible of hers. His aunt tried to discourage him and only reluctantly sent the letters. One patient asked his uncle why he and other Jews in this country didn't protest more vigorously, go on hunger strikes, or demonstrate. His uncle responded with accusations of his own: "Why did so many of you go to your death like sheep? Why didn't you fight? You had nothing to lose, why didn't you commit suicide?" These survivors have been made to feel that they were responsible for what they went through—these are unmistakable and open expressions of contempt for the survivor. By far more devastating were the more subtle expressions and unconscious expressions of contempt. For these patients, the free world became another prison with invisible barbed wire erected by a profound lack of understanding. They isolated themselves, chose their own kind, and often became depressed, suspicious, and distrusting, stating: "You can't possibly understand me—there is always going to be an 'us' and a 'you.' You can never know what we know. We saw how thin the veneer of civilization is and how easily it is dissolved." Another patient stated: "I've seen you naked: I've seen what human beings are capable of. I saw my 'respected' rabbi shave his beard and collaborate with the Germans. When hostages were taken to be executed, all previously repected people pushed others in front of them."

These individuals had a great deal to teach us, and they wanted to share it with us, but we missed the opportunity. I think, because they made us feel guilty and ashamed, and because we turned them off and turned them away with our pity, hostility, and contempt, that the gap has remained unbridgeable. They were treated like poor sick relatives by our giving them handouts (compensation?). This attitude confirmed their reason for despair. However, one cannot even generalize in the case of this despair, even though it was not an uncommon occurrence. There were many survivors who, because of a combination of factors, were able to avoid falling into states of despair, depression, and other pathologic manifestation. These survivors were relatively young at the end of the war, in their mid-adolescence, and they had had a fairly normal prewar adjustment. They came from families in which education and intellect were highly regarded. Because of their age, they could more easily resume their interrupted education. Furthermore, on coming to this country, they were received by loving relatives or even strangers who were truly interested in them and were not disturbed by the survivor's grief. The survivor felt understood and cared for. Only in this type of receptive environment could the survivors begin to mourn their losses. Meerloo (1968, p. 74) states:

> I was amazed and surprised to hear from people who had gone through the horrors of concentration camps that their greatest com-

> plaint was that they had not been *permitted* to mourn their dead, those they had lost in these very camps. *Not the torture, not the famine, not the humiliation kept them down* now, but this lack of cathartic ceremonial [Emphasis added]. . . .

Indeed, in the treatment of survivors one rarely hears from them of the aftereffects of torture, starvation, humiliation, or any other inhuman condition as contributing to their symptoms. In fact, the aftereffects of these are frequently expressed as a hyperawareness of the freedom and some of the physical comforts they now enjoy.

The most profound effect of the Holocaust on those who survived invariably revolves around the loss of libidinal objects. In concentration camps, mourning would have been impossible even if it had been permitted. Grief in itself threatens the integrity of the ego, and under circumstances in which the intensity of the affect is too great or the ego has been so weakened—both of which were the case in the Holocaust—mourning cannot take place. Thus, the attachment to the lost objects remains unresolved. Even under average conditions, I doubt if mourning is ever complete. It certainly is not in the case of a parent for a child.

Freud, for example, in his letter to Binswanger (1957) on the anniversary of Freud's daughter's thirty-sixth birthday, wrote:

> We know that the acute grief we feel after a loss will come to an end, but that we will remain inconsolable, and will never find a substitute. Everything that comes to take the place of the lost object, even if it fills it completely, nevertheless remains something different.

In a subsequent letter to Binswanger, Freud refers to this daughter's son, who died of military tuberculosis. He writes:

> To me this child has taken the place of all my children and other grandchildren, and since then, since Heinele's death, I don't care for my grandchildren anymore, but find no joy in life either. This is also the secret of my indifference—it was called courage—toward the danger to my own life.

In the case of survivors, numerous obstacles interfered with the mourning process. Death was in most cases catastrophic, brutal, and not expected. Frequently death was presumed but most often not definitely confirmed. There were no identifiable burial places, no dates of death. This leads to one form of pathological mourning in which the person strives to recover the lost object, especially when the individual is one in whom self and object are poorly differentiated. The survivor's mourning extended beyond the objects; he also had to mourn his past and his external world, which no longer existed and to which he could not return. He had to establish new links to a new external world.

The degree of maturity of the psychic apparatus of the mourner determines the capacity for mourning. Ego defects, distortions, or arrests make healthy mourning impossible. Here, the pretraumatic personality is extremely influential in the symptomatic outcome. Even under normal circumstances, there is a tendency toward aggression toward the lost object that varies from individual to individual. In the survivor, this aggression is frequently found to have been repressed, displaced onto the self, and displaced onto the second generation. The survivor who harbored unconscious destructive aggressive fantasies of childhood experienced those losses as wish fulfillments. This makes mourning almost entirely impossible. In some cases, the death of the object was denied. This greatly influences the survivor's capacity to recathect new objects, often resulting in miserable marriages and unhappy family relationships in which the unresolved conflicts that might have been discharged in the actual relationships in the original family are now acted out in the new family. This process is also misunderstood by those who have devoted great energy to the establishment of the equivalent of a "survivor syndrome" for the second generation, albeit with another name. This discussion is thus more than an historical footnote, for despite the fact that most survivors are approaching the end of their lives, the problem is perpetuated in the literature on their children.

SUMMARY

The Holocaust was an unprecedented event in modern history. Those who survived the concentration camps were individuals who returned from the dead. They had witnessed and learned about life, death, and the nature of humankind as no one ever had. They possessed information which they wanted to share with those who were spared the experience. The fact that they managed to survive made them valuable objects for study as to the nature of and capacity for survival under such extreme conditions. Undoubtedly there were different reasons and circumstances for survival.

Instead of reasonably meticulous studies, the psychiatric literature is filled with generalizations, such as that all survivors suffer from the same syndrome, which is not only invalid but is also a disservice to the survivor. Such a generalization disregards individual differences that are crucial to the understanding of the way the survivor was affected by the Holocaust experience. Furthermore, the experience itself is not necessarily pathogenic for everyone. Actually, it is the trauma of the libidinal object losses and the inability to mourn them during and following the Holocaust that has the highest pathogenic potential. It is the disturbance in the work of mourning that interferes with the individual's subsequent human relations, not necessarily the physical pains he endured in the concentration camps. The capacity to mourn object losses varies greatly among individuals and is determined by the degree of maturity of the psychic apparatus.

The psychiatrists' efforts in obtaining restitution compensation for the victims have negatively affected any therapeutic possibility. Furthermore, when a psychiatrist has a "survivor syndrome" entrenched in his mind, it makes it difficult for the survivor to be treated objectively. The survivor senses this lack of empathy; he despairs and feels not understood. The psychiatrist's attitude is the result of his own unresolved conflict associated with the Holocaust, and may also be a result of the contempt for the victim that is present in the unconscious life of all of us. When the survivor experiences this unconscious contempt from professionals who are "helping" him, it becomes another trauma—perhaps the most painful of all.

REFERENCES

Bergen, M. D. 1958. "The Effect of Severe Trauma on a Four-Year-Old Child." *Psychoanalytic Study of the Child* 13:407–429.

Binswanger, L. 1957. *Sigmund Freud: Reminiscences of a Friendship*. New York: Grune & Stratton.

Eissler, K. R. 1967. "Perverted Psychiatry?" *American Journal of Psychiatry* 123:1352–1358.

Freud, A. 1958. "Child Observation and Prediction." *Psychoanalytic Study of the Child* 13:112–116.

Gyomroi, E. L. 1963. "The Analysis of a Young Concentration Camp Victim." *Psychoanalytic Study of the Child* 13:484–510.

Krystal, H., ed. 1968. *Massive Psychic Trauma*. New York: International Universities Press.

Meerloo, J. 1968. In *Massive Psychic Trauma*, ed. H. Krystal. New York: International Universities Press.

Niederland, W. G. 1968. In *Massive Psychic Trauma,* ed. H. Krystal. New York: International Universities Press.
Sterba, R. 1968. In *Massive Psychic Trauma,* ed. H. Krystal. New York: International Universities Press.
Waldhorn, H. F., and Fine, B. D., eds. 1974. *Trauma and Symbolism.* Kris Study Group of the New York Psychoanalytic Institute, Monograph V. New York: International Universities Press.

III

A GENERATION AFTER

INTRODUCTION

Laub (a survivor) and Auerhahn (a daughter of survivors) are concerned with the role of the reality of the Holocaust as an unconscious organizing principle for future generations; that is, the manner in which this historical event can shape one's internal representation of reality, including interpersonal relationships. They focus not on survivors but rather on those not directly affected by this event and propose that subsequent generations may construct inner psychic representations which are reflective of this external massive trauma.

There is a continuum between a real trauma and an imagined trauma so far as pathogenic effect is concerned. The authors believe that the Holocaust, to those who have not experienced it, may create an in-between state where, although the trauma did not occur (to the individual affected), the virulence of the individual's traumatic fantasy (due to the magnitude of the event imagined) approaches in potency a real event. For example, among other effects, a trauma such as the Holocaust will sensitize witnesses to the potential for human brutality and aggression, and inevitably evoke in them, through fleeting identifications, imagery of their own potential for extreme aggression.

Laub and Auerhahn illustrate their thesis by an examination of the reverberations of the Holocaust in the imagery, fantasy life, psychological conflict, and mechanisms of defense and adaptation of psychotherapy patients. They show the manner in which the Holocaust may leave an everlasting psychic imprint.

Reverberations of Genocide: Its Expression in the Conscious and Unconscious of Post-Holocaust Generations

DORI LAUB and NANETTE C. AUERHAHN

Once upon a time there were gas chambers and crematoria; and no one lived happily ever after.

—"A Modern Fairy Tale"
(Langer 1975, p. 124)

INTRODUCTION

At the 1972 midwinter meeting in New York, the outgoing president of the American Psychoanalytic Association, Dr. Robert S. Wallerstein, observed that although Freud's theoretical reformulations repositioned the ego "at the crossroads where the drive demands of the id, the moral constraints of the superego, and the requirements of the outer reality all met and were mediated," the psychoanalytic study of reality has been "relatively neglected or taken for granted in usual psychoanalytic discourse." This neglect, Wallerstein asserted, is implicit in the time-honored perspective of a fixed world "out there," of an unvarying "average expectable environment." Yet recent historical events have irreversibly shaken such a stable, understood, and mutually agreed upon conceptualization of reality, of what "out there is really all about, how it hangs together, and what we can expect of it." These historical events have demonstrated that the actual human environment, far from being average and expectable, is "systematically varying, and highly differential and differentiated in its impact" and therefore must be treated scientifically as a variable too.

Wallerstein proceeds: "the realities with which psychoanalysis concerns itself . . . are created, evolved, and constructed realities, given meanings in ways comparable to the [other] psychic instances, also to be comprehended as both functionings of and products of the mind of man." The psychological impact of reality on the individual varies according to what a human being makes of it, consciously or unconsciously. There is no objective reality per se that carries psychological weight of its own.

In considering these attempts at revision of psychoanalytic theory, a more thorough acquaintance with psychic constructs, as well as reflections about what did take place in the world, seems in order. This paper will focus on the psychological reverberations of one cogent aspect of the reality of our times—external massive trauma. We shall focus on the Holocaust, for as Yale's President Giametti said in his recent Baccalaureate Address (1982), by contemplation of this event, "one may have, as I had, one's certainties challenged and one's faith shaken in a radical way by confronting a reality that is now part of the inheritance of the human species." Specifically, we shall address the question of how the inner psychic "evolved and constructed realities" reflective of external massive traumatic events affect early object relationships, drive derivatives, and representations, and especially the vicissitudes of aggression and of self-preservative psychological defenses against them.

One of the central problems in considering the impact of actual trauma is evaluation of the relative contribution of actual trauma versus that of fantasy. This issue is similar to the dilemma that Freud faced in his thinking about external sexual traumatization in 1897. Up to that time, he had thought his patients had been seduced by their fathers. After that, he discovered the potency of fantasy in childhood and concluded that in most cases real tauma had not occurred; the child had not been sexually seduced by his parent, but wishes for and fantasies of such seductions were enough to act as traumatogenic factors. Since then, we have come to know that sexual seduction and incestuous relationships, especially between fathers and daughters, are not that infrequent. This, of course, does not detract from the potency of the infantile fantasy but underlines the fact that in many cases an actual occurrence might have played a role. Indeed, there is a continuum between a *real trauma* and an *imagined trauma* as far as pathogenic effect is concerned (as well as a crucial difference between the two conditions).

Our question is *whether there can exist intermediate states wherein the trauma did not occur but the virulence of traumatic fantasy approaches in potency that of a real event.* In particular developmental conditions one can find such situations—when boundaries between object and subject are blurred, fantasy and reality are confused, and the urgency of drives is matched by the weakness of their controls, as happens in many schizophrenogenic families. Also included under such circumstances are family situations in which expressions of violence and erotic ties approach a level of uncontrolled realness. Does an *external reality* in which such instinctual expression occurs, and where the parents cannot assimilate it, act in a similar fashion? The temporary inability of parents to master highly intense instinctual states in response to brutal and atrocious events in real life may be just the sort of precipitate a child finds himself unable to master. It is as if the child internalizes the precarious ego/instinct balance that the parent experiences. In such circumstances, the matter of timing seems of secondary significance. It is not crucial whether the parent is traumatized while the child can observe it or whether the parent carries with him the undigested memory of past severe traumatization. Transmittal to the child will occur under either condition, albeit varying in intensity. Under such circumstances, we find conditions wherein children imagine traumas or, rather, experience them through identification. Although substantially different, there also exists a certain continuity between situations in which parents themselves were directly traumatized and situations in which they experienced traumatization by passively witnessing it in others.

Political events of historically unprecedented magnitude, such as the two world wars, Hiroshima, and the various genocides of our century (to which millions of people have been exposed), may constitute the traumatic ambience for these parents and thus become the cultural heritage of our times.

THE HOLOCAUST AS AN UNCONSCIOUS ORGANIZING PRINCIPLE

In the following essay, we shall address the role of the reality of the Holocaust as an unconscious organizing principle for future generations, that is, the manner in which this historical event may shape one's internal representation of reality, including interpersonal relationships. We shall focus not on survivors but rather on those not directly affected by this event and propose that subsequent generations may construct inner psychic representations which are reflective of this external massive trauma. We shall illustrate our thesis by an examination of the reverberations of the Holocaust in the imagery, fantasy life, psychological conflict, and mechanisms of defense and adaptation in the clinical material of analytic patients and discuss the manner in which the Holocaust can leave an everlasting psychic imprint.

Our focus, for purposes of illustration, is on children whose parents were *not* survivors but, instead, the contemporaries of survivors, Jews and non-Jews alike. Many of our current adult patients belong to this group. As were the survivors, these parents were too overwhelmed by the awesomeness of the event to give it conscious expression. Nevertheless, parents who were distant witnesses to the apocalyptic events—to a reality in which aggression surpassed anything predictable or even imaginable—could not but be profoundly affected by it despite their outward silence; their innermost psychological structures were shaken. The more profound the outer silence, the more pervasive was the inner impact of the events. They could not but perceive (even if not openly acknowledge) that all the certainties and givens that they had grown up with and lived by no longer existed. Suffering and annihilation were total, merciless, and anonymous. Those who did not participate had to struggle with or defend against their real or fantasized involvement and deal with guilt about their survival. The Holocaust, not surprisingly, compellingly found its way into their children's imagery and character structure.

The mechanisms employed in the transmission of the Holocaust to children of survivors and of nonsurvivors are early unconscious ego identifications which carry in their wake the parents' perception of an everlasting life-threatening inner and outer reality (Axelrod, Schnipper, and Rau 1978; Barocas and Barocas 1973; Kestenberg 1972; Klein 1971; Laufer 1973; Lipkowitz 1973; Rakoff 1966; Sonnenberg 1974). These children were not free to assimilate their immediate life experience in harmony with the external reality in which they grew but, rather, were chained to their parents' versions of reality, albeit with neither parent nor child being consciously aware of it. This became the matrix within which normal developmental conflict took place.*

The children of survivors and of the latter's contemporaries were both more heavily burdened (from early on in their lives) and less immediately constrained from giving expression to their parents' conflicted themes. Their distance from the experience itself, as well as the compelling quality of their heritage, make them inevitable spokesmen for it.

*Ritvo and Solnit's (1958) views on early identifications as part of the evolving mother/child interaction are helpful in understanding this phenomenon, as are Erikson's (1964) views on development.

It is the child who finds himself compelled to experience more fully and to amplify the parents' suppressed themes. The child echoes what exists in his parents' inner world; his inner reality thereby reveals the indelible marks left by the events of our time. The particular style the child adopts—whether it be acting out, neurotic symptomatology, character traits, artistic expression, or occupational endeavors—is subtly and complexly determined by a myriad of psychological and reality factors. That is, the Holocaust heritage, though leaving its unique imprint, does not operate in a vacuum. It leaves its mark on survivors and nonsurvivors alike and is intricately interwoven in each case with a uniquely personal history. A discussion of what is most particular to the Holocaust culture, in order to clarify the latter's impact in the mosaic of forces that determine development and character formation, will be attempted in this paper.

EFFECTS OF THE HOLOCAUST: METAPHORICAL EXPRESSIONS AND STRUCTURAL CHANGES

The impact of such a major event as the Holocaust may be seen in at least two ways: first, as "mere" imagery and metaphor in which normal development themes and conflicts can be couched; second, as an impetus for pervasive structural changes. Regarding the former effect: Those not directly affected by the event may be precisely the ones capable of having the distance necessary for the use of metaphor. Sadomasochistic impulses are, as we would expect, the ones that borrow most commonly from Holocaust imagery, but they are not alone in this. Oral strivings, phallic and exhibitionistic impulses, and reaction formations against them are equally likely to find expression in such imagery. Fantasies of military exploits, of victories and conquests, or of courageous D-Day operations are some typical examples of the latter. Beyond this, oedipal conflicts with yearning for lost objects, dread, and evidence of damage and castration gain frequent expression. One is impressed by the ubiquity of the fantasy of the guardsman-rival-opponent who, by his cruel modern machinery and police, replaces the age-old witch-dragon.

Regarding the latter effect: A basic question is whether Holocaust themes go beyond providing appropriate manifest content to time-honored developmental conflicts, whether the metaphors acquire a life of their own, subtly changing the actual objects and processes they stand for. Our clinical experience leads us to believe that fantasy contents alone do not encompass the impact of a historical event. The events of the

Holocaust not only provide metaphors that symbolize developmental conflicts, but they also shape these conflicts as well. The presence of Holocaust metaphors often covers more profound psychic changes which are subtle and difficult to demarcate. These changes involve primarily ego and superego functions, the sense of self or of reality, modes of adaptation, as well as certain superego manifestations which reflect the awareness of the actual occurrence of unbridled aggression.

The mechanism by which such changes occur is complex to outline. Early superego and ego identifications account for some. Also, Holocaust metaphors can become actual components of infantile developmental conflict, contributing to it more than mere content, affecting various aspects of infantile development—primitive urges, reality representations, and superego content. A fantasied version of a real extermination camp includes all of the above for the young observer, and in the analytic reconstruction of the infantile conflict, all this has to be taken into account. A clinical vignette may help to enlighten us here.

> After a considerable amount of work on her defensive characterological reaction formations (depressive moods, endless mourning, phobic avoidances, inhibitions of creativity) was accomplished, patient A became more directly aware of her intense oedipal feelings towards the men in her life. This included yearning, loyalty, and murderous, castrating wishes. In one session, while touching on her adoration of the men-heroes, she angrily complained of how unfairly she felt treated by every one of them, from the President of the United States to her analyst. Her next association was to the Hansel and Gretel story, which led to the following exchange: "You are the witch today [in a later session she elaborated on how frightened she had once felt, watching this play on the stage, with the part of the witch played by a man] and I would like to push you into the fire. Only, to say such things to you about ovens and burning or even think of them is so terrible." The analyst responded here with a question—"After the Holocaust, by thinking of it, you became a Nazi?" —to which she responded with an outcry, "Yes, and I do not want to be one."

Knowledge about the historical reality of the Holocaust intensely colored the infantile conflict and its recrudescence in the transference neurosis in this patient. If the metaphor had been in the Hansel and Gretel story alone, the intensity of the experience and defenses it necessitated would probably have been of a different order.

Knowledge of the particular qualities of the Holocaust metaphor and their reflection in ego functioning is therefore essential to the understanding both of the choice of particular defensive operations (like the strong inhibition of aggressive and phallic strivings and their replacement with a life of asceticism and mourning, as we shall see in another patient) and of certain pervasive qualities common to all defensive and adaptive mechanisms and styles (e.g., patient A's propensity to externalization, projection, abrupt repressive shifts, and equally abrupt realignments of defensive operations, mobilized to deal with threatening mortal dangers).

Our hypothesis of structural changes resulting from knowledge of the Holocaust is a variation on Erikson's thesis that cultural institutions and processes reflect as well as shape the development of the ego ("ego virtues," as Erikson [1964] calls them). We believe that the emergence, for instance, of a sadistic wish in the context of knowledge about real atrocities alters the affective and cognitive process set in motion in experiencing and mastering such wishes—that is, phallic, aggressive, and other strivings imagined in terms of Holocaust metaphor (either of being an SS commandant, Hitler himself, an American or Russian liberator, or a Jewish David who takes vengeance, for example). These impose a particular style of ego experience and awake particular superego responses that differ from normative and genetically determined developmental phenomena in their harshness and overinclusiveness.

What is crucial in causing these changes is the fact that an identification with, for example, the fantasied monster Hitler carries with it the critical awareness that this figure actually existed in the very recent past, that he really was responsible for momentous victories and unimaginable atrocities, and that these profoundly affected people surrounding the child. There is no escape into the protective sense of this being only a fantasy or bedtime story (a maneuver Bettelheim [1976] considers useful in the mastering of aggressive impulses). In addition, this often leads to severe ascetic reaction formations and changes in superego functions to satisfy a need to atone for having survived and thereby feeling that one has abandoned the victim or joined the ranks of the persecutors. Subtle ego and superego identifications with various participants of the Holocaust drama take place, once Holocaust metaphors become the language and symbols by which developmental conflicts are experienced within a culture.

A second example may further help to illustrate our point. It comes from the analysis of Mr. B, a brilliant Jewish doctoral candidate in his twenties studying history. This man tried to sabotage both his academic career and his social life. He led a barren life in an unfurnished apartment to which he would invite neither male nor female friends. His father had died suddenly when he was an adolescent. The father, who had suffered from a chronic but not debilitating illness, had had a close brush with death five years earlier, just after the boy achieved a remarkable scholastic success and developed a crush on a beautiful Gentile teacher. At that time the boy had also become fascinated with the speeches of historical figures—in particular those of Adolf Hitler—which he used to recite from memory before his class. This activity would make his father livid with rage. Mr. B's upbringing had been traditionally Jewish, with much pleasure taken in the observance of holidays. The tie between father and son seems to have been particularly close.

Following his father's death, things changed radically. Mr. B completely abrogated Judaism and the traditions he had grown up with, practiced with fervor, and enjoyed. Not only did he abrogate them, but he adopted politically militant anti-Jewish and anti-Zionist views, parallel with a scholastic interest in the subject matter. Despite his vociferous ideological explanations for his behavior, this drastic turnabout possessed the distinctive quality of asceticism, self-exile, and punishment.

The motivation for this reaction-formation became clearer in light of his fascination with the fascist hero of the movie *The Conformist*. This character, driven by an unconscious sense of guilt about an unknown crime, kept up his fascist activities, including murder, thus fueling a pervasive self-hatred. At the end of the movie, it becomes clear that he believed he had long before killed a man who had made homosexual advances toward him. He now discovers that the supposed victim is alive and well. The spectator is left to imagine what goes on in the mind of the hero. As with our patient, his sense of primal sin drove him into further sinning. He never made peace with his original victim so as to be able to regain his home, origin, and roots but continued living in solitary self-exile, tortured by self-hatred, compulsively repeating the original sin. Our patient did likewise through political radicalism, openly parading PLO sympathy, as well as through asceticism in the form of social, sexual, and professional abstinence.

It is true that we are dealing here with fantasies of parricide (cf. Freud 1928) and also true that the father died suddenly during the patient's adolescence. But was it not the identification with the killer of all fathers, this little boy's recital of Hitler's speeches, and the *reality* of the occurrence of such monstrous events, that gave an inescapable *real* sense to the son's crime, to its enormity, and to the deserved punishment? How could he ever have stood up to his father if that meant following in Hitler's footsteps? Could he ever hope to deserve the yearned-for reconciliation if he felt that he had committed such a crime? The only resolution he was able to conceive of was becoming a damned fugitive.

THE HOLOCAUST AS PROVIDING A REALITY REFERENCE FOR AGGRESSIVE FANTASIES

What is essential about the Holocaust is its purely man-made origin—the fact that it was not a natural catastrophe and that it was perpetrated deliberately by people, often without the use of technologically sophisticated machinery. Such an event sensitizes witnesses to the potential for human brutality and aggression and inevitably evokes in them, through fleeting identifications (Moses 1978), vivid imagery of the extremity of their own potential for aggression—an imagery they cannot avoid. To prevent guilt and deny any identification with the aggressor, nonsurvivor parents were limited in their capacity for continued emotional availability and guidance in the face of their children's primitive aggression. Such empathy is necessary for the growth of the ego and the use of aggression in the service of development.

Indulgent parents unable to respond to their children's aggression were not the exception but the rule; social phenomena in the young during the last decades may partly have reflected this fact (Lasch 1979). Many of the next generation picked up their parents' guilty identifications with the victims and came to see the parents as exquisitely vulnerable to their aggression. They sensed their parents' self-perceptions as survivors/aggressors, and the ensuing inhibition of all aggression and assertiveness, and so came to regard their own aggression and growth as potentially so destructive that it had to be avoided at all costs. Parental reactions, together with the totality, extremity, and savagery of Holocaust imagery, and especially together with the event's historical actuality and proximity, its *realness,* all made the Holocaust ultimately compelling and inescapable to children of that generation.

Nonsurvivors' children were often unable to detach the savagery of their fascinating sexual and aggressive fantasies from the realness of the atrocity that occurred. Children, after all, are often unable to distinguish between reality and fantasy. Should misfortune occur (as in the example of patient B previously cited), how could a child regard it otherwise than his own omnipotent wishes having come true? Was not the realness of the

Nazi savagery an indisputable fact too? Patient B was plunged into an inauthentic and theatrical perpetual state of mourning which generalized into a sense of deceit and inauthenticity in all his human contacts and which seemed but a restatement of his original sin—the fact that the savagery he had identified with, had occurred. A real trauma may contribute to the ultimate validity of the child's Holocaust imagery. Patient B's precipitous loss of his father while he was an adolescent became a pivotal event after which all that was playful in his fantasy was lost. The fantasy crime became real, the atonement and punishment mandatory. There was no place for further fantasy elaboration. It was as though a curtain had fallen and the outcome was determined. The occurrence of a real death (importantly in adolescence) added a final element of realness to developmental conflicts experienced in Holocaust metaphors.

A proximity to raw aggression is to be regarded as part of the normal childhood traumata of today through the (subliminal at least) awareness of modern atrocities. Such exposure leads to particular types of internalizations, which though well-isolated and not grossly impeding further personality development, nevertheless remain as weak spots, foci of regressive potential, for both drives and ego. Such ego states, deriving their power from the realness of the events, inflict a certain degree of instability on all subsequent developments involving aggression and its manifold expressions. Whenever this state of instability is characteristic of mental functioning, primitive defenses must be brought into play because of the ego's fear of aggressivity. This will occur whenever development partakes of the imagery of atrocity; whether consciously—as reflected in rather hazy, obscure, elusive, and flighty fragments of a daydream, or unconsciously—as a continuous, compelling flow of startling yet imageless affect—uncontrollable rage and utter destructiveness. These defensive operations are not intended to ward off superego or reality anxiety, despite the sense of realness of the atrocity imagery, but, rather, internal aggressive stirrings that reach all the way into the earliest and most primitive layers of aggressive experience.

These early feelings are defensively projected onto others in order to purify the ego and rid it of the intolerable tension of containing the destructiveness in itself. They have been objectified and given reality reference by the realness of the atrocity events which is assimiliated via the parents' perceptions of the genocide and the child's identifications with it (Moses 1978). When such primitive or raw aggressive stirrings come to be experienced as real, further maturational processes, such as drive fusion, neutralization, and the building of psychic structure, can be impeded, and repression may prematurely set in. Repositories of such primitive aggressiveness will remain as unconscious (even preverbal) repressed memories. These will be readily rearoused by the very force that was instrumental in originating them—the imagery of atrocity. What follows such reawakening is a process of ego regression—the reexperience of early feeling states of helplessness and absence of control. Such regression also involves primitive identifications with the image of a malignant, all-powerful parental figure. Thus, the patient views himself as evil and monstrous. To avoid the painful feelings of anxiety accompanying the inner resonance to the imagery of atrocity, a series of defensive operations are urgently mobilized. These can be instantaneous and acute, reflecting an intensification of anxiety and transference feelings in the treatment situation itself. Examples of such acute defenses in one patient were: instant forgetfulness (which seems like the process of repression occurring *in vivo*), abrupt interruptions of the fantasy flow and shifting of themes (as though thought itself was discontinuous), abrupt flights into mourning or seductiveness (especially from themes of sexuality and activity), and dread and phobic avoidance of fantasy and the spoken word (e.g., trying to get the analyst to speak and thus assume responsibility for both), as though they were real events. These experiences may reach their peak in sensations of a nonverbal, often visual nature and at such times are communicable only affectively.

There can also be a second group of defenses which are more continuous and characterological, producing the picture of a fate neurosis. Foremost among the latter, for example, are restrictive phobic avoidances as well as counterphobic leaps into health, amnesia extending over many years of childhood and adolescence, a paucity of dreams, manifold inhibitions, and a defensive use of carefully structured language that highlights the dread of free association and of the disastrous regression and loss of impulse control the latter activity might entail.

ADDITIONAL PSYCHIC REVERBERATIONS

Sensitivity to the unconscious Holocaust imagery that permeates our current daily life may express itself in additional ways besides a vulnerability to aggressive ideation and affect. We shall enumerate some of the themes we have noticed in our patients, acknowledging that, of course, all trends are not found in all patients. Each person presents a unique constellation of symptoms and attitudes arising from his particular circumstances. While most of these themes are universal and not specific to the Holocaust, it is, nevertheless, of utmost importance to grasp the unique quality the Holocaust experience has imparted to them. These themes are:

1. Pervasive castration themes and fear of the loss of bodily integrity. One's self is experienced as having been injured, and there are feelings of envy as well as vengeful wishes.
2. The feeling that there is no external brake to urges, that one must establish them internally to prevent excess of any kind. An especially harsh superego develops, one which clamps down on the id with a harshness equal to the strength of one's desires.
3. Superego "lacunae." Paradoxically, since the superego adapts to an abnormal reality (one in which all rules were broken), it develops what has superficially been labeled as lacunae. The individual believes that customs, rules, or contractual agreements cannot be taken with seriousness in a world in which survival is at stake. Therefore, what really counts—perhaps the only thing that counts—is staying alive. His commitment to life (his own, that of those close to him, that of Israel, or that of people in danger anywhere in the world) overrides every other consideration.
4. Tenuousness of object relationships. A mournful loneliness and forlorn quality is experienced when dealing with the absences of significant others. Relationships are viewed as ever-threatened by potential loss and sudden disruption as well as being threatened by the slightest show of aggression or ambivalence. Separations are feared and viewed with deathlike finality.
5. Nurturance of others and identification with victims.
6. Outer world experienced as unstable. The individual is haunted by the sense that the world can suddenly change, without reason, into an atrocity-producing atmosphere and that people are not what they seem. Civilization is seen as a veneer covering a potential for violence and corruption. As a result, the individual is perenially on guard, hypervigilant to any sign of betrayal by another. Distrust and alienation characterize relationships, as does sensitivity to duplicity.
7. Fluidity of boundaries between self and other, past and present, reality and fantasy. Also there is an incomplete neutralization of aggressive with libidinal urges.
8. A view of the parental generation as damaged, victimized, and unable to protect one from others' and one's own aggression. The

parents' presence, or for that matter anyone's presence, is not a safe enough one in a world containing mortal dangers. Nevertheless, there is a wish for a savior, a life-sustaining relationship with a powerful other. There may be an attempt to forge mutually protective dyadic relationships.

9. A sense of helplessness, crisis, and doom, and the feeling that nothing can provide a guarantee against the occurrence of an apocalyptic event (next time arriving, possibly, in the form of a nuclear holocaust).
10. The need to continually rescue oneself and a tendency to adopt a number of techniques common to survivors (e.g., appearing Aryan, not arousing anger, or avoiding notice). Disguises and strategies of escape are developed and practiced to elude the anticipated disaster. One may present, for example, a fragile, cautious, subdued, and well-behaved image to evade the Gestapo's watchful eye and be especially careful not to take chances. (At the same time, one may often perform counterphobic, assertive acts to convince oneself that the danger is surmountable.)
11. Fantasies of rescuing others.
12. Inhibition of fantasy. Holocaust atrocities are vividly imagined, but otherwise there is an inhibition of fantasy and curtailment of pleasure and excitement because of their element of realness and the potential for abusive excess.
13. Hypervigilance focused internally to prevent oneself from becoming a Nazi. Overt competitiveness, accomplishment, or self-assertion may be experienced as tantamount to pushing rivals into destruction and hence curtailed, for winning is seen as surviving while others are dying, and thereby moving closer oneself to being a Nazi. There is, likewise, a fear of the primitive and chaotic within oneself, as if they could allow a breakthrough of destructiveness.
14. A defect in the idealized self and object representation. This stems from the child's narcissistic omnipotent imagery having been compromised by the extinction of any hope for perfection in the post-Auschwitz era. Not only does the child, now adult, despair of ever personally attaining perfection, but the very existence of perfection becomes inconceivable to him.

CLARIFICATION

We would like to put the foregoing in context. Our point of view is in no way intended to replace the centrality of psychic reality or of psychosexual developmental themes. Rather, our purpose is to supplement them by acknowledging the significance and permanence of the permeating metaphors and images in which these themes are couched and take shape in the post-Holocaust era. It is to appreciate, too, the extent to which reality may confirm fantasy and to recognize that whenever fantasy is given reality reference, an acknowledgment of the reality is required before one can analyze its use as a defense. If such acknowledgment does not take place—that is, if profound, conflict-laden perceptions of the patient are ignored or regarded as fantasy only—then the patient will feel that his sense of reality is assaulted. He will need to protect himself from feeling crazy by closing off communication and insight all together.

A second point must be clarified. In most of our patients, the intensity of their dread and the urgency of their defenses possessed a somewhat dissonant quality—that of scotomata amidst an unusual degree of insightful clarity in highly intuitive, creative, intelligent, and courageous patients. This lends support to the speculation that we are dealing here with a rather distinct element of neurosis, an area of potential regression that by far outdistances other areas of regression. It is advantageous to differentiate such disharmonious, profound, yet circumscribed pathological enclaves from the consistent, diffuse, and encompassing neurotic picture. These areas of disturbed functioning in the mosaic of an otherwise synthetically operating ego, inexplicable to patient and analyst but commented on frequently in the professional literature on survivors, are the survivor's heritage in the directly affected victim and the not directly affected witness alike.

CONCLUSION

The imagery of atrocity not only reflects but also impacts on reality, shaping both one's experience of reality and one's personality adaptation to it. The outer world becomes permeated with a sense of evil; likewise one's inner world is experienced as contaminated as well. Despite its importance, this impact is rarely made explicit; the Holocaust is a subject that is discussed only with great difficulty. Too much of the primitive, of the unformed, which in this instance is tied to undeniable, real experiences, is brought into play. The full comprehension of the post-Auschwitz reality—a paradoxical and intensely charged mixture of life proceeding undisturbed in its natural rhythms alongside experiences of bleak terror and glimpses of life's disruption—is not easily contained in any interpersonal encounter, be it between patient and therapist, among family members or friends, or in a political forum. But beyond the withdrawal evoked by the particular affects and conflicts that are stirred up, the mutual recognition of this highly charged and paradoxical reality, of these shared cultural metaphors and their inner resonances, makes for a uniquely intimate experience. Individuals who discuss it daringly remove the veil from a tenaciously kept secret, arousing intense dread of intimacy and stirring up defenses against exhibitionistic and voyeuristic gratifications in narrator and listener alike. Therefore a general, pervasive trend in today's generations of adults is a reluctance to deal with the topic. This reluctance exists, too, among analysts who have failed to be receptive to the full impact of Holocaust themes in survivors (De Wind 1974), in their children, and in patients who have not been directly affected by the event. Contemporary witnesses of genocide are often unaware of its impact and may well be unknowingly inhibited by it (Levitas 1974; Lipkowitz 1973).

Nevertheless, the subtle yet quite thorough process of transmitting information from the witness of an atrocity event to subsequent generations can be perceived when one allows oneself to be open to this material. It behooves us to understand subsequent generations' sense of unsafety and their identification with the Holocaust survivor and his shattered world. An acknowledgment of a shared historical reality and its impact on psychic reality is called for to free-up fantasy life. One must acknowledge the compelling, reality-confirmed aspects of fantasy elements; otherwise, the fantasy formation retains its power.

In order to move beyond the Holocaust and free ourselves from its awesome constraints, its manifold realities must be explicated and shared. Otherwise, interpersonal barriers will remain, as they do whenever there is an unspeakable family secret. Furthermore, sharing limits the power of the Holocaust to arouse internal fantasies by establishing its existence outside oneself, so that it is no longer experienced as internally caused and as an actualization of one's aggressive drives. The shared remembrance and owning, as well as the detailed examination of the Holocaust, no matter how painful or awkward, is the only way to reexternalize and objectify the inner demons that must resume their appropriate place in outer historical fact. Only in this manner will we be able to proceed with life in the face of the contaminating, overwhelming evil that is part of the experience of our generation.

REFERENCES

Axelrod, S.; Schnipper, O. L.; and Rau, J. H. 1978. "Hospitalized Offspring of Holocaust Survivors: Problems and Dynamics." Paper presented at the annual meeting of the American Psychiatric Association, Atlanta, May 1978.

Barocas, H. A., and Barocas, C. B. 1973. "Manifestations of Concentration Camp Effects on the Second Generation." *American Journal of Psychiatry* 130:820–821.

Bettelheim, B. 1976. *The Uses of Enchantment: The Meaning and Importance of Fairy Tales*. New York: Knopf.

De Wind, E. 1974. "Psychotherapy after Traumatization Caused by Persecution." *International Psychiatry Clinics* 8:93–114.

Erikson, E. H. 1964. *Insight and Responsibility*. New York: Norton.

Freud, S. 1928. "Dostoevsky and Parricide." In *The Complete Psychological Works of Sigmund Freud,* vol. 21. London: Hogarth Press, 1961.

———. 1940. *An Outline of Psychoanalysis*. In *The Complete Psychological Works of Sigmund Freud,* vol. 23. London: Hogarth Press, 1964.

Furst, S. S. 1978. "The Stimulus Barrier and the Pathogenicity of Trauma." *International Journal of Psycho-Analysis* 59:345–352.

Geerts, A. E., and Rechardt, E. 1978. "Colloquium on 'Trauma'." *International Journal of Psycho-Analysis* 59:365–375.

Kestenberg, J. S. 1972. "Psychoanalytic Contributions to the Problem of Children of Survivors from Nazi Persecution." *Israel Annals of Psychiatry* 10:311–325.

Klein, H. 1971. "Families of Holocaust Survivors in the Kibbutz: Psychological Studies." In *Psychic Traumatization: Aftereffects in Individuals and Communities,* ed. H. Krystal and W. G. Niederland. Boston: Little, Brown.

Langer, L. 1975. *The Holocaust and the Literary Imagination*. New Haven: Yale University Press.

Lasch, C. 1979. *The Culture of Narcissism: American Life in an Age of Diminishing Expectations*. New York: Norton.

Laufer, M. 1973. "The Analysis of a Child of Survivors." In *The Child in His Family: The Impact of Disease and Death,* vol. 2, ed. E. J. Anthony and C.Koupernik. New York: Wiley.

Levitas, D. E. 1974. "A Discussion of the Paper by Shelley Orgel on Fusion with the Victim." *International Journal of Psycho-Analysis* 55:539–541.

Lipkowitz, M. H. 1973. "The Child of Two Survivors: The Report of an Unsuccessful Therapy." *Israel Annals of Psychiatry and Related Disciplines* 11:2.

Moses, R. 1978. "Adult Psychic Trauma: The Question of Early Predisposition and Some Detailed Mechanisms." *International Journal of Psycho-Analysis* 59:353–363.

Rakoff, V. 1966. "Long Term Effects of the Concentration Camp Experience." *Viewpoints* 1: 17–21.

Ritvo, S., and Solnit, A. J. 1958. "Influences of Early Mother-Child Interaction on Identification Processes." *Psychoanalytic Study of the Child* 13:64–85.
Sonnenberg, S. M. 1974. "Children of Survivors: Workshop Report." *Journal of the American Psychoanalytic Association* 22:200–204.
Wallerstein, R. S. 1973. "Psychoanalytic Perspectives on the Problem of Reality." *Journal of the American Psychoanalytic Association* 21:5–33.

INTRODUCTION

In this essay Dr. Luel, a son of survivors, addresses some of the psychological problems facing the second generation with the Holocaust as an unavoidable, ofttimes painful, facet of their consciousness. He is particularly concerned with the problems of hedonic impairment and a self-flagellating, conflict-laden involvement with the Holocaust legacy. Luel also comments on the emotional issues relevant to rearing a healthy third post-Holocaust generation. He offers suggestions that could contribute to a diminution of such Holocaust-related turmoil as obsessive rumination over the past, including one's parent's persecution, self-injurious cynicism, distrust of "the other," debilitating anger and fearfulness. Through a decisive shift in attitude and feeling—away from painful self-absorption—the second generation can create the optimal conditions for self-renewal and effective child-rearing.

Living with the Holocaust: Thoughts on Revitalization

STEVEN A. LUEL

The true value of a human being is determined primarily by the measure and the sense in which he has attained liberation from the self.

—Albert Einstein[1]

I approach the Holocaust, in this essay, as a son of survivors and as a developmental psychologist and educator. In attempting to comprehend the impact of this event on the second generation I have wrestled with innumerable observations and characterizations—my own and those of others. One recurring impression regarding the Holocaust's psychological impact on the second generation has far-reaching psychosocial implications, and I hope to be able to shed some light on it in this essay. I am referring to the impact of this event on the way we think and feel and to both the loss of innocence and the impaired capacity for self-abandonment that are part of its aftermath. Des Pres introduces the problem well: "We are entirely innocent but innocence, the blessedness of simple daily being, no longer seems possible." Earlier he observes: "We live, that is to say, in the unrest of the aftermath and we inherit the feeling that something has been taken away that cannot be restored. . . . The self's sense of itself is different now, and what has made the difference, both as cause and continuing condition, is simply knowing that the Holocaust occurred."[2]

I will attempt to place Des Pres's thoughts into a psychological framework and explore the relationship between the Holocaust and a diminished capacity for liberation from self. I see a conflict-laden involvement with the Holocaust in an individual who did not experience the horrors directly as one in which an awareness of what took place is eventually followed, not only by an objective tragic comprehension, but by an interruption in the normal process of psycho-physiological reinvigoration. In simpler terms, Auschwitz has made it much harder for many to play. What transpires is that disturbing Holocaust-related associations and affects intrude and lead to painful self-consciousness, obsession, difficulties with flexible ego regression, and, in extreme cases, nihilism and psychosis.

A brief illustration may elucidate the problem under discussion. In December 1980, at the Meeting of the Second Generation, convened in New York City, Henry Krystal, an analyst and survivor, shared some of his ideas concerning the facilitation of integration and self-healing in light of the Holocaust. Following the talk, which was made to a small audience of children of survivors, there was a question-and-answer period. Krystal was angrily challenged and criticized for daring to discuss the consequences of the loss of faith after the Holocaust and the need to memorialize the dead—particularly through the building of monuments and ecclesiastic edifices. He referred to the "pain-addiction" and diminished hedonic potential observed in many survivor families, and this too was met with anger and incredulity. He reminded the group that "they could do noble things without pain, anger." The meeting affected me deeply. What was it that made Krystal's description of the path to integration and self-acceptance after the Holocaust so troublesome for my cohorts?

My answer was that for those who angrily rejected Krystal's views, a shift to a less personally tormenting involvement with the Holocaust would represent both a symbolic desecration of the memory of the millions slaughtered and an affront to their parents. I will argue that such a transformation is neither a sacrilege nor a profanation. Rather, I conceptualize it as a post-Holocaust obligation to ourselves and certainly to our children—the third generation.

SELF-ABANDONMENT AND THE NEED TO BE "ORDINARY"

It is self-evident that life presents us with a steady flow of challenges. The organism mobilizes to meet the external or internally-mediated demands, and normally a quiescent state is reached. Seyle has identified this ongoing self-regulatory process as the General Adaptation Syndrome, or G.A.S.[3] The G.A.S. is made up of the three stages: alarm, followed by adaptation and exhaustion. The perpetuation of this process throughout the life-cycle is dependent on numerous factors, not the least important of which is the capacity to forget oneself and one's difficulties and thereby acquire solace and renewed vitality. These periodic "adaptive regressions" can be viewed as a natural adult effort to re-create the sense of bliss and comfort that characterized the oneness of the "symbiotic orbit" which comprised mother and infant. This fusion (oceanic feeling) accompanies immersion in a wide range of activites: sexual love, communion with nature, meditative states, involvement with art, music, humor, and for the believer—a oneness with God. Such experiences allow us to transcend our awareness of bodily pains and unavoidable psychic discomforts. In addition to the specific pleasure-providing activities mentioned above, we have the small "ordinary" diversions that are a part of daily life. In the long run, access to these activities has the cumulative effect of leading us to view our days as either relatively pleasant or predominantly burdensome. I refer to the cat that jumps into our lap, the smile of a child, the meal with loved ones or close friends, the walk on the beach—in other words, activities which come under the rubric of what the French refer to as *le petit bonheur,* "the little happiness," an important component of the art of living.

The health-enhancing and curative benefits of possessing a strong "pleasure economy" is the subject of current medical research and clearly beyond the scope of this essay.[4] The Holocaust, however, has, as I mentioned earlier, contributed for many to making it much more difficult to experience the pleasures of self-abandonment. Moreover, intellectual attempts are made to justify one's suffering and to see something noble in one's anger and disenchantment. I understand but have no sympathy with this outlook. It is, as Bertrand Russell observed, "a malady, which it is true, certain circumstances may render inevitable, but which none-theless, when it occurs, is to be cured as soon as possible, not to be regarded as a higher form of widsom."[5]

MANIFESTATIONS OF PATHOLOGICAL HOLOCAUST INVOLVEMENT

It would be unduly reductionistic to assert that the Holocaust is the sole catalyst leading to the state of impairments in hedonic functioning described thus far. However, I think that it would be fair to admit that the psychological impact of the Holocaust has been profound and should never be underestimated. I am in full agreement with Laub and Auerhahn in their impression that with the post-Holocaust generation we are dealing, more often than not, with professionally successful, intelligent, and caring individuals. However, "pathological enclaves" are present within "the mosaic of an otherwise synthetically operating ego."[6] How could it be otherwise when the same researchers report that numerous anxiety-producing themes play a significant role in the lives of many of their second-generation patients (even those whose parents were *not* Holocaust survivors). Examples of such themes include a view that relationships are ever threatened by potential loss and sudden disruption; a perception of the outer world as unstable, resulting in hypervigilance, distrust, and alienation; a view of the parental generation as damaged; and feelings of helplessness, crisis, and doom. With the Holocaust and its associated imagery serving as a backdrop in the creation of the above stress-producing *weltbild,* how could a reduction in hedonic potential and an impaired capacity for self-abandonment not follow?

The disruption of normal pleasurable functioning can be further characterized as a flaw in the self-preservative functioning of the ego. This formulation makes sense within the context of a psychology of health and adaptation which views pleasure and play as lifelong necessities, not luxuries. Such a flaw leads to unpleasant mood disturbances and is part of a larger picture of neurotic suffering. More important, as I see it, is the undesirable effect it has on the individual's life-philosophy particularly, in relationship to the rearing of the third post-Holocaust generation. The literature on the psychological effects of the Holocaust on the second generation contains many examples which illustrate the problems of Holocaust obsession, "pain-addiction," and pleasure intolerance.[7] The various defensive strategies employed to justify the existence of such patterns of response have also been discussed. Helen Epstein's *Children of the Holocaust* is a keen portrayal of such unhappiness.[8]

A presentation of clinical vignettes illustrating pathological involvement with the Holocaust is beyond the scope and intention of this essay. I prefer to offer a fresh perspective that may lead to some measure of resolution of, and freedom from, the psychological dilemma with which we are confronted.

LIVING WITH THE HOLOCAUST LEGACY

We of the second generation are rearing or are about to rear the third post-Holocaust generation. How do we wish to present the Holocaust to them? To what extent do we wish them to share our anxieties, rages, and hurts? On the one hand, we want to remind through remembrance and transmission of the horrific truth. On the other hand, the second generation will be best equipped to rear the third if, in preparation, they extract themselves from a self-injurious attachment to the Holocaust. How to achieve this and how to encourage remembrance and vital awareness while minimizing further pathological reverberations will be our challenge.

This will mean, first, that the Holocaust must become less of a painful emotional problem for us and remain predominantly in historical, philosophical, and intellectual contexts for our children. They will see the photos, read the poems and diaries. They will make their pilgrimage to Yad Vashem, and some will listen to the tales of "night and fog" from grandma and grandpa. We will try to sensitize our young to human anguish. But our obligation, unless we choose to remain wedded to masochism, is to promote healing and to foster wellness in our young. We must find a *via media* between the obligation to remember, with its unavoidable sadness, and the obligation to lessen the obsessive rumination, the corrosive cynicism regarding human possibilities, the distrust of "the other," the anger, the apprehensive expectation and its accompanying hypervigilance—all of which point to damaging links to the Holocaust.

We can gain some insight as to how this can be accomplished by taking note of Klein's observations of kibbutz survivor families.[9] He has described how their post-Holocaust adjustments have been better than those of their city-dwelling counterparts. This was and remains due to their secure supportive environment, which allowed for collective mourning, and the profound organic satisfaction these people derive from their contact with the land. This shows itself at their Holocaust commemorations. Flowers and fruits are displayed, along with the burning of the six candles, to embody the element of hope and rebirth and to affirm the meaning of past experience as a positive force for the future. The flowers and fruits are highly significant in light of their absence, to the best of my knowledge, from such memorial gatherings in the United States or elsewhere.

As one kibbutz Holocaust survivor, who lost his entire family, told me in this regard: "Israel is my mother." There is much psychological value in fostering such an attitude. From a psychoanalytic perspective, it could be compared to the successful resolution of the Oedipus complex. The post-Holocaust Jew turns, under the threat of another Holocaust (read castration), from a fixation on the Diaspora (e.g., the German Jews' inability to perceive the political changes in Germany realistically, stemming from their futile yearning for and expectation of acceptance) to the new, nonincestual, "achievable mother": Israel. The psychological benefits accruing from care for and deep involvement with the homeland may be one outgrowth of an approach that aims to transform Holocaust-related problems into Holocaust-related achievements.

In addition to the salutary and balanced kibbutz approach to the Holocaust, we can learn much that will help us in our efforts at revitalization from the Oriental and Sephardic Jews. For example, let us look at the Yemenite community. They have known tragedy and have lived under terrible conditions. Yet they made a remarkable adjustment to their new lives in Israel.[10] I believe that they have access to sources of refreshment and renewal that have not played as central a role in the cultural life of the Ashkenazic Jews (with the possible exception of the Hasidim). Dance, craftsmanship, intergenerational transmission of inspiring myths and traditions, extensive creative ritualization of experience, emphasis on the pleasures of the senses, and a deep appreciation of beauty are examples of such aspects of Yemenite life that have contributed to their highly developed cultural adaptability. There is also an institutionalized concern with health enhancement through the application of folk-medicine. Des Pres, in the paper cited at the beginning of this essay, maintains that the Holocaust has thwarted our ability to celebrate and to "experience a rapport with the world as a sacred living whole."[11] I believe that he is addressing a Western audience numbed by oft-repeated exposure to the imagery of atrocity. The emotional distance from the Holocaust has enabled the Yemenites and others in the Oriental and Sephardic community to retain the genuine affirmation and "blessedness of simple daily being"[12] that, he argues, we in the West are now denied.

Philosophical outlooks will also need modification. A post-Holocaust metaphysics will, as Eissler has observed, call for the replacement of archaic concretizations and magic with "highly refined sublimations in which the self becomes absorbed in the cosmos and loses itself in the infinity of time and space."[13] This feeling of union with nature and the cosmos, coupled with a view of life *sub specie aeternitatis,* has spared many the miseries that accrue from too intense a responsiveness to the vicissitudes of life and painful realities such as the Holocaust. It would behoove us to cultivate such an attitude and encourage it in our children. This will call for the development of a more tolerant view of detachment and philosophical self-resignation—attitudes which are in many ways antithetical to the spirit of Hebraism: "Hebraism contains no eternal realm of essences, which Greek philosophy was to fabricate, through Plato, as affording the intellectual deliverance from the evil of time. Such a realm of eternal essences is possible only for a detached intellect, one who, in Plato's phrase, becomes a 'spectator of all time and all existence.' "[14] Again, a difficult midpoint will have to be located between needed commitment, "the passionate involvement of man with his own mortal being," and needed detachment, which provides us with a desirable impartiality and sense of proportion.

Denial, in moderation, has its place in my view as well.[15] In the kibbutz study referred to above, denial of the more traumatic details of the Holocaust experience allowed the members to "regard it as a positive force linked to the rebirth of the Jewish people in the state of Israel."[16] The kibbutz members do not deny the past as such. Denial persists in the sphere of feelings, or "the affective quality of their past experiences," and this serves adaptive purposes. It has played, in my judgment, a decisive role in Israel's survival and growth by partially freeing its citizens from thoughts of prior humiliations and brutalization.

I believe that the modification of our thinking and attitudes toward the Holocaust in the direction outlined above will strengthen our adaptive capacity and enhance the pleasure of existence. Moreover, it is the direction we must take if we are to provide our children with that which we may have lost at too early an age: the illusion of invulnerability. In this regard, trends in early education emphasizing stark realism at the expense of make-believe need to be examined. Fantasy activity in childhood is a crucial coping mechanism, and this function needs to be protected and enhanced. Introducing children to overwhelming horrors must be done with the utmost care lest we impair the tension-reducing fantasizing and play. Moreover, it would be prudent to avoid exposing children to Holocaust materials until they have acquired a sense of inner security based on the oft-repeated experience of an outside world that proves to be reliable and loving. This "basic trust" needs to be accompanied by cognitive attainments in logical thinking and concept formation that generally do not appear until the onset of late latency (approx. 7½–8½ years of age).[17]

Postman has commented on the hazardous trend of making certain facets of life—its mysteries, its contradictions, its tragedies, its violence—so accessible to children. This leads to "homogenization" of adulthood and childhood.

> The invention of childhood was one of the most humane inventions of the Renaissance. What it did was to make it a cultural principle that we had to nurture and protect children. It promoted ideas throughout society that are important, such as curiosity and malleability and innocence and a sense of continuity and re-creation. These are the qualities that we've come to associate with childhood that are necessary prerequisites for developing into mature adulthood.[18]

All this means that we of the second generation should be mindful of the psychoanalytic caution that imposition of the truth on others is more often an act of violence and aggression than the generous sharing of truth that it purports to be.

I am not willing to go so far as Camus with his remark: "Man is face to face with himself: I defy him to be happy."[19] I value introspection and self-scrutiny; but I have attempted to explain the need and benefit of greater liberation from self, both for ourselves and for our offspring. Our children will then have the possibility of identifying with parents who have turned trauma into opportunity and whose humanity and altruism are built upon a solid foundation of self-tolerance and self-preservation.

Our greatest resistance to our efforts to develop a less oppressive relationship to the Holocaust is the frightening and usually unspoken acknowledgment that we can, if we allow ourselves, experience much joy and pleasure in its aftermath. It is the searing dichotomies of orgasm and Auschwitz, the smiling infant we hold today and our image of a burning one then, that must be mourned over and accepted.[20] It is a reconciliation that we know "they" would have wanted us to make.

REFERENCES

1. Albert Einstein, *Ideas and Opinions* (New York: Crown, 1954), p. 12.

2. Terrence Des Pres, "The Dreaming Back," *Centerpoint* 4, no. 1 (Fall, 1980): 13.

3. Hans Seyle, *The Stress of Life* (New York: McGraw-Hill, 1956).

4. For a full discussion of the relationship between pleasurable states and individual health and disease, see Norman Cousins, *Anatomy of an Illness as Perceived by the Patient: Reflections on Healing and Regeneration,* (Boston: G. K. Hall, 1979).

5. Betrand Russell, *The Conquest of Happiness* (New York: Bantam, 1968), p. 113.

6. See the paper by D. Laub and N. Auerhahn in this volume, above, p. 151.

7. Martin Bergman and Milton Jucovy, eds., *Generations of the Holocaust* (New York: Basic Books, 1982).

8. Helen Epstein, *Children of the Holocaust* (New York: Putnam, 1979).

9. Hillel Klein, "Children of the Holocaust: Mourning and Bereavement," in *The Child in His Family,* ed. E. J. Anthony and Cyrille Koupernik, vol. 2, International Association for Child Psychiatry (New York: Wiley, 1973), pp. 393–409.

10. Reuven Feuerstein, *The Dynamic Assessment of Retarded Performers* (Batimore: University Park Press, 1979), pp. 38–39.
11. Des Pres, op. cit., p. 14.
12. Ibid., p. 15.
13. Kurt Eissler, *Medical Orthodoxy and the Future of Psychoanalysis* (New York: International Universities Press, 1965), p. 281.
14. William Barrett, "The Hebraic Man of Faith," in *The Dimensions of Job*, ed. Nahum N. Glatzer (New York: Schocken, 1969), pp. 275–276.
15. For an excellent discussion of the topic of stress and denial, see Shlomo Breznitz, ed., *The Denial of Stress* (New York: International Universities Press, 1982). Breznitz points out that although in extreme forms denial may be pathogenic, often it serves as a "protective veil of illusion," allowing us to cope with strain.
16. Klein, op. cit., p. 407.
17. For a psychoanalytically based discussion of Holocaust education, see Israel Charney's paper, "Teaching the Violence of the Holocaust," in *Jewish Education* 2 (1968): 15–24.
18. Neil Postman in *U.S. News and World Report,* January 19, 1981, p. 45.
19. Albert Camus, "Death in the Soul," in *Lyrical and Critical Essays* (New York: Knopf, 1968), p. 44.
20. I have found George H. Pollock's views on the significance of the mourning process as it relates to adaptation and post-Holocaust living to be particularly helpful. See, for example, Pollock, "Mourning and Adaptation," *International Journal of Psycho-Analysis* 42 (1961): 341–361.

INTRODUCTION

In this essay, Dr. Marcus discusses the impact of the Holocaust on Jewish self-concept from the viewpoint of an American Jew personally untouched by the events in Nazi Europe. Drawing on the existential, theological, and psychoanalytic literature, the author presents his post-Holocaust conception of Jewish identity. Using the existential notion of authenticity as a focal point, Dr. Marcus offers his portrait of the authentic post-Holocaust Jew. This individual does not shy away from confronting the significance of Nazi brutality, nor does he deny that Auschwitz has posed difficult and painful dilemmas for his Jewishness. The authentic Jew, however, attempts to create a Jewish identity based on a positive framework of meaning—albeit with now necessary modifications.

In the latter part of the essay, Dr. Marcus discusses these ideas as they relate to current criteria of mental health and with reference to the outcome of a successful psychoanalysis. He argues that such an analogy not only can be made but that the therapist's sensitivity to the Jewish component of the patient's self-representation has important implications for the therapeutic process.

Jewish Consciousness After the Holocaust

PAUL MARCUS

The Holocaust represents the most traumatic Jewish experience in the Diaspora in modern times. For the Jew it has meant facing up to the most painful realities of what it means to be a Jew in a post-Holocaust world. As Elie Wiesel has suggested, the modern Jew's problem after Auschwitz is an existential one. It is the question of his being and not of his thinking. During the Holocaust, Jewish existence as such was at stake. Wiesel speaks about the totality of the experience and the universality of the failure—of all men, including Jews themselves.[1] "Everybody concerned was totally committed to his condition. The murderer to his crime, the victim to his fate, the bystander to his indifference."[2] It is this extraordinary experience which forces the Jew to ask anew: "By what values are we to act among ourselves and in relationship to the world at large in the future."[3]

In this essay I want to discuss some of the ways the Holocaust has had a decisive influence on Jewish consciousness as viewed from the perspective of an American Jew personally untouched by the catastrophe. Therefore, I will not be considering survivors or their offspring, since this subject has received considerable psychological attention and deserves special consideration.[4] I will be discussing the significance of the Holocaust as an example of Jewish destiny, and the meaning to the Jew of this unprecedented brutality. I will also be commenting on the impact of the catastrophe on Jewish self-concept, with reference to the victims and survivors. Finally, I will discuss the implications of these ideas for psychotherapists.

JEWISH AUTHENTICITY

The notion of the authentic Jew is given heavy weight in this essay, since one of the central dilemmas for the Jew after the Holocaust is to decide whether to be or not to be a Jew. This truly is the question. The Holocaust has threatened the Jewish people with near extinction such that the present choice to be (or remain) a Jew, as well as the search for Jewish meaning, has become inextricably bound up with the survival of the Jewish people as a distinct ethnic-religious group.

Authentic existence is the modality in which a man assumes the responsibility of his own existence insofar as he can distinguish between acts which are done in good and bad faith and which are true and false to the self. Following Sartre, "Jewish authenticity consists in choosing oneself as Jew—that is, in realising one's Jewish condition."[5] "The authentic Jew makes himself a Jew, in the face of all against all."[6] "To be a Jew . . . is to be responsible in and through one's own person for the destiny and the very nature of the Jewish people."[7] The authentic Jew, like the authentic man, must freely choose his identity; "he is what he makes himself, that is all that can be said."[8]

Inauthentic existence, on the other hand, is the modality of the man who lives under the tyranny of the crowd, i.e., the anonymous collectivity. Sartre says that "the inauthentic Jew flees Jewish reality."[9] More specific to our present discussion, the Jew who says he is a Jew only because the *Goyim* will not let him forget it is being inauthentic, because he accepts a definition of himself imposed by the crowd. The Holocaust, in a paradoxical way, has highlighted the inauthentic response of some Jews. In Europe there were many Jews who didn't choose themselves as Jews, but Hitler's pronouncement that "a Reich citizen is only that subject of German or kindred blood who proves by his conduct that he is willing and suited loyally to serve the German people and the Reich"[10] made the Jewishness of these individuals largely determined by external forces without their consent. I think Sartre expressed this commitment to self-definition when he refused the Nobel Prize and told the correspondent of *Life* magazine, "I don't align myself with anybody else's description of me."[11]

The nature of an authentic Jewish response to the Holocaust has been the subject of considerable discussion by Jewish theologians, some of them with considerable psychological sophistication (e.g., Emil Fackenheim, Richard Rubenstein, and Eliezer Berkowitz).[12] All of these courageous scholars stress the need for the Jewish people to survive as a distinct group making a unique ethical, religious, and intellectual contribution to civilization; however, they differ in their views of what should specifically constitute the Jewish response after the Holocaust, especially from the theological point of view.

In the wake of the Holocaust, Fackenheim, for example, maintains, the former distinction between secular and religious Jews is obsolete. Now the distinction is between inauthentic Jews, who flee from their Jewishness, and authentic Jews, who affirm it. "The latter group includes religious and secular Jews. They are united by a commanding Voice from Auschwitz." Fackenheim claims that the Voice from Auschwitz, like the Voice from Sinai, is a revelatory voice. "The voice issues a commandment, now grafted onto the 613 commandments of the Torah." This 614th commandment forbids Jews—secularist and religionist alike—"to hand Hitler posthumous victories," and orders Jews to survive as Jews, lest the Jewish people perish.[13]

Fackenheim's approach has its difficulties, especially from the theological point of view. Suffice it to say, his conclusions indicate that a commitment to communal survival is an act of collective life-affirmation. After the catastrophe in Europe, what could be a better sublimation than rebuilding one's community and strengthening one's commitment to the group? Freud, in a different context, had a similar idea when he wrote in *Reflections upon War and Death,* "To endure life remains, when all is said, the first duty of all living beings."

The survivalist mentality can always be challenged from a moral point of view, since there are moral values that are greater than sheer survival. Even within the framework of Jewish morality there are things worth dying for. But this survivalist view is reinforced by others who have suggested that the group transmits certain imperatives to its members, rooted in what may be described as the individual's "quasi-mystical coenesthetic, primary organic involvement with an ancestral community."[14] Furthermore, this view asserts that the Jews are bound together by sentiment, religion, and culture, and that the demand after the Holocaust is for greater loyalty to the group, especially in times of danger, to ensure its survival. It seems, then, that after Auschwitz the absolute demand for Jewish survival is intimately bound up with the perennial search for Jewish meaning.

WHITHER JEWISH DESTINY?

Upon learning the brutal and horrifying facts about the Holocaust, many Jews find themselves consciously and/or unconsciously grappling with the question of whether to continue being part of a people that is so vulnerable to attack and destruction, as was the case in Nazi Europe. I think a significant anxiety among some Jews, young and old, is based on the perception that another Jewish Holocaust can happen almost anywhere in the world, including America. America is, after all, one of the most nationalistic countries in the world and has its own history of anti-Semitism, and racist and totalitarian currents are latent in American society.

One avenue of flight from this anxiety-inducing situation is assimilation into the non-Jewish world. In this way the fear of being attacked and discriminated against is diminished, and one escapes the intensity of the demands of the Jewish community; demands engendered by belonging to a threatened group. Obviously, the reasons for assimilation are much more complicated, but assimilation can be one way of reducing the associated anxiety connected to the perception of yet another hostile attack lurking down the road—all amidst the historical backdrop of the Holocaust.

The issue becomes even more complex since there is a tendency among Jews to blame themselves for any tragedy that befalls them. This is not unique to the Holocaust, since self-reproach is probably the guilt that prevails among surviving Jews for having failed to rescue European Jews from the Holocaust.[15] This guilt can contribute to new or preexisting feelings of self-hatred, anger, shame, and a desire to flee from Jewish reality so common among those American Jews who lived during the Holocaust and feel they did not do enough to help. When contemplating the fate of the victims, many Jews use arguments that the Jewish community contributed to its own demise through self-destructive compliance on the part of the Jewish victims.[16] This becomes another reason for fleeing Jewish reality and the community.

The reaction to thinking about the fate of the victims is not always flight from the Jewish reality or assimilation. There are some whose identification with the fate of the victims contributes to a more generalized bonding to the Jewish community as well as to the survivors. The existential dilemmas faced by the concentration camp inmates (and those in hiding), and their responses, can reverberate in the Jew and intensify the identification with the victims and survivors. There may be the objective realization that if one had been a Jew in Nazi Europe, one would probably have suffered the same fate as the victims. A survivor friend of mine reported a conversation he overheard between a father and his teenage son during a selection in Auschwitz. The young son asked his father in a whisper probably one of the most distressing questions a son could ask a father: "Why is this happening to us?" And the father replied: "Because the Nazis, fear, hate, and *envy* us." This idea of envy is an important one because it points to the need for a positive basis for remaining a Jew and not one primarily determined by the distorted characterization of the anti-Semite.

The fact that there were Jews who survived in the concentration camp by using a Jewish framework to maintain their dignity in the face of wicked degradation seems to make the issue of a positive basis for Jewish survival a central one. Jewish spiritual resistance—through maintaining one's Jewishness (some Jews actually studied Talmud and heard lectures on Jewish philosophy in the camps, others celebrated the festivals and regularly prayed, and some even got married in a Jewish ceremony)—suggests that Judaism, broadly defined, can be and was a source of spiritual and psychological strength which contributed to enduring the horrors.[17] And if some Jews could actually go into the gas chamber while proclaiming the *Shema* and singing *Ani Maamin,* in defiance of the Nazis and in affirmation of their Jewish faith, then it is quite comprehensible why some Jews today feel it imperative to take their Jewishness seriously and attempt to understand (and perhaps cultivate) what this remarkable attachment to Jewishness was all about. These are illustrations where the group can transmit certain adaptive imperatives to its members via confrontation with tragedy that befalls the group, in order to perpetuate its survival.

FROM POWERLESSNESS TO POWER

Feeling oneself vulnerable to attack and not capable of significant self-defense, as was the case of the Jews in Nazi Europe, must be connected with the issue of Jewish powerlessness. George Steiner put it poignantly when he wrote, nearly twenty years ago, that when he listened to his children breathing in the stillness of his house, he would grow afraid. This has not changed. "I am utterly trying to teach my children the sense of vulnerability," he now says, "and keep them in training for survival."[18] Richard Rubenstein has pointed out that the Holocaust demonstrated the ultimate conclusion of Jewish powerlessness. Jews must now be involved in a "power struggle" for existence. Since the strategy of Jewish survival by powerless appeasement has been proven specious by the Holocaust, the contemporary Jew, he argues, must forge a new image, from powerlessness to power. For Rubenstein, the modern Israeli is the prototype of this new image. The way of attaining this goal is by reasserting a pagan theology, rooted in Nature (i.e., earth's fruitfulness, its cycles, and its engendered power). The God of Nature must replace the God of History so that the image of the potent Jew can replace the image of Jewish impotence.[19]

The issue of Jewish powerlessness and its relationship to Israel has implications for Jews in the Diaspora. Israel is no longer a refuge for Holocaust survivors. It is a power unto itself. Sometimes power can make victors out of victims. The American Jewish community (and the non-Jewish world) has great difficulty in accepting a Jewish capacity for aggressive pursuance (especially militarily) of their cause and the ability to destroy the enemy with the use of offensive power. During the 1948, 1967, and 1973 wars, for example, Israel had her back up against the wall. She was clearly the underdog, and her survival was at stake. This image of the Jew-Israeli fighting with great courage and success against overwhelming odds makes Jewish expressions of power more acceptable to Jews because it is unambiguously and manifestly self-defensive and reactive. More recently, one Israeli official offered a wry illustration to account for international criticism of Israel's invasion of Lebanon,* but I think it also reflects the attitude of many Jews in the Diaspora.

> Three men, one an Israeli, are captured by cannibals, and while the cauldron of water is heating, they are each granted a final wish. After the others' conventional wishes have been met, the Israeli makes his request—that the cannibal chieftain kick him in the behind. The wish fulfilled, the Israeli pulls his Uzi submachine gun from under his shirt, kills his tormentors and sets his companions free. "But why did you ask him to kick you?" They ask. "Because otherwise, no matter how justified my shooting him, I will be accused of aggression," comes the reply.[20]

Some Jews have unrealistically insisted that Israel remain morally a kind of superhuman state, one that exists outside nature and normalcy and whose conduct is to be compared to an ideal rather than to the conduct of other nations. This is certainly a severe and even bizarre requirement for any nation to fulfill and one that would require a separate essay to explain.

The point is simply that the capacity to help shape Jewish destiny through military power and negotiations from a position of strength runs counter to the familiar pattern of the Jew as scapegoat or the "nice Jewish

*This essay was completed before Israel decided to go beyond the twenty-five-mile "security zone" and make its incursion into Beirut, with all the ensuing tragic consequences.

boy." It is perhaps the fear and begrudging respect that this power evokes that may be necessary for Jewish survival and normalization in a post-Holocaust world.

ATTITUDES TOWARD THE NON-JEWISH WORLD

There are some Jews whose Jewishness is largely determined by negative feeling states (e.g., anger) directed at the non-Jewish world. This is an inauthentic (and self-destructive) way of defining oneself, since it is reactive and a consequence of hostile non-Jewish actions toward the Jew rather than primarily an autonomous self-definition rooted in a framework of positive Jewish meaning.

One of the earliest psychological reactions upon learning about the Holocaust is intense conscious or unconscious anger directed at the non-Jewish world. The anger is perhaps better described as narcissistic rage. It reflects, as Henry Krystal pointed out, "love outraged." The Jew has experienced the Holocaust as the most devastating narcissistic wound; the result of Gentile assault and indifference. It is especially painful because the Jew for thousands of years has been persecuted by and marginal to the Gentile world. Someone once said, "No matter where you touch a Jew you find a wound." In the modern world since the emancipation (about 1815), the Jew expected to be treated like everyone else, with all his rights protected under the law. The Holocaust snapped the backbone of European humanism, and the Jew felt and still feels enraged, because his expectation of a decent world where he would be shown respect and given equal rights (read: love) was shattered into pieces by the most civilized people of the world—the nation of poets and thinkers. It is likely to take a very long time before this narcissistic rage can be significantly worked-through and transformed into a revitalized fellowship with the Gentile world.

Not only will it take a very long time for this wound to heal, but I think there has been a near irreversible rupture in Jewish-Christian relations. There has always been anti-Semitism, but it was generally limited in scope and intensity (e.g., pogroms in Russia), and its expression and consequences however brutal, never resembled the Holocaust in magnitude and in devastation and horror. In previous anti-Semitic regimes the Jew could either convert, assimilate, or flee his persecutors, but during the Holocaust there was no escaping the executioner. The lack of ambivalence on the part of the Nazi social policy of genocide,[21] and the world's silence, smashed the Jewish belief that Gentiles could and would restrain themselves from total expression of hate, whether it be the pure destructiveness of the Nazi or a derivative of the death instinct—the conscious indifference of the onlooker.

Some Christian theologians have written that in order for any true dialogue and reconciliation to occur between Jew and Gentile, there first must be a ruthless self-scrutiny on the part of the Christian world regarding its behavior during the Holocaust, which includes a severe challenge to Christian theology.[22] This would seem to be a necessary first step (which is already underway) to rebuild the connectedness and human solidarity between Jew and non-Jew that was severed during the Holocaust.

Finally, it is worth mentioning that for some Jews the Holocaust has been used to confirm, once and for all, that the "world hates the Jews and wants them dead." In its extreme, this perception can take on a paranoid flavor. However, it could be argued that this view is partially based on reasoned historical analysis; that is, it is not merely a Jewish projection but has an objective basis in the history of anti-Semitism.

GOD'S SILENCE AND JEWISH DESPAIR

The problem of Jewish authenticity after the Holocaust does not necessarily imply a faith in God. One can be an authentic Jew and not believe in a transcendent being or the God of History, especially after Auschwitz.

The concept of God is so open to perverse distortion that it almost seems pointless to bring it into the Holocaust landscape. This is best illustrated by a statement by Himmler to his masseur, Felix Kersten: "Some higher Being . . . is behind Nature . . . If we refused to recognize that we should be no better than the Marxists . . . I insist that members of the SS must believe in God."[23] The notion of God can be so grotesquely disfigured, subjective, and unverifiable that it becomes a futile effort to center a Jewish response to the Holocaust on understanding His behavior. Greenberg implied this point when he wrote: "Let us offer this fundamental criterion after the Holocaust. No statement, theological or otherwise, should be made that would not be credible in the presence of burning children."[24]

Theologians have struggled with the question "Where was God?" This is perhaps the most radical religious question after the Holocaust. Elie Wiesel points out that the Holocaust "can be explained neither with God nor without Him." To Wiesel it seems that for the first time in Jewish history the covenant was broken—this is theodicy in the extreme.[25]

Rubenstein in *After Auschwitz* argues that after the Holocaust the belief in a redeeming God who is active in history and who will redeem mankind from its troubles is no longer possible. Belief in such a God, and an allegiance to the rabbinic theodicy that attempted to justify Him, would imply that Hitler was part of a divine plan and that Israel was being punished for her sins.[26] Eliezer Berkowitz, on the other hand, asserts that affirmations of Jewish faith may be made after the Holocaust, as they were made after other catastrophes in Jewish history.

I am not going to review the enormous literature on theodicy but rather want to offer a few brief remarks on Jewish faith after the Holocaust. The fact that God was not able or willing to redeem the victims of the Holocaust has raised some terrible questions about the viability of believing in a transcendent God. No doubt every Jew who takes God seriously has to confront the painful reality that God's "chosen people" were mercilessly and nearly completely wiped out while He looked on in silence. And every believing Jew must protest to God His indifference and argue it out with his own conscience. Some Jews have emerged believers, others are nonbelievers, and still others are sometimes believers interspersed with nonbelief in Him, what Irving Greenberg calls "moment faith." I, however, agree with Kafka, who told his Gentile admirer Gustav Janouch, "He who has faith cannot talk about it; he who has no faith should not talk about it."[27]

The problem of faith after the Holocaust is clearly an individual decision, and every man must face the problem with the inviolate indestructible core of his conscience being his guide. Never before has the Jew had to grapple with so much despair, despair concerning the human condition, the ontological foundation of the universe, and the possibilities for redemption.[28] I agree with Wiesel, who believes that overwhelming despair need not lead either to ineffectiveness with respect to the human situation or to the end of Judaism. Despair may even act as a powerful motivating force. For example, despair regarding their fellow men and other nations has led the American Jewish community and the State of Israel to a necessary self-reliance, and may provide the only possibility for survival.

Perhaps a Jew's faith after Auschwitz must be like a mirage that exists only through the force of his own will. When that disappears, so does he. Wiesel has given the best rationale for going on, with or without God, but always with hope, which is one response to tragedy: "Out of despair, one creates. What else can one do? There is no good reason to go on living but you must go on living. There is no good reason to bring a child into the world but you must have children to give the world a new innocence, a new reason to aspire towards innocence. As Camus said, in a world of unhappiness, you must create happiness."[29]

RESPONSIBILITY TO THE SURVIVOR

The attitude of Jews personally untouched by the Holocaust to the survivors reflects in many fundamental ways on their own sense of Jewishness. For many, the survivor of Auschwitz personifies what is quintessentially Jewish in modern times—he was vilified and victimized for one reason only: being Jewish. This may become associated with the feeling that the victims and survivors have suffered *for me,* and therefore I am obliged to affiliate myself with and be loyal to the Jewish group.

Survivors by their very nature point the finger at all of us and reminds us of our responsibilities to the Jewish group and to humanity. They are like messengers from the martyred dead, witnesses to the wicked treatment of the Jewish people by the Nazis, and by much of the world through its indifference.

For some Jews these feelings become associated with guilt. Ostow points out that some American Jews, influenced by the current mode of social activism, believe that they could have made more aggressive efforts to protect their brothers. It is not guilt that the individual has personally victimized the one who perished; but guilt that he has not offered to make an equivalent sacrifice for the group. It is a manifestation of the individual's tie to the group rather than an interpersonal transaction.[30]

Sometimes this unresolved guilt contributed to an unconscious contempt for the survivor which was expressed through the unkindness, indifference, or shame of relatives and others within the Jewish community when the survivor returned to the community to make a new life for himself. In addition, as Jack Terry points out in his essay in the present volume, the unconscious contempt for the survivor expresses itself via the so-called psychiatric experts. They study survivors and denude the particular survivor of his individual identity by applying a rhetoric of rejection composed of prepackaged categories like "survivor syndrome" to describe him.

The Jew after the Holocaust may also harbor a degree of envy towards the survivor. He feels amazed at the survivor's capacity to endure such agonizing treatment for so many years without going insane. This perception dwarfs his own personal conflicts and contributes to minimizing his own personal pain. The fact that some survivors showed a stubborn will to live that partially rested upon Jewish-oriented spiritual considerations adds to one's admiration for the survivor's social and psychological resources. It also encourages exploration of the dynamics and meaning of Jewish spirituality—spirituality that enabled survival amidst tragedy.

IMPLICATIONS FOR PSYCHOTHERAPISTS

For psychoanalysts the problem of authenticity has always been a troubling one, and the problem of Jewish authenticity has never to my knowledge been dealt with in the psychoanalytic literature. Rycroft points out that psychoanalytic theory has no means of making a distinction between acts which are done in good and bad faith, true and false to the self, nor between acts that are "sincere" and "insincere," even though psychoanalytic practice largely depends on the therapist's ability to make these distinctions.[31] However, inauthentic behavior is regularly interpreted as defensive, the implication being that the patient's "real" feelings or motives are other than he himself realizes, or alternatively, that he was insincere to avoid confronting some aspect of the situation or of himself which would have aroused anxiety. The criteria for deciding whether behavior which is based on identification is authentic are obscure, though Rycroft suggests that identifications based on a loved object are more likely to be authentic than those based on identification with a feared or hated object. A further criterion would be whether the identification is a true one or an "as if" identification.

Since these distinctions are difficult to make, the problem of Jewish authenticity after the Holocaust becomes a very complex matter to determine in the consultation room. One practical way to apprehend a Jew's authenticity when in psychoanalysis is for the analyst to ask himself: Is the patient comfortable in his own skin? If the patient seems excessively anxious, defensive, evasive, or alienated in regard to his Jewishness, then one can probably assume that there is an unresolved issue operative. Manifestations of self-hatred and the "Uncle Jacob" orientation (i.e., behavior toward Gentiles that is fawning or abjectly servile) are always indications of psychopathology and inauthenticity.

In addition, one would have to question a Jew's authenticity when he disavows his common history or identity with the Jewish people. Noam Chomsky, for example, whose father was a Hebrew scholar, collaborated with a French author who claims the Holocaust never happened:[32] I won't speculate on the significance of Chomsky's behavior to himself, but in less illustrious people whom I have worked with in psychotherapy, the motivation almost always seemed to be a patricidal wish of an intense nature.

The patient's quest for Jewish authenticity becomes even more problematic when one considers that some Jewish analysts have not adequately dealt with various Jewish issues in their own training analysis. Ostow has pointed out that when he "was a student at the New York Psychoanalytic Institute, there was an unspoken gentleman's agreement that in psychoanalysis one does not discuss Jewishness, except to demonstrate to an occasional religious patient that his piety is a sign of neurosis.[33] Only recently has this begun to change. The early pioneering analysts, many of whom were Jews, were trying to move away from their particular Jewish past into more universalist concerns via psychoanalysis, and the training analysts of that generation, and subsequently their students, never had their Jewish complexes fully analyzed.

Thus the Jewish patient struggling with painful issues concerning Jewish identity and self-definition after the Holocaust may have to work-through these conflicts without the empathy or insight of the analyst whose Jewishness is a blind spot in his own personality. Colleagues have told me about Jewish analysts who have reacted with considerable countertransferential aggression toward Jewish patients whose Jewishness is a central issue in the analysis. Usually the patient suppresses these concerns to avoid the painful counteraggression of the analyst, and the issue is never properly analyzed. Therefore, it is essential to view the Jewish aspect of the patient's identity, including attitudes toward the Holocaust, as valuable grist for the analytic mill. This will require an openness on the part of the analyst toward the Jewish component of the patient's self-representation.

There is no doubt that for some patients (and analysts) the Holocaust can serve as a pathological mooring point for the expression of sado-masochistic and voyeuristic wishes, as well as obsessional, depressive, and existential problems, to name but a few. The Holocaust can be used to disavow the more personal determination of depressive conflicts by being superimposed onto familial issues which are then forced underground and not directly dealt with in the analysis. Suffice it to say that there are numerous ways one can have a neurotic involvement in the Holocaust, and this should be a subject of a separate paper.

There are Jewish patients for whom the Holocaust is *not* primarily used as a symbolic medium to express personal conflicts but rather a profound issue related to the quest for authentic Jewish identity and meaning in and of itself. In other words, for some an involvement in the Holocaust can be a non-neurotic concern and one that reflects a healthy grappling with a monumental event that has far-reaching psychological, theological, and social consequences for the Jew personally, for the Jewish community (i.e., survival of the group), and for mankind (i.e., survival of the species).

It does seem that analysts today are much more attuned to the patient's use of the Holocaust as a sign of psychopathology. There can be a flight into reductionism on the part of the analyst where the patient's legitimate post-Holocaust concerns are reflexively translated into neurotic categories and denuded of deeper meaning, meaning which refers to an irreducible datum which is of great importance to the patient's search for truth and integration.

A final implication of the Holocaust for the psychoanalyst is best captured by the Freudian analyst Kurt Eissler, who wrote: "The resistance a person can put up against the onslaught of strong mass sentiments is an index of the degree of personality integration."[34] Hence, the cultivation in the Jewish and non-Jewish patient of greater social responsibility, rooted in the realization of the need to speak out against evil, should be included in any criteria of a successful analysis.

CONCLUSION

One version of the authentic Jew after the Holocaust may be described from a depth-psychological viewpoint as follows: He freely chooses to be a Jew and has a clear awareness of his Jewish situation in the world. He does not disavow his common history or identity with the Jewish people. He is not defined by the negative identity conferred by anti-Semites but creates his own Jewishness rooted in a positive framework of Jewish meaning drawing from the best of the ethical, intellectual, and cultural resources of the Jewish heritage. He is committed to Jewish survival both in Israel and the Diaspora and accepts his responsibilities toward preserving the integrity of the group. He recognizes the need to develop and rationally use Jewish power in order to ensure that the anti-Semites of this world won't rise again and to secure his group's continued existence. He is committed to dialogue and reconciliation between Jew and Gentile but understands that this demands a painfully honest self-scrutiny for the Gentile and willingness to forgive, without self-righteousness, on the part of the Jew. He uses his unique Jewish history of suffering as a basis for empathy, and then action, on behalf of others who are victims of injustice and violence. The authentic Jew may or may not believe in God, but under no conditions does he surrender to despair—he affirms life and eternally hopes.

The skeptical reader may question this apparently value-laden description of the authentic Jew, particularly when offered by a psychoanalytically oriented psychotherapist. However, on closer examination of some of the currently accepted criteria of mental health, there seems to be a high degree of compatibility with the authentic Jew as described in this essay.

For example, the notion of freely choosing one's Jewishness and creating one's identity is associated with the development of true autonomy and nonpathological identity formation (e.g., without self-hatred) as well as positive self-acceptance. By not allowing one's identity to be a negative one conferred by the anti-Semite, one is taking responsibility for one's self-definition; this implies the ability to maintain self-esteem largely independent of others, based on one's own internal criteria and value system. Through drawing on the best of the Jewish heritage to shape one's Jewishness, one shows the capacity to effectively use the environment for personality enrichment and growth. A lucid consciousness of the Jewish situation in the world, and the acceptance of one's common history or identity with the Jewish people, indicates the capacity to think independently, to accurately perceive and clearly judge reality without the excessive use of defenses (e.g., denial, avoidance), which are always maintained at the expense of one's reality testing.

In a commitment to Jewish survival, sometimes expressed through the rational use of power, one is demonstrating a feasible combination of ethical standards with a life-preserving code of conduct—thus, constructively using aggression in the service of self-preservation, neither turned against the self nor expressed in unprovoked violence.

Through the ability to forgive the Gentile and use the unique history of Jewish suffering as a basis for helping others, one is not being strictly determined by narcissistic rage. Rather, the primary motivating force is a desire for positive object relationships within and outside the group coupled with a self-protective wariness. Also being expressed is a human solidarity rooted in a faith in man's capacity for repairing damage done. There is the wish to universally share one's value system, based on empathy, drawing upon the powers of Eros, and in the service of humanistic ideals. In addition, when the Jew refuses to give in to despair, this implies the existence of an "ego virtue"—hope, which is a human attitude that is a basic ingredient of all strength (Erikson).

Finally, the authentic Jew after the Holocaust, like the authentic man after undergoing psychoanalysis, sees the past as an opportunity to accept events, and to integrate and use his history in order to fulfill his potentialities and to gain satisfaction and security in the immediate future. The authentic Jew and the authentic analysand both strive against the forces of psychic repression, since to repress or deny (e.g., denying the impact of the Holocaust on one's Jewishness) amounts to blotting out a piece of one's self, which then impoverishes the ego and impairs self-realization. The Jew who authentically works-through the implications of the catastrophe called Holocaust for his Jewishness is similar to the analysand who tries to comprehend and integrate an early personal trauma into his life. Both are occupied with overcoming the negative impact of the trauma, to turn obstacle into opportunity, so as to live a more meaningful and pleasurable life; both are, to quote Nietzsche, concerned with "how one becomes what one is."

REFERENCES

1. L. Yahil. Israel Pocket Library, Holocaust (Jerusalem: Keter, 1974). p. 191.
2. "Jewish Values in the Post-Holocaust Future," *Judaism* 16, no. 3 (Summer 1967): pp. 218-282.
3. Ibid., p. 268. From Steven S. Schwarzschild's introductory remarks to the symposium with Emil Fackenheim, Richard H. Popkin, George Steiner, and Elie Wiesel.
4. See M. S. Bergmann, and M. Jacovy, eds., *Generations of the Holocaust* (New York: Basic Books, 1982) and H. Epstein, *Children of the Holocaust* (New York: Putnam, 1979).
5. J.-P. Sartre, *Anti-Semite and Jew*. trans. George J. Becker (New York: Schocken, 1948), p. 136.
6. Ibid., p. 137.
7. Ibid., p. 89.
8. Ibid., p. 137.
9. Ibid.
10. Nuremberg Law, September 15, 1935. Quoted from *The Facts About the Destruction of European Jewry by the Nazis* (London: Holocaust Remembrance Group).
11. *Life,* November 6, 1964, p. 88.
12. See Fackenheim, *God's Presence in History* (New York: New York University Press, 1970) and *The Jewish Return into History* (New York: Schocken, 1978); Rubenstein, *After Auschwitz* (Indianapolis: Bobbs-Merrill, 1966) and "God

as Cosmic Sadist,'' *Christian Century* 87, no. 30 (July 29, 1970); Berkowitz, *Crisis and Faith* (New York: Sanhedrin Press, 1976) and *Faith after the Holocaust* (New York: KTAV, 1973).

13. B. L. Sherwin, ''Encountering the Holocaust: An Interdisciplinary Survey.'' B. L. Sherwin, and S. G. Ament, eds. (Chicago, Impact Press, 1979), pp. 421-22.

14. Alan Miller, review of *From Oedipus to Moses: Freud's Jewish Identity,* by Marthe Robert, *Psychoanalytic Review* 16, no. 1 (Spring 1979): p. 146. In his discussion Miller summarizes Robert's suggestion that on a conscious level Judaism was for Freud a quasi-mystical, coenesthetic, primary organic involvement with an ancestral community.

15. M. Ostow, ''The Jewish Response to Crisis,'' in *Judaism and Psychoanalysis,* ed. Mortimer Ostow (New York: KTAV, 1982), p. 256.

16. See H. Arendt, *Eichmann in Jerusalem* (New York: Viking, 1963); Richard Rubenstein, *The Cunning of History,* (New York: Harper & Row, 1978); George Kren and Leon Rappoport, *The Holocaust and the Crisis of Human Behavior* (New York: Holmes & Meir, 1980); and Howard Stein's ''The Holocaust, the Uncanny and the Jewish Sense of History'' (Unpublished manuscript, 1982).

17. See Yaffa Eliach's *Hasidic Tales of the Holocaust* (New York: Oxford University Press, 1982).

18. *Time,* March 29, 1982, p. 71.

19. B. L. Sherwin, ''Encountering the Holocaust: An Interdisciplinary Survey.'' p. 413.

20. *New York Times,* August 4, 1982. ''The Week in Review,'' p. 1.

21. I first heard this formulation of unambivalent Nazi hatred of the Jew during a discussion with Martin S. Bergmann.

22. See Harry James Cargas, ed., *When God and Man Failed: Non-Jewish Views of the Holocaust* (New York: Macmillan, 1981).

23. Quoted in Roger Manvell, *SS and Gestapo* (New York: Ballantine, 1969), p. 109.

24. I. Greenberg, ''Judaism and Christianity after the Holocaust,'' *Journal of Ecumenical Studies* 12 (Fall 1975): p. 525–526.

25. L. Yahil, Israel Pocket Library, ''Holocaust,'' p. 192.

26. M. G. Berenbaum, ''Elie Wiesel and Contemporary Jewish Theology,'' *Conservative Judaism,* (Spring 1976): p. 26.

27. Quoted by Alfred Kazin in *New York Review of Books,* June 24, 1982, p. 4.

28. M. G. Berenbaum, ''Elie Wiesel and Contemporary Jewish Theology,'' p. 25.

29. *New York Times,* April 7, 1981, p. C11.

30. M. Ostow, ''Psychological Determinants of Jewish Identity,'' *Judaism and Psychoanalysis,* pp. 181–182.

31. C. Rycroft, *A Critical Dictionary of Psychoanalysis* (Middlesex: Penguin, 1968), p. 9.

32. *Newsweek,* August 2, 1982, p. 68.
33. M. Ostow, "Discussion of Martin S. Bergmann's Paper," in *Judaism and Psychoanalysis,* p. 150.
34. K. Eissler, "Objective (Behavioristic) Criteria of Recovery from Neuropsychiatric Disorders," *Journal of Nervous and Mental Disease* 106, no. 5 (November 1947): p. 501.

INTRODUCTION

Dr. Wangh begins his essay by noting that even after thirty-eight years the Nazi Holocaust remains in the forefront of discussion at social science and other gatherings. His essay is concerned with what obstructs the needed working-through of the Nazi experience. Wangh argues that the main obstacle rests with the psychological shock caused by the confrontation with the utter evil evoked by the death camps. It was not only the individual victims who arrived at the camps who suffered this shock, but to some degree all of us, for we were all affected when we learned of the Holocaust. The reactions to the shock consisted mainly in the mobilization of "psychic numbing" and other defenses. The witnesses to the disaster remained silent and passive. This defensive stance led to a general attitude of indifference to what happens to the person next-door to us (e.g., the "bystander syndrome"). Once such defenses have been fostered and evoked, they are apt to be used repeatedly in the face of any new threat. Wangh observes that the reality of the overwhelming threat of an all-destructive nuclear holocaust hangs over all of us and makes us most reluctant to give up the "protection" which such narcissistic withdrawal offers. Hence, the author concludes, the working-through of the past Holocaust, the reperception, even in memory, of the anxiety and shock which such remembering necessarily involves, is constantly impeded by its linkage to anxiety about a future holocaust which now faces all of mankind. Wangh concludes his essay by briefly describing the contribution psychoanalysis can make toward the amelioration of this perilous state of affairs.

On Obstacles to the Working-Through of the Nazi Holocaust Experience and on the Consequences of Failing to Do So

MARTIN WANGH

Papers are still being published, and scientific meetings on the issue of the Nazi Holocaust, as well as the prosecution of Nazi war criminals, are *still* taking place. Thus, the issues of the Holocaust *still* take up much time in the sociological, psychological, and juridical fora of the Western world, which, of course, includes the State of Israel. The traumata experienced through detention camps, death camps, concentration camps, prisoner-of-war camps, labor camps, *still* live on in the minds and bodies of the survivors. We are also discovering that their offspring are *still* affected by the experience of their parents. In what is to follow, I shall try to demonstrate that the shock waves of the Nazi Holocaust continue to impinge upon the world at large as well.

What are these waves, and what has stood in the way of setting aside the Holocaust experience?

I shall begin with a description of the mental state of the Holocaust survivors themselves and then go on to describe that of the rest of us in the postwar world.

Profound psychic shock enveloped those who newly arrived at the death camps as they faced the vestiges of humanity of the prisoners who had preceded them.[1] What had been rumor became truth. Shock was followed by apathy. Recovery from these two states could occur only by means of psychic splitting. This meant that some form of "denial," of "psychic numbing," "derealization," or "depersonalization" took over mind and/or feeling. Also, in order to survive, a predominantly egotistical stance had to prevail. As one survivor put it: "Will you survive or I?"[2] In general, one lived like a hunted animal, constantly alert to mortal danger. Yet any aggressive, vengeful impulse had to be utterly suppressed, thereby deeply rooting a permanent paranoid attitude. But as paranoid projection distorts clear vision of reality, any new or conjured-up danger causes catastrophic alarm. This again reconstitutes the defensive cycle of shock–apathy–splitting–narcissistic withdrawal, paranoid alertness, etc. Thus, each of these defensive steps, mobilized as it is for the sake of survival, would, if enduring, lead surely to the very opposite—to renewed danger.

Let me illustrate. I begin again with the death camp survivor himself and then will show how—differing in order of magnitude—similar sequences can be found in the postwar world in general. If the new arrival at a Nazi death camp, already exhausted by the dehumanizing conditions of his transport, remained in shock for any length of time, he surely would soon be killed. The same was true for one who remained apathetic. Elie Cohen writes: "[Apathy] . . . was a period fraught with extreme danger. For many prisoners this period proved too long, so that they never had any opportunity to engage in the struggle for adaptation."[3] Then Cohen refers to the psychic split within himself: "I felt as if I did not belong, as if the business did not concern me."[4] Yet even such retreat upon oneself, i.e., to solipsistic narcissism, had its limits. One who only thought of himself was soon shunned by other prisoners and hence deprived of their support. Unless he became a kapo, he too soon died.[5]

Let us now go outside the camps, to the ghettos. Here the mental split involved in "denial" operated more heavily in the direction of death rather than of survival. Walter Laqueur thinks that a good many of the Warsaw Ghetto inhabitants might have saved themselves had "denial" not held sway for too long.[6] Three of the Jewish gravediggers who had to bury the corpses of the thousands murdered at Chelmo succeeded in fleeing. Escaping to a nearby, still-untouched shtetl, they were urged by the local rabbi to make their way to Warsaw to warn the ghetto. There, however, their report was not believed. This, despite the fact that the ghetto had already heard of the mass murders of the Jews of Lithuania and elsewhere. This earlier news had been warded off with such ratiocinations as, "[These were] manifestations of German revenge against Jewish Communists in the former Soviet territories," or with the argument that "this is Warsaw, in the centre of Europe, there are 400,000 Jews in the ghetto; a liquidation on this scale is surely impossible."[7]

Yet shock and denial of what was happening to the Jews in Poland extended to the world at large and the American Jewish community in particular. The result was a failure to adequately respond, which was a significant impediment in the process of mobilizing help. Laqueur gives us as an example the reaction of Felix Frankfurter.[8]

At the end of 1942 a most courageous Polish Christian came to speak with Justice Felix Frankfurter. (He finally got all the way up the governmental line to President Franklin Delano Roosevelt himself.) The man's name was Jan Karski (Koziclewski). He was a fighter in the Polish underground. He had had himself smuggled into a concentration camp (Belzec) to be able to report as an eyewitness. He then made his way across Nazi-occupied Europe to England and thence to the United States. He related to the judge at length and in detail the fate of the Polish Jewry. When he finished, the justice said some complimentary things but ended with: "I don't believe you." Only after the Polish ambassador, who had accompanied Karski, vouched for him, did Frankfurter explain: "I did not say this young man is lying. I said I cannot believe him. There is a difference." From the awkwardness of this wording, one can see what was happening to the usually so eloquent justice: his wish to *deny* what he heard is evident—his initial *shock* is not recorded.

Hitler's Holocaust of the Jews brought to the world's attention the possibility that man is perfectly capable of *unambivalently* eradicating selected others of his own species. As the next step, the invention and use of nuclear weapons made it even more clear that the reign of pure Thanatos—i.e., a panholocaust—is, in fact, realizable. Thus, ever since the conclusion of World War II, "end-of-the-world" fantasies have acquired realistic dimensions.

Since then, too, defensive and presumed self-preservative, narcissistic behavioral manifestations (as outlined before) have been seen throughout the industrialized world.

The events of March 13, 1964, illustrate this vividly. On that day, at 3:20 A.M. in the borough of Queens, New York, thirty-eight persons listened and watched, over a time span of thirty-five minutes, as a knife-wielding man assaulted and stabbed—in three separate acts—a young woman (Kitty Genovese) while she was returning home from work. Her loud cries for help went unanswered. Only after it was too late did someone call the police. This inaction by the thirty-eight people soon came to be labeled the "bystander phenomenon." Dr. Renée Clair Fox, professor of sociology at Barnard College, called it a "disaster syndrome."[9] "Witnessing a prolonged murder under their own windows had destroyed their feeling that the world was a 'rational, orderly place.' . . .

[this] deeply shook their sense of safety and sureness." The result, she ventured, "was an 'affect denial' that caused them to withdraw psychologically from the event by ignoring it."*

A not too dissimilar story from present-day Russia was recently recounted on the radio: two thieves murdered a woman whose outcries were heard by many of the inhabitants of the apartment complex—without their coming to her aid or immediately alerting the police.[10]

What is to be stressed here is that a pessimistic sense that the world is no more a "rational, orderly place" has been increasingly with us ever since World War II. It precedes and underlies the Genovese incident. The formerly assured statement "It can't happen here" has become an unconvincing slogan for the inhabitants of the industrialized world. The repeated wars, threats of war, and anarchic terrorism that have come to pervade daily life and awareness almost everywhere since the Second World War are, in my opinion, the main obstacles to the working-through of the Holocaust and of the vast need to mourn for the 30,000,000 dead of the war.

While "working-through" is a term coined specifically for the process of overcoming resistance in the quiet stability of the psychoanalytic situation,[11] the insights that emerge from it may occur during ordinary life as well, at least in regard to "normal traumatization," in "normal" development during a "normal" life span. But this therapeutic working-through process cannot be accomplished when the whole gamut of narcissistic self-preservatory withdrawal reactions are constantly reinforced by the steady and actual recurrence of terror.

Krystal and Niederland relate how a child of a survivor described a shopping trip taken with her mother.[12] The two were in a car when they were stopped by a policeman, who accused them of passing a red light. The officer demanded to see the mother's driver's license and also asked her to turn off the motor. In sudden panic the mother bit the hand of the policeman, then stepped on the gas and attempted to escape. A chase ensued. Her car was soon surrounded by policemen, but she apparently conducted herself in such a manner that she evoked sympathy and was charged with no more than a minor traffic violation. The sudden eruption

*The "bystander syndrome" is of governmental concern. A recently passed law in Minnesota makes it illegal for people to fail to aid a person in an emergency where there is exposure to grave physical harm. This 'Good Samaritan' law, the first in this country, was prompted both by the Genovese case and by the rape of a woman in a Massachusetts poolroom while a group of bystanders watched. *New York Times,* August 3, 1983, p. A10. (eds.).

of Holocaust memories and the equally sudden and amazing recovery are characteristic of many survivors. The comment of the patient who told the story in treatment was: "In our home there are no small dangers, only catastrophes."

How much the deteriorating and thereby actual threatening social circumstances in the urban centers of today chronically aggravate the phobic disposition of survivors may be illustrated by an example from my own psychiatric practice. An elderly woman was seen by me for the purpose of a *Gegengutachten.** She had lived in hiding in a Western European capital throughout the Nazi occupation. Ever since the liberation she had been suffering from agoraphobia; she only felt safe at home with the doors securely locked. Upon arriving in the United States, she settled in the Bronx. Since that time this area of New York City has grossly deteriorated. Her agoraphobia and her persecution complex have thus found renewed justification. Her life may be in actual danger in her present surroundings.

In recent years the recurrent and unexpected bombings of Jewish places of worship and offices, as for instance in Belgium and France, have caused widespread symptom aggravations in many Holocaust survivors. They rekindled psychic depressions and panic attacks among the survivors of the death camps.

Freud used the analogy of the unconscious wish as being the capital which finances the day-residue-entrepreneur to form the dream.[13] In the instance of the traumatized survivors living in the present-day world, we have to modify the metaphor. Both the early traumatizing Holocaust experience and the present-day living experience require the containment of large amounts of anxiety. These, added one to the other, form an enormous capital-reservoir which is prevented from overflowing only by staunchly held defensive barriers.

The last of the defenses against overwhelming threat which I enumerated at the beginning of this essay is paranoid suspiciousness. It severely impairs correct judgments of reality. Here one's own revenge-born aggression is projected and refound in the enemy. Actions undertaken against him are unconsciously aimed at undoing the initial traumatization. The resulting effect, alas, is that rather than laying to rest the earlier trauma, new traumatization is induced. The attempt to undo what was

*I.e., an evaluation to counter the evaluation of a German psychiatric (or medical) expert attached to the German restitution courts.

suffered in passivity through becoming the active agent always fails of its goal.

Active reenactment of what was endured may seek to heal a previous traumatic experience. Its results, however, are almost always nocuous. They prevent the healing process. Actions by terroristic groups, such as the Baader-Meinhof gang, the Red Brigades, or the Neo-Fascists, belong here. The blowing up of the Bologna railroad station, filled with masses of innocent people, is a most poignant example of the senseless ruthlessness of these acts. But one only has to look at the birthdates of the leaders of these loose organizations to see that they were raised under the brutalizing conditions of the Nazi domination and that they had as children suffered under the devastating bombings of the war. Aside from being organized for violence, these groups offer no coherent societal plan. Although, compared to the Nazi model, they are minuscule in number, they have succeeded in keeping the Western world under constant tension. The consequent absence of respite from threat has vastly stood in the way of the working-through of the Holocaust experience.

One may postulate that not too dissimilar psychological mechanisms are at work in nations as well. Especially the need to carry to completion a once-awakened impulse, for instance one aroused by feelings of rage or revenge, plays a formidable role here. Thus, one might hypothesize that the abrupt victory over Japan did not sufficiently work-through the trauma of Pearl Harbor. The rage created by the surprise attack was not laid to rest. Japan's surrender was too rapid. (We now know that even the bombing of Nagasaki was unnecessary to bring about the surrender.)[14] The pressure of incompletely discharged vengeful aggression may, I suggest, have led by displacement, and by paranoid projection, to subsequent wars against two other yellow races: the Koreans and the Vietnamese. The unfortunate result—produced by misperceiving the political situation through the distorting lenses of past experience—was not resolution but renewed traumatization. Similarly, the intense response of Israel to the repeated attacks by its neighbors, the desperate courage of its soldiers, may find its explanation in the Jewish Holocaust experience. The "Never Again" slogan, so often used by Mr. Begin, the former Premier, points clearly to this compulsory motivating source.

Thus, crises may spring from judgments that were correct for past experience but which, applied in the here and now, impede clear sight of present reality. To discern causalities within the nexus of past and present is essential for any good psychoanalytic procedure. Psychoanalysis helps to separate our anxiety which belongs to a past experience. It shows how it may bias a view of the present, and how it may add inappropriate emotional weight to present-day anxiety. Unclarified, this interwoven circuit may result, on the one hand, in grossly inadequate reactivity, and on the other, in excessive action. "Working-through" means continuously confronting, *in full awareness,* these perceptual and emotional comminglings. A measure of control over the combination of past-present anxiety is thereby achieved. The psychohistorian hopes that such knowledge of, and alertness to, this intertwining circuitry can help the social scientist, the people at large, and thence the decision-making politician to obtain self-understanding and thus get a clearer vision of present-day reality.

In my earlier papers on Nazi anti-Semitism, the recurrence of war, and the youth rebellion of the sixties,[15] I have tried to demonstrate how psychogenetic and psychodynamic psychoanalytical considerations can contribute to the understanding of political and social events.[16]

For any kind of curative relief that aims at keeping a rational social stance in an irrational world, the sensitizing past trauma *together* with the stimulating present-day residue have to be simultaneously lifted into full consciousness, and separated out from each other. This is a basic psychoanalytic procedure. The nexus of past-present sequences, their facts and affects, should be taught as a basic sociological principle from every cathedra in history, philosophy, and political science, and conveyed from every pulpit. Awareness of the sources of one's anxiety—as diluted as such consciousness-raising may seem by the measure of clinical analytical experience—is the most valuable weapon for control of the compulsion toward reenactment, with its consequent renewal of traumatization. This means, which has its roots from insights gained in the realm of individual psychoanalytical therapy, should become a necessary political science tool as well.

One Holocaust-survivor author, in particular, who attempts to do just this is Samuel Pisar. In his book *Of Blood and Hope,* he courageously faces the awful memories of his own concentration camp experiences and also the awesome danger of nuclear war in our day. He writes: "We live for the first time in an age where the crises are almost too numerous to count and where the means exist to demolish the entire planet."[17] He confronts our temptation to react to these crises with shock and denial, defenses that prevent the working-through of past Holocaust experiences, and also prevent us from facing the pan-holocaust before us. To quote Pisar again: "The precondition of survival in the face of deathly peril is *clarity of mind* [my emphasis]. To avert a holocaust on a universal scale, an awareness is urgently needed that Mankind is entering a new historic phase."[18] He overcomes his own enduring personal bitterness toward Communist Russia, the Russia which oppressed and failed him and his family in his childhood, by declaring: "Nothing constructive can be undertaken on a global level unless a way is found to defuse the fundamental and unmitigated hostility between the East and West; a hostility which exacerbates tensions everywhere and plunges us ever more deeply into a spiraling vortex of armed confrontations, political terrorism, social anarchy and economic warfare."[19]

What then is the contribution which we "mental health workers" can make to alleviate the nefarious effects of the past social trauma, and to help us face the present crises with reason and courage? We must, so it seems to me, help "civilized" humanity to understand the psychogenetic sources and dynamics of its paranoia, which if allowed to flourish, will lead, as is ultra-clear now, to the end of humanity itself. Paranoia always has its source in the unresolved anxieties of past experience. We must work against withdrawal in the face of anxiety. Working-through a trauma demands an even-balanced focus on the present stimulus as well as on the past experience. Without the recognition of the one, sole awareness of the other becomes an intellectual defense, and hence, yet another obstacle to achieving clarity of mind and purpose. Simultaneous double focus increases our ability to stay conscious of the components of our anxiety. In this way, we allow our minds to *stay clear*—i.e., to keep our reactions appropriate to the dangers at hand. The Nazi Holocaust and the bombing of Hiroshima both command us to stay aware that we not only possess the physical means but also have the psychic ability, driven on by narcissistic and paranoidal defenses, to override all of our ambivalences and plunge ourselves toward absolute death, the reign of Thanatos.

REFERENCES

1. Cf. Terrence des Pres, *The Survivor: An Anatomy of Life in the Death Camps* (New York: Oxford University Press, 1976; Simon & Schuster, 1977), pp. 83–107.

2. Ibid., p. 178.

3. Ibid., p. 92.

4. Ibid.

5. Samuel Pisar, in *Of Blood and Hope* (Boston: Little, Brown, 1979), describes how many of the kapos, when the end was coming, were done away with at the hands of the survivors whom they had tortured.

6. Walter Laqueur, *The Terrible Secret* (Boston: Little, Brown, 1981; New York: Penguin, 1982), pp. 3, 237.
7. Ibid., p. 127.
8. Ibid., pp. 3, 237.
9. *New York Times,* March 28, 1964, pp. 21, 49.
10. Radio Station WINS, New York, N.Y., March 29, 1982.
11. Burness E. Moore and Bernard D. Fine, eds., *A Glossary of Psychoanalytic Terms and Concepts* (New York: American Psychoanalytic Association, 1967).
12. In Martin S. Bergmann and Milton E. Jucovy, eds., *Generations of the Holocaust* (New York: Basic Books, 1982), p. 54.
13. S. Freud, Standard Edition, vol. 5, p. 561.
14. Cf. the unpublished recent paper by Lawrence J. Friedman, "Nothing Happened They Say. . . .! (from Hiroshima to Amchitka)."
15. Martin Wangh, "National Socialism and the Genocide of the Jews: A Psychoanalytic Study of a Historical Event," *International Journal of Psychoanalysis* 45, pts. 2–3 (1964): pp. 386–395; "A Psychogenetic Factor in the Recurrence of War," *International Journal of Psychoanalysis,* 49, pts. 2–3 (1968): pp. 319–323; "Some Unconscious Factors in the Psychogenesis of Recent Student Uprisings," *Psycohanalytic Quarterly,* 41, no. 2 (1972): pp. 207–223.
16. Cf. also Martin Wangh, "The Psychological Fallout of Surface Nuclear Testing," *American Imago* 38, no. 3 (Fall 1981).
17. Pisar, op. cit., p. 293.
18. Ibid., pp. 292–293.
19. Ibid., p. 293.

IV

PSYCHOANALYSIS and the HOLOCAUST: A ROUNDTABLE

INTRODUCTION

On May 2, 1982, four distinguished psychoanalysts were invited by the editors to participate in a wide-ranging, informal discussion about psychoanalysis and the Holocaust. The purpose of the meeting was to create a forum for the sharing of ideas on questions that seemed troubling to psychoanalysts both professionally and theoretically, and sometimes personally. The uniqueness of the meeting was that analysts were being asked to express views concerning issues that they had not systematically and comprehensively explored. The emphasis was on idea generation and constructive debate, so that the readership could observe a responsible and thoughtful group of analysts wrestle with some of the most disturbing and difficult questions about the Holocaust.

The purpose of the roundtable, therefore, was to promote dialogue and intellectual searching, without expecting any solutions or prescriptions. In a sense, then, the nature of the roundtable discussions resembled the analytic process, in that the analysts, like their patients, initially focused on one subject and ended up exploring others that seemed more compelling, and perhaps more illuminating.

Participants

Martin S. Bergmann
Sidney Furst
Frances Grossmann
Martin Wangh

Moderators

Paul Marcus
Steven Luel

Psychoanalysis and the Holocaust: A Roundtable

1. *Has the Holocaust forced you to reexamine any of the constructs that underlie psychoanalytic theory or technique? What has such a reexamination led to?*

Wangh. I would say it has, in major ways, focused our attention on the issues of "self" and "self-preservation." The preoccupation with "narcissism" is, in my opinion, an outgrowth of the experience of the Nazi Holocaust as well as of the menace of a future global nuclear holocaust. Intrapsychic conflict, the issue which psychoanalytic investigation usually scrutinizes, has paled in comparison to our fairly recent theoretical shift to "self," "self-preservation," and narcissism. The question "Shall man exist?" "Can man exist?" is to be faced.

Bergmann. The Hitler experience was the central one in our adulthood, and the significance is undoubtedly very great, but I would not see it particularly in terms of psychoanalytic technique.

The Holocuast has a very prominent place in my mind and in my view of Jewish history. If anything, I would say that psychoanalysis was a better preparation for the Holocaust than anything else that I know of. It's not that Freud really foresaw the dimensions of what was going to happen, but there was something in his theory, in his belief in the uneasy truce between libido and aggression, and the possibility that the aggressive drive could win, that made it a little easier, at least intellectually if not emotionally, to deal with the dimensions of the problem.

When, for example, anti-Semitism is considered, we know that to some extent the Jews survived throughout history because the Catholic church never treated the Jews as a heretic sect. These are the views of Professor Yosef Hayim Yerushalmi.* The church had a certain Oedipal rivalry, Oedipal hostility toward the Jews, but also a certain amount of Oedipal

*Personal communication. Yerushalmi is Salo Wittmayer Baron Professor of Jewish History, Culture and Society and Director of the Center for Israel and Jewish Studies, Columbia University.

respect. Therefore, they did not quite go out to exterminate the Jews, as with Hitler's "final solution." Hitler showed us that it's possible for at least a segment of Western society to lose its ambivalence toward Jews and become utterly nonambivalent.

The question of the value of ambivalence as a positive, protective issue is very significant. The loss of ambivalence is very, very serious. Among the various psychologies and philosophies available, it was Freud that in some way, at least, enabled us to cope with it.

I would not say that the Holocaust has influenced psychoanalytic technique. Rather, it has greatly influenced the psychoanalytic patients, or their outlook on the world—perhaps even providing rationalizations for depression, or genuine depression based on the fact that if this could have happened, then there is no guarantee of goodness. It does not seem, to my knowledge, that it affected the technique per se, apart from the general development which psychoanalytic technique has undergone based on changing conditions.

Grossmann. From a conceptual point of view what troubles me is the notion of survivors' guilt. I would like to question the concept of guilt, in the Freudian sense of repressed death wishes to important people in one's life. What is the meaning of guilt when one prisoner is forced at gunpoint to bury alive another prisoner? Or when a seventeen-year-old girl is forced to load sick people on a truck going to the gas chamber, and some of these people whom she loads on the truck are her friends. What is the meaning of personal guilt when prisoners themselves are forced to decide which prisoners are to be sent to the gas chamber? The magnitude of these events transcends personal guilt.

Marcus. I want to add that the question "Why was I allowed to survive?" is not necessarily responded to by guilt—that is the wrong word—but by responsibility. The survivor feels he has to tell what happened. This responsibility is not motivated by guilt but by human relatedness to the dead. Perhaps the term "existential guilt" is a more accurate formulation, would you accept this?

Grossmann. I might accept the term "existential guilt," but the Freudian guilt concept, which is based on a fantasy wish, is inadequate.

Furst. In general, I think I would say that the Holocaust has not resulted in major modifications in analytic theory and technique. I think what it has done is it has posed some very important challenges to psychoanalytic theory and technique.

On the theoretical level, for example, it has directed our attention to group processes and the broader sociologic variables, which, of course, psychoanalytic theory has been struggling to add to itself. This has been the focus of any number of contributions and conferences, but so far we still haven't been able to go too far beyond Freud's remarks in *Group Psychology* and *The Analysis of the Ego*.

This is the great frontier that psychoanalysis is standing on now. Some say that it does not rightfully fall within the realm of psychoanalysis.

As far as technique goes, I would say the challenge is primarily in the technical problems in therapy of Holocaust victims and the children of Holocaust victims. However, it has again posed more of a challenge to our technique than added to it. The challenge is in dealing with individuals who are different from other patients in that they suffered a very severe, massive trauma—a rare thing. The big question is, "Is the original psychoanalytic model of trauma applicable to these people?"

In psychoanalytic theory the main focus has been on the intrapsychic effect of trauma, such that in infantile trauma, the weak ego of the child is faced with a problem that the infantile apparatus can't handle, leading to repression and other defenses which affect the total personality. The Holocaust, however, was a massive psychic trauma which distinquished itself not only from infantile trauma but also from war neurosis and battle trauma, because of the duration and intensity of the external stimuli. Therefore, even the strongest ego will fail to protect the psychic apparatus from being traumatized. In terms of technique the notion of bringing the repressed to consciousness with a now more highly developed and better equipped ego, as in the case of an infantile trauma, is not applicable to the Holocaust-induced trauma.

I think the Holocaust has caused us to make certain modifications in technique in handling these patients, whom I don't think we truly understand as well as patients who fall into the more classical patterns of neurosis, and even those who present borderline pathology. But I don't think psychoanalytic technique has modified itself in any way which is specific to a Holocaust victim. The modifications are ones which would be used to handle a patient who has certain very special vulnerabilities and ego weaknesses, which do not usually stem as far back as patients with serious ego weaknesses who fall in the categories of borderline and other severe personality disorders. When one treats Holocaust victims, one finds that there are certain areas where one has to be a little more supportive, a little less rigid in technique, because a serious weakness exists primarily on the basis of the external experience.

2. *In light of the Holocaust, what are your thoughts on the conceptual validity of Freud's death-instinct theory and its connection to the problem of aggression?*

Furst. I suspect the Holocaust could be used—depending on theory, or your patient—to confirm or disconfirm the death-instinct theory. It can, of course, be used to confirm a later vicissitude that death-instinct theory has undergone, namely, attributing spontaneous, unprovoked aggression as a manifestation of the death instinct. But I think, as far as analytic theory and the Holocaust goes, the closest Freud came to it really was in *Civilization and Its Discontents*. There he spoke of civilization as something that the human race can maintain and continues to maintain with great difficulty. It is never firmly established; it is always in danger of breaking down. And this is obviously what happened in the Holocaust.

The degree to which it broke down in the Holocaust, such that genocide became accepted government policy, suggests that the Holocaust was really different from any of the other historic persecutions of the Jews—the pogroms, the Inquisition, etc. The reason why—as has been mentioned already—is that the Nazi Holocaust involved the absence of ambivalence as reflected on a government level. Professor Yerushalmi* argues that in the past, Jewish persecutions were never part of formal government policy—including church policy—and that very often it was the church who protected the Jews. Much of the Jewish persecution was mob action and triggered very often by economic adversity. But it was never adopted as a major policy. He insists that modern Germany under Hitler was the first time this had happened.

Now, what effect this had on causing the breakdown in civilization that Freud spoke of—it looks as though for a while this was the final straw, the straw that broke the camel's back, and pure instinct erupted without compassion and with unprecedented magnitude. But as far as death-instinct theory goes, I don't think the Holocaust gives us any crucial body of evidence to argue in favor or against it.

Wangh. The Nazi Holocaust seems to affirm the death-instinct theory in that it was possible that pure and absolute aggression could predominate in a society. However, it might be strange to hear that the libido still played a role with the Nazis, regardless of their sadism. If they really had wanted to, they could have killed the Jews within a very short time span. All the techniques were there, and yet it took them time. They had to wait until there was a war process going on. As shocking as it is, remember

*Personal Communication.

they were shooting first before they could gas. So in that sense some degree of libido was still in existence. Robert Lifton reported this recently at a meeting of the American Psychoanalytic Association. He had learned from the twenty or so Nazi doctors whom he interviewed that 20 percent of the Nazi Einsatzgruppen who killed Jews by gunfire became psychiatric casualties. When that occurred, the mechanization of the killing gas ovens, preferably operated by "non-Germans," became routine.

Grossmann. I don't think it was a matter of libidinal investment, I think it was a matter of what the Germans thought the world would allow them to do with the Jews. When they came to the conclusion that the world did not care what they did to the Jews, they could do anything they wanted to, they did. They were very sensitive about the world's attitude toward their treatment of the Jews, but when they saw that they met no resistance they simply went ahead.

Wangh. Even the idea of what the world would think means there is a consideration of somebody else's opinion, and this implies some kind of awareness of the world and libidinal attachment. It depends on which level we are speaking.

Bergmann. In Germany I would say that it was not so much the libidinal factor which was effective but the distinction between a paranoid personality and the psychotic. The former is a good reality tester. I doubt that Hitler ever had any ambivalence toward Jews, but what he did have was a very shrewd recognition of how far he could go. So I agree with Dr. Grossmann on this one.

I also want to comment on the death-instinct issue. There was already a development away from the death-instinct theory of Freud in psychoanalysis independent of the Holocaust, because more analysts did not accept the death-instinct theory than did. The modification that was brought about after Freud's death was to transform the whole death instinct into the recognition of the role of aggression.

The question here is not whether or not the aggression toward the self is primary, but rather, returning back to the earlier idea of Freud, that when aggression is turned inward it becomes bound. The whole question is whether or not the death drive is first of all directed toward the self, or directed toward others. I think that most analysts today would say that normally and originally it is directed outward; it is already a perversion to direct it onto the self. It's a kind of development within psychoanalysis itself.

In connection with the Holocaust, there is, however, one point which is important and surprising. By and large we have always thought that if the aggression can be directed outward onto someone or something it would not need any particular target group for its expression. There was a kind of general rule that in those countries in which witches were persecuted there was no anti-Semitism. Thus, there was always a search for a victim, but who the victim was, was not relevant; every victim could satisfy the same social needs. However, this was not the case with Hitler; his entire outlook was dominated by narcissistic rage of psychotic proportions. This rage of the psychotic differs from the neurotic's in that the psychotic's rage has greater object constancy and less displaceability. Thus Hitler was less able to displace the Jews as the object of his aggression; no other "enemy" would gratify his need for a victim. There is an astonishing fact about Hitler which also implies that his whole system was psychotic: the "final solution" was formulated for the first time after there was good reason for Hitler to believe that he would not win the war. There are statements by Hitler that if he could not conquer the world, he wanted to go down in history as the exterminator of the Jews. It is only in light of this that one can understand the remarkable fact that even though railroad links were needed for the front, the railroad that transported Jews to the concentration camps had a higher priority.

Actually, Hitler fought two wars simultaneously, the war against the Jews and the war against the Allies. It seems as though he gave more emotional attention to the war against the Jews than the outside war. This suggests the psychotic dimension of this problem, for which we were not prepared; neither as analysts, Jews, nor as human beings. We did believe, somehow or other, in the limited expression of aggression, whereas Hitler has taught us that it can be without limits.

Wangh. I wish to add here that to ascribe a "psychotic dimension" to the one person, Hitler, does not suffice. The whole German nation was involved—admittedly with some exceptions. But this is the most striking phenomenon: that a whole cohort (a cohort, according to modern historians, are all generations which have been touched by the same social events) regressed more and more to a more-than-psychotic process (where there is still ambivalence) of thinking and acting. The defusion of Thanatos from Eros became almost complete.

3. *Political scientists, historians, and economists offer differing views to explain why the Holocaust was possible—generally deemphasizing the role of intrapsychic factors. What does the application of psychoanalytic insight teach us regarding the conditions that made a Holocaust possible?*

Wangh. This is the most difficult question, because so many things are involved simultaneously. One must not think the Holocaust was caused by one stimulus producing a necessary effect. For example, if we say "These six elements determine a particular patient's behavior a certain way," we are inevitably going to omit some important elements. We thus guess at twelve others, while we only mention six. The same must be true of sociological and historical explanations for the Holocaust.

I have tried to throw some light on this question of psychogenetic and psychodynamic factors in two of my papers: one was on the specific quality of Nazi anti-Semitism,* and the other on the recurrence of war.† My main theme in these papers is that both generations, those who were children in World War I and shortly thereafter, and those who were young German soldiers in World War I, were deeply traumatized by this lost war. The *regressive* revival of these traumatizations and their complex structure was immensely stimulated by the psychological impact of the economic crisis of the early 1930s. For a more comprehensive exposition of the complexities of this development, I do recommend a reading of my papers on the subject.

Bergmann. I agree that this question is extremely complex and there are many factors operative. There was the hard-core minority that followed Hitler. Their character was similar to his in that they were, among other things, profoundly narcissistic. There were no limits to Hitler's hunger for victims. In fact, as the amount of victims increased so did his hunger and insecurity. There was a thirst for victims that even overshadowed the military security of Germany. Hitler was also an unbelievably good strategist. He knew how to win over German capitalists who thought they could support him and control him. He misled them into believing that he would be a pawn in their hands, and he wasn't. He also appealed to a certain division between Communists and Social Democrats that was extremely powerful, so that many Communists, with their own apocalyptic vision, thought, "Well, so Hitler will last for a few months, and after Hitler we will come to power." They thought that they would use Hitler for their own purposes. But once he managed to win the majority, although not by much, he then used systematic terror to put himself in total power.

There are also certain unquestionable tendencies in the German char-

*"National Socialism and the Genocide of the Jews: A Psychoanalytic Study of an Historical Event," *International Journal of Psycho-Analysis* 45 (1964): 386–395.

†"A Psychogenetic Factor in the Recurrence of War," *International Journal of Psycho-Analysis* 49 (1968): 319–323.

acter toward obedience, toward excessive anality, toward cruelty, etc. One can't understand what happened in Germany without mention of the German character. Although this is a kind of psychoanalytic reductionism, one can generalize and speak of a predominant constellation in a nation, as there are variations in each culture.

In a way, then, we are not quite able to answer your question. For one thing, we only have a very rudimentary social psychology as psychoanalysts. It's not the psychoanalytic forte. It is very interesting how little psychoanalytic group studies have contributed to our basic psychoanalytic data on the phenomenon of man.*

I am afraid that we are asking psychoanalysis to do here more than it can. It can contribute its share, but it is presumptuous for us to think that we have a psychoanalytic theory that accounts for the Holocaust.

Furst. Your question is a tantalizing one, because it is asking, "Could it have happened anywhere else besides Germany?" And as psychoanalysts you have to try to reduce group processes to individual processes, and there is the problem that we are confronted with: For whatever reason, the German people as a whole came to support Hitler. Why did they do it? How many of the factors which led them to support Hitler were the result of group processes, and how much had to do with the individual contribution to the group?

You would think that as psychoanalysts we might be able to make some contribution to it. There are factors which others have mentioned, with which I concur, regarding certain German character traits. They have been accused of being less libidinal and more aggressive and obsessional than those in Western European countries. One can take any of the basic psychoanalytic determinants of personality organization and find some connection to speculate—to it and the Holocaust. But they all bend the basic question, Could it have happened elsewhere, and can it happen on such a scale again?

The McCarthy era is a case in point. Yes, McCarthy missed, but did he miss by all that much? If the snowball had kept rolling a little further, would it have become unstoppable?

4. *From the point of view of superego formation and moral development, how is the same individual capable of loving poetry and crying when*

---

*Some pioneering efforts have been made to address this gap, most notably Alexander Mitscherlich and Margarete Mitscherlich, *The Inability to Mourn* (New York: 1975), Grove Press; Martin Wangh's "National Socialism and the Genocide of the Jews"; Kurt Eissler's "Death Drive, Ambivalence, and Narcissism," *Psychoanalytic Study of the Child* 26 (1972): 25–78; and "The Fall of Man," *Psychoanalytic Study of the Child* 30 (1975): 584–646.

listening to Mozart, as so many Germans did, and on the other hand murdering children, without recognizing any contradiction in his personality or being affected by it?

Furst. Theoretically that question is not difficult to answer, at least in the basic sense. After all, the superego is considered to be the introjection of parental demands and attitudes. All one has to have are parents who maintain certain values, inculcate them into their children, and ultimately that forms the core of the superego.

If cleanliness, orderliness, admiration of certain kinds of beauty, music, or whatever, is characteristic of the parent, it eventually forms the core of the child's superego. In addition, with a parent for whom compassion for other human beings is not considered to be of value, the child is left without it in the superego. There are one or two other considerations. Firstly, one never sees what one might call a consistent superego structure in anyone. I've never seen it in any patient I've analyzed. There are lacunae. There are exceptions for everything. Secondly, certain structures in the mind, including the superego, are maintained only at the cost of the expenditure of a good deal of psychic energy, particularly the higher superego demands. Occassionally one allows oneself an area where id needs are permitted expression within a circumscribed area. These are the lacunae. You cannot find a compulsive neurotic who is fastidiously clean, where the original wish doesn't break through in some form. I remember the patient who showered four or five times a day and changed his clothes completely each time he showered, except that he changed his underwear every two weeks. He was rather surprised when I called this to his attention. "Well," he said, "underwear, you just don't change that."

You can also see this where aggression is allowed, it is allowed to break through in a certain area. It appears clinically, as a contradiction or inconsistency in the superego. But superegos are no more consistent than egos.

Bergmann. The superego is not necessarily connected with morality along the lines implied in the question. It can be perverted for other purposes.

For example, there is the statement of Himmler. How, in spite of the fact that they had to commit all of these cruelties, they managed to preserve within themselves the image of man. Unlike pogroms, which were mass expressions of impulses, the German ideal was extermination without the sense of disorder. To be sure, there were pogroms, but by and large extermination of the Jews was the fulfillment of duty with the help of the perverted ideal of Himmler. The capacity to separate the two—the "image of man" and exterminating children—became exalted into a very high principle. Documents that we have of concentration camp commanders show that they elevated cold-blooded murder without mercy into a high moral commandment. Moreover, when they went home they could play with their children; thus, splitting became the cultural ideal.

Grossmann. I agree with what has been said regarding the superego, but I think that your question raises more general issues about German child-rearing methods which contributed to such Nazi brutality against innocent people. My research suggests that there was a lot of repressed rage in the average German due to brutalizing child-rearing. Certainly then, and even today, their upbringing is rigid, the father is primarily a punitive agent, the child receives little affection—there is little speaking at the dinner table, the mother rarely interferes when the child is being punished by the father. "Be clean and obey" is the message. An important part of German childhood are the Grimm's fairy tales. These bedtime stories contain much that is horrible, brutal, and sadistic, e.g., people being burned in ovens, boiled alive, etc. Many of the atrocities depicted in these fairy tales were practiced against the prisoners in the concentration camps. Interestingly, the Danish and Scandinavian fairy tales are more gentle and less violent. And the Danes were the ones who did so much to help the Jews.

Wangh. Apropos superego formation and its faulty moral development, I wish to add the following ideas. True, German child-upbringing may have been a shade harsher than, let us say, the French upbringing. I say this although I am not utterly convinced of this. The cruelties executed against each other by successive groupings during the French Revolution, or the brutal killing in 1871 of 20,000 citizens of Paris, members of the Commune, by their own compatriots, were not acts of euthanasia, to put it mildly. Were these deeds due to "French upbringing," or were they not, rather, due to sadistic mass regressions evoked by certain historical sequences of the sort I have mentioned earlier. In my paper on Nazi anti-Semitism I say that "prejudices" are "superego vents" of which any society is possessed and by which it often stabilizes itself.* Parents indeed transmit their prejudices to their children and get very upset when the children, in the course of their lives, may free themselves of these prejudices.

---

*"National Socialism and the Genocide of the Jews: A Psychoanalytic Study of an Historical Event," *International Journal of Psycho-Analysis* 45 (1964): 386–395.

5. *Some Germans, albeit few, were relatively immune to the impact of constant genocidal propaganda. From a developmental perspective, what was different about the upbringing of these Germans?*

Grossmann. David Levy did a study of German anti-Nazis.† This is one of the few systematic studies of German anti-Nazis in existence. He found that the critical difference between Nazis and anti-Nazis lay in their experiences in childhood. The anti-Nazis had a more permissive, less authoritarian, generally more humanistic upbringing. Corporal punishment was minimal or absent.

My own findings in a study of Gentiles who saved the lives of Jews during the Holocaust are very similar to Levy's.* I found that these Gentiles did not have more contact with Jews in their childhood than other Gentiles. They were also neither particularly religious nor political. On a test entitled "The Study of Values," they scored low on political values, very low in the area of religion, but they did quite well on aesthetics. In addition to having had a more humanistic and less authoritarian upbringing, there was greater communication and affection between parents and children. In such an atmosphere, there were greater opportunities for the development of self-expression, independence, and critical thinking. There was an absence of corporal punishment as well. When confronted with a choice of helping or not helping Jews, they tended to respond to an inner authority and value system rather than an external one. When asked why they undertook the very dangerous work of helping Jews, the response in most cases was, "It was the decent thing to do. My neighbors' rights were being violated, and I felt a personal responsibility to help them."

6. *Were the Nazi officials who perpetrated the Holocaust by and large sadistic psychopaths, or as some argue, notably Arendt, were they in some way ordinary men and women trapped in a situation which forced them to behave in ways inconsistent with their personalities, perhaps in ways they found abhorrent?*

Grossmann. I do not believe that the Nazi officials behaved in a way which was inconsistent with their personalities, nor was the Final Solution abhorrent to them, judging by the fanatical zeal with which they

†"Anti-Nazis, Criteria of Differentiation," *Psychiatry* 2 (May 1948): 125–167.

*"A Psychological Study of Gentiles Who Saved the Lives of Jews During the Holocaust" (Paper presented at the International Conference on the Holocaust and Genocide, Tel Aviv, 1982).

hunted down Jews. On the basis of psychological projective tests* as well as other sources of information, it would appear that men like Himmler, Goering, Goebbels, Eichmann, and of course Hitler, did constitute a society of misfits suddenly catapulted into positions of enormous power. Whom else would a man like Hitler, with the weakness of ego and low self-esteem that he possessed, choose as his associates? To these people Hitler could offer the fulfillment of their wildest dreams and most pathological fantasies in exchange for their loyalty.

On the other hand, there was a man like Albert Speer, who was neither a psychopath nor a sadist nor paranoid, as were some of the leaders. Speer was a highly educated man and a fine architect, who nevertheless, as head of the munitions industry, employed a half a million slave laborers under the most inhuman conditions in order to supply the Wehrmacht with its military requirements. Judging from Speer's book, his major drive was to win Hitler's love and friendship.† He sadly concluded that Hitler was incapable of love or friendship.

Although it is difficult to generalize, it may be said that many of the Nazi leaders reflected in their own personalities the pathology of the time and nation which they ruled.

Bergmann. I would say that the Nazi officials were not forced into a leadership role, because they could have selected other occupations. Many of them didn't survive as members of the hierarchy and were transferred to other places. There were also some who showed acts of kindness, which was not tolerated by the regime. But there were also those hard-core dedicated sadists. However, their sadism was different, since they were "adjusted sadists." They were not given to uncontrolled expression of aggression. They were well disciplined and killed on command. And their sadism was, on the whole, under very tight reins and expressed in a highly controlled manner.

One could say, therefore, "Yes, they were killers." But if you look at it from the point of view of their adjustment to society, you would say that their adjustment to the German society was excellent.

Furst. One other way of conceptualizing the behavior of the Nazi officials—not the German people in general—is to ask, were they sadists or opportunists? The sadism can undoubtedly be accounted for in terms

*See Florence Miale and Michael Selzer, *The Nuremberg Mind: The Psychology of the Nazi Leaders* (New York: 1976), Times Books.

†Albert Speer, *Inside the Third Reich: Memoirs of Albert Speer* (New York: Macmillan, 1970).

of strong, unmodified aggressive-drive derivatives, the erotization of aggression, and in some cases as a defense against masochism. (It had been reported that Hitler was a masochistic pervert.) The opportunism was probably in the service of wishes for power, status, and self-aggrandizement. In most instances it was probably a combination of both and constituted a classic complementary series. The more you had of one, the less you needed of the other. But certainly, nobody was forced to be a Nazi official.

Wangh. My answer to this question shifts its focus from the leader to his followers. It may well be that all sorts of psychological tests show that indeed the highest Nazi leaders and officers were psychopathic personalities. But I don't think we have gained very much if our diagnosis stays limited to these persons. What and who brought them into the leadership position; what and who allowed them to pursue their nefarious aims and deeds; what ideas made them flourish, and why did they flourish at a given point in historical time? These are the questions to be asked. There are many Hitlers standing at the various Hyde Park corners of the world—why do some of them gather a following and some not? That is the question. Only those become leaders, in other words, whose perorations correspond to the wishes, ideas, and feelings dormant or alive in the crowd that listens—that stays listening to them. Once one accepts this perspective, then one can easily see that even if one of these "leaders" falls, someone else from among the many psychopathic characters in the audience—that is, in the people—may take his place. Ultimately, the question is: what has carved the mind of the cohort in a certain way at a given time? And from here we have to come to an even graver question: could we ourselves, given our history, be among these people or leaders?

7. *Some scholars like Arendt, Hilberg, and Rubenstein argue that there had to be some kind of masochistic and/or self-destructive compliance on the part of the Jewish victims. Every assault requires at least two actors. Even the most innocent victim is part of the process of his undoing. To think otherwise is to maintain what Kren calls the "fallacy of innocence."* Psychoanalytically speaking, to what extent, if any, did the Jewish victim contribute to his own undoing and destruction?*

Furst. To say that the Jews were responsible or played a central role in their destruction in the Holocaust is an untenable argument.

The question, however, of why certain Jews foresaw what was happen-

*See G. Kren and L. Rappoport, *The Holocaust and the Crisis of Human Behavior* (New York: Holmes & Meir, 1980).

ing and managed to escape, while others did not, is quite interesting. I think that there would be different reasons for different individuals. There were some, for example, who were more suspicious, more frightened of the outside world. We see this today. There are people who are optimistic and get along with everyone. There are people who see danger lurking around every corner. This is part of personality organization, and I'm sure that it applied to many individuals during the Holocaust.

It could also stem from a need to deny. Many people, because of their personality organization, need to deny certain deep-seated fears and anxiety. These Jews denied what was coming and therefore did nothing about it.

Perhaps this can be considered a kind of secondary masochism, as some have suggested. But I'm not sure that it invariably has to be even that. It can be another character trait, such as optimism, which ultimately brings about the same terrible result. However, this is not masochism in the sense that the motive is to suffer or to be humiliated.

There is one other relevant point to the Jewish response to crises. Historians refer to the analogy of the oak versus the willow tree. There is a bad storm; the oak is big and strong, and it stands up. The willow is weak, but in the face of a storm it bends. Which tree has the better chance of survival?

Should the Jews have stood up and given more resistance to the Nazis, or should they have bent? When one reviews Jewish history, I think what the historical chronicle shows was that the willow usually fares better. This was typically the response of the Jews in most of the crises with which they were faced throughout history. In several crises where they didn't bend they did not do well. The rebellion of Bar Kochba, and Masada are very good examples of this.

In bending, in trying to adjust until it was too late, the Jews during the Holocaust, in general, would have been following a typical pattern, typical for eons of Jewish history. As I said, I think it would be pretty hard to argue that this was a real masochistic component, the masochism being the motivation which led them to respond to the crisis as they did. Perhaps, however, there was a passivity in the Jewish response.

Grossmann. I totally reject this whole argument which says the Jews were responsible for their destruction or that they were masochistic and wanted to suffer. The Jews died because the most powerful nation in Europe waged a war of genocide against them. The whole idea of blaming the victim for his own misfortunes, whether it's Jews, a woman who has been raped, an abused child, is a copout. It's just not assuming responsibility for what you've done to other people.

Wangh. There are group phenomena that should be considered to explain the Jewish response to the Nazis. One's response depended on where you were in the whole circle of Jewish culture; the extent to which you were on the border enabled you to escape. Also, you had less opportunity as time went on. Another factor was one's attitude toward the predominant German culture. It was detrimental if you felt that because you received an Iron Cross you would be spared. Many in the Eastern Jewish community in Germany saved themselves. They were also more affiliated with international Jewry; many of them were Zionists. I also want to say that the fact that Jews are different makes them an obvious target of hatred and prejudice. But to completely assimilate and vanish as a distinct group is a kind of collective suicide which is a pathological response to a crisis. The anti-Semite who cannot tolerate the existence of someone different is equally disturbed.

Bergmann. I agree with Dr. Grossmann that to believe that the Jew is responsible for the Holocaust, and not the Nazis, is a psychological perversity. However, I realize that the answer to your question defies easy classification because it involves complex group phenomena—the interaction between the Jewish and Christian communities across the ages. Take the Jew's idea of being chosen, for example. It is not, as it first appears to be, a purely narcissistic idea—that we were chosen because we were better. When this idea was conceived, Jewish ideology coalesced. There was a mixture of what we would today understand as narcissism together with a certain acceptance of obligation. This pure narcissism came very quickly under superego domination. "Chosenness" meant being morally better. Historically speaking, when other nations lost a war they would change their god. The Jews showed a significant transformation in that they didn't reject their god as powerless in the face of their enemy but rather said to themselves: "He chose to punish us because of our sins. If we want redemption, then we have to change ourselves for the better." This is an autoplastic rather than an alloplastic solution.* Obligation also becomes increasingly stronger in the prophets, and this is associated with their having to say, "You were only chosen to fulfill God's commandments." This represents a kind of mitigation of a basic narcis-

---

*Autoplastic modification affects the organism alone. Alloplastic modification affects the surroundings.

sism by an ever-increasing superego. However, the Gentiles don't believe we are superego narcissists, they believe that we are pure and simple narcissists. And there may be a bit of truth in this.

Much of the Jewish-Christian hostility is due to the extent to which we are envied for this original idea of believing ourselves to have been chosen. But even more than this, the Christians, insofar as they accepted Christianity, also had to accept the previous election of the Jews. In that sense, anti-Semitism is different from any other prejudice, as it contains all the other elements of every other prejudice, plus something extra.

Grossmann. I also think that anti-Semitism is a unique kind of prejudice and is not the same as being anti-black or anti-Japanese. Freud wrote that anti-Semitism is a result of man's ambivalence toward his gods, more specifically the Christian's love-hate relationship with Christ. Freud stated that Christianity is a difficult religion to follow. To love one's neighbor as oneself is all but impossible, as it is to turn the other cheek.

Over the centuries Christians have resolved this ambivalence by loving Christ and hating his people. In other words, anti-Semitism represents a repressed hatred of Christianity.

An interesting case in point is Friedrich Nietzsche. Nietzsche, the patron saint of the Nazis, was not an anti-Semite. Nietzsche despised anti-Semites. He said anti-Semites are always lying. The only thing he had against the Jews is that they produced Christianity, which he loathed. He said that Christianity was a religion of slaves. All are equal in the sight of God, the meek shall inherit the earth, these are very un-Germanic ideas. Because Nietzsche did not repress his hatred of Christianity, he did not have to be an anti-Semite.

8. *Henry Krystal has written that "desperate attempts are made by survivors to restore and maintain their faith in God. However, the problems of aggression, and the actual destruction of basic trust which resulted from the events of the Holocaust make true faith and trust in the benevolence of an omnipotent God impossible." As psychoanalysts, what are your thoughts on Krystal's conclusion?*

Wangh. In general, man tries to find reasons, even irrational reasons, to things, particularly when he can't explain something. He must find explanations in order to exist; he must find some consistency in his experience, some meaning to his suffering. That's why we observe these very great efforts in all survivors to answer the question: "Why did I survive?" The general fact is, some survived because they had a strong-enough body which could endure the horror. In the main, *most* survivors survived because of luck, not because of their capacity to be adaptive.

The belief in God after the Holocaust is another effort to give a meaningful framework to one's experience, to give value to one's life. Interestingly, after every major Jewish catastrophe in history there was a renewal in the belief in God. I see this as an activity of Eros against Thanatos. By the way, Inge Fleischhauer and Hillel Klein described this in an interesting German book entitled *Ueber die Judische Identitat*.*

Luel. Regarding the question of faith after the Holocaust, the late Hans Morgenthau said that scholars from diverse disciplines had failed to adjust to the realities of living in a postmetaphysical world—in an ethically indifferent universe.

Wangh. Morgenthau comes from a left-wing, liberal, rationalistic background, and when he criticizes those who have religious faith after Auschwitz he may be right. But remember that those who were committed to rationalism and scientism were as stumped as the religious believers.

Bergmann. I have very little to add except one point. It's part of the Passover ritual to remember that in every generation there are persecutors out to exterminate us, but God saves us from them. The question is, how long can you keep on saying that? How many Jews must die in order to still consider God as saving us?

Personally, it is much more logical to say there is no God after Auschwitz, but I wasn't sure there was one even before. But I think, as psychoanalysts, we have to say that the effort to reinforce one's orthodoxy and to recreate one's community is as good an adaptation, as good an answer to the catastrophe as one could hope for.

As I mentioned earlier, in Jewish history, when the Jews lost a war, they did not, like other nations, turn upon their God and accept the gods of their victors. Rather they interpreted their defeat by saying to themselves, "It is because of our sins that we are being punished." This was an enormous step in internalization. Can we trust this process of internalization to go on and on? Is it still possible for a Jew to say, "It wasn't God who was responsible, but we with our sins, and our sins were so great that we deserve six million dead"?

Some people can do it, and others can't. As psychologists we can only say that there is a very powerful process of internalization that maintains the idealization of God at all costs, the way a young child maintains the idealization of a parent.

---

*I. Fleischhauer and H. Klein, *Ueber die Judische Identitat* (Berlin: Athènaum Kno, 1978).

When Krystal is entering into this controversy, he is entering into it as a feeling Jew, but not, in my opinion, as a psychoanalyst.

Furst. I would add one more thing to what Martin Bergmann said about the internalization. One great Jewish historian, Y. Kaufmann,* presents a very interesting thesis, that what really distinguishes the Jewish religion from all those that preceded it is not just that they were polytheistic religions and that the Jews were monotheistic. But that the one God didn't have a genealogy. He had no parents, as it were. In ancient times, there were old gods, warlike gods, nice gods, love gods, hate gods, etc. These gods had all sorts of relationships with one another—love, hate, lust, and genealogies as well as human physical characteristics and attributes. The Jewish god was spiritual and possessed no physical attributes at all. This is the major difference between the Jewish religion and the pagan religions which preceded it.

This is, of course, part of what permitted God to be internalized. This is what made the difference.

Grossmann. In part I agree with Dr. Wangh about man's need for consistency and to rationalize what happened to him. Obviously, different people respond in different ways whether they are laymen or theologians.

The problem of faith in God after the Holocaust is a complex one. I was thinking of the meeting of survivors which took place in Israel. I wasn't there, I saw it on television. Gabe Pressman, the reporter, went around asking various survivors, "Do you believe in God in view of what happened?" Most of them said no—reluctantly, thoughtfully. He asked Moshe Dayan, who said, "I believe in the Jewish people." Then he asked Begin, who replied, "Sure I believe in God. You see, God didn't let the Nazis win. He saved the Jewish people."

There are others who became very religious because they felt very mystical about the fact that they survived. There are theologians, Jewish and Christian, who feel that the Holocaust was redemptive because it led to the State of Israel. There is an incredible range of responses to this question of faith after Auschwitz, and as analysts we should begin to examine this area more systematically.

9. *Optimists such as the late biologist Renée Dubois argue that despite ominous trends in the political, economic, and ecological realms, humans possess the imaginative and adaptive resources needed to reverse such potentially lethal conditions. Others, including Kurt*

---

*Yehezkel Kaufmann, *The Religion of Israel,* trans. Moshe Greenberg (Chicago: University of Chicago Press, 1960).

Eissler, B. F. Skinner, and Hyman Rickover, see the future of mankind in far bleaker terms. Eissler, for example, when referring to nuclear weaponry wrote that "one does not need to be a hypochondriac to suspect that such an accumulation of destructive forces that now exists must lead one day to an explosion."

In light of the Holocaust and your lifelong involvement with psychoanalysis, what outlook do you have regarding the future of mankind and our ability to prevent another Holocaust, nuclear or otherwise?

Furst. How one feels on this question will usually be determined by one's personality—the optimist, pessimist, or the realist.

There are, however, some interesting considerations. Man changes at an evolutionary pace, very slowly. Technology changes at a geometric pace. The more war, the faster technology is developed. Look what has happened to technology in the past one hundred or two hundred years compared to how much man has fundamentally changed in that same period. For that matter, how has he changed basically in the last five hundred or one thousand years?

However, when viewed against the background of human history, man was in a certain sense the master over technology. He produced the technology, and up until this time, man has always used his technologic progress essentially for his benefit: to produce more, to live more comfortably, etc. For the first time in the history of man, we are in a position where we have evolved a technology which can very easily destroy us. This confronts man with a problem he never had before, which is *not* to use the technology which he has developed.

Wangh. The Chinese invented gunpowder somewhere in the twelfth century or earlier and did not use it for aggressive purposes as far as I know.

Furst. I think that would prove an exception to the general rule that man has always utilized the technology he has produced. Once gunpowder got to the West, they were rather quick to use it for aggressive purposes.

With regard to prevention of another Holocaust, I don't have much to say on specifics. Prediction has never been a strength of psychoanalysis. Firstly, there is a danger in making a parallel between the Nazi Holocaust and a nuclear Holocaust. The Nazi Holocaust required the broad support of millions of people, while the nuclear Holocaust can be brought about by a few people. This is what makes the nuclear possibility so worrying.

A second consideration concerns the nature of aggression. A lot of aggression stems from xenophobia. I am sure it has a biological basis, and it is one of the deepest motives in the psychic structure. The truly destructive acts in history have often been made possible because the enemy was different, alien, and unknown. When you get to know someone, libidinal forces are activated and fear is reduced. Prevention, then, must involve the encouragement of as much cultural exchange and personal contact as possible.

Wangh. One hopes that the species has an innate command to perpetuate itself. In a sense, the anxiety about the nuclear threat is helpful, since it can be used to mobilize people to act in the name of species perpetuation. But one must face and work-through the Nazi Holocaust in order to deal effectively and realistically with the nuclear threat.* They are connected phenomena, as is the nuclear bombing of Japan. In fact, many of the people in the antinuclear movement are Americans born during World War II or right after. These are young people who have experienced as children the first atomic threat. They were taught to go into the shelter and had to deal with the possibility that much of humanity can be erased in a few minutes.

Grossmann. I agree with all that has been said. As for prevention, I think new systems of child-rearing and education are essential. It must be based on the assumption that it is not so much *what* you teach the child, but how you treat him, which will determine what kind of human being he will be.

In general, I tend to be an optimist like Dubois. The brain is an untapped organ with enormous creative potential and the capacity for choice. Maybe man will make the right one.

Bergmann. If you ask me in sober thought, let's say if I was an insurance salesman, to predict the chances of the world surviving, given the piles of atomic bombs in the two camps, given the possibility of error, given the possibility of a paranoid personality leading the superpowers, I would say that my thinking tells me that our chances of survival are slim.

If you ask me if I believe in that, I would say no. I believe in our survival, because I could not live my life with such an attitude.

There are some intrapsychic changes needed to bring about the new morality that can turn things around. We need a superego with a primary loyalty to humanity as a whole rather than to one's country or group. We have to put an end to the justification, "I was only following orders." By applying the lessons of the Nuremberg trials to the nuclear threat and other genocidal attacks, we may help create this new morality.

---

*See Wangh's essay in the present volume (above, pps. 196-205) for further details.

I also think we must recognize the degree of hostility and aggression that is prevalent in those in authority. Such that nobody is good enough to be entrusted with the fate of the world by having available the nuclear option. We need a less trusting and more critical attitude toward authority.

Finally, a word about Jewish survival. I think the Nazi Holocaust must be remembered and comprehended, for not to do so would be a huge and dangerous denial. But a group that only dedicates itself to the past is traumatized and never allows complete mourning to take place. To be traumatized and in mourning inevitably affects a group's ability to assess current threats and deal with them effectively and realistically. Therefore, we have to steer a careful line between not forgetting and excessive remembering.

Too much stress on remembrance is an oppressive way to live. It is often overlooked that the process of mourning should ultimately lead to some measure of resolution and resignation without despair.

Epilogue

Psychoanalytic comtemplation of the Holocaust, like all other examinations of this event, takes one into an ineffable world in which a sense of chaos and incomprehension prevail. Yet the analytic observer, like his counterparts in literature, theology, and history, must boldly face the paradox of speaking about the unspeakable and thinking about the unimaginable. Attempting to make sense of what George Steiner argues was a literal staging of "hell on earth"[1] is a Sisyphean task, one which calls for us to grapple with absurdity, renounce the unattainable, and yet seek constructive possibilities. Thus, we think it unwise and even dangerous to avoid struggling with and understanding the Holocaust, since it is only in this way—without self-deceptive mythologizing and distortion—that we can prevent future genocide. Fortunately, nearly everyone involved in Holocaust studies and commemoration opts for pragmatism while seeing the need to understand the Holocaust within the larger scheme of things.

This book has dealt with the Holocaust from the vantage point of psychoanalysis, and so we need to limit our parting remarks on the future relationship between the Holocaust, a decisive turning point for mankind, and a discipline whose founder viewed "all mankind as his patient."

The foregoing essays and roundtable discussion have shown that contemporary psychoanalysis has contributed its share of insights to the understanding of the Holocaust and its legacy. Psychoanalysis has offered a framework for understanding the psychohistorical conditions that made a Nazi regime possible and, as well, has suggested why Hitler psychologically appealed to the German nation. Analysts have offered thoughtful observations on the superego formation and individual psychodynamics of the anti-Semite, the psychotic and unambivalent hater, and the bureaucratic killer. Most importantly, psychoanalysts have described the psychological preconditions that contribute to making an individual vulnerable or invulnerable to genocidal propaganda.

Psychoanalysts have also been pathbreakers in understanding the effects of massive psychic trauma on the survivor, the transmitted sequelae to the second generation, and the psychotherapist's key role in either exacerbating or ameliorating the survivor's pain. Issues as wide-ranging as the loss of faith and the psychological meaning of repeated victimization on the individual (and group) have been intelligently and sensitively explored using psychoanalytic constructs.

Finally, psychoanalysis has suggested a direction for the future with its views on the promotion of prosocial behavior in childhood and the means of averting genocidal outbreaks. Analysts have also offered novel viewpoints on the nuclear threat in light of the Holocaust. Yet there remains a need for a more systematic study of the Holocaust through the application of psychoanalytic constructs coupled with interdisciplinary cooperation.

Contemporary psychoanalysis, we found, cannot be viewed as unaffected by the boundless assault on life and love that characterized Nazi-dominated Europe of 1933–45. For example, Kohut's self-psychology, which currently shares the professional spotlight, focuses on the patient's inordinate concern with the "self."[2] Kohutians argue that this is due to chronically cold and unfulfilling early-childhood experience. These individuals are impulsive, attention-seeking, lack empathy, and are shallow in interpersonal relations. We would argue that the current emphasis on narcissism and the "culture of narcissism" is, in part, a reaction to an event so cataclysmic as to call into question much that we know and feel about human existence. Who would doubt that libidinal forces would be drawn away from such a mad outer world in order to strengthen a fearful and depleted post-Holocaust self? Moreover, the Holocaust serves as a stark reminder that uncontrolled violence and dehumanization in society never fail to make their way into the microcosm of neighborhood and home and thus affect child-rearing and personality formation.[3]

Theoretically, we would hope that the Holocaust would lead analysts and others to a renewed respect for our biological roots, since it is the raw human instinctuality that has made a mockery of our notion of culture and civility. Yet contemporary theorists, in many quarters, seem to have given less than sufficient attention to the instinctual core of man. In the Freudian lexicon this is known as dual-instinct theory. Attempts to ignore or underestimate the centrality of Freud's theories concerning the drives diminishes the radicalism of psychoanalytic theory and limits our understanding of genocidal eruptions and the threat of global nuclear destruction.

Perhaps the most important influence the Holocaust has had on psychoanalysis is in pointing the direction for the future. Violence and psychopathic behavior have received comparatively little attention in the psychoanalytic literature; the Holocaust has forced analysts to study not only the individual persecutor but also group violence. It is with this problem in mind that psychoanalysis must develop its social psychology so as to be better able to extrapolate from the individual to a catastrophe on the scale of the Holocaust. Thus, there is a need for analysts to consider the impact of the Holocaust on psychoanalytic theory and technique and to respond to the challenge that the Holocaust raises to all theories of human behavior.

In light of the preceding observations, we would argue that an immersion in the Holocaust Kingdom (the ultimate expression and now the symbol of absolute evil) is essential for the aspiring mental health worker. We would urge that psychoanalytic institutes as well as graduate training programs in the mental health field require coursework in the psychological dynamics and consequences of the Holocaust, genocide, and nuclearism. The mental health professional seeking to treat and prevent psychic dysfunctions will be aided immeasurably by a guided consideration of the Holocaust. When one has been sensitized to human tragedy of such a magnitude as to bring many to view global civilization as a near failure, anguish and empathy are heightened, and one's humanity is strengthened. One also becomes more capable of fighting for life and dignity for oneself and for others. Moreover, the therapist who has confronted the world of extermination camps and "Final Solutions" will better comprehend the psychological ramifications of grappling with an awesome historical event, and thus will be better able to detect and constructively work with the conscious and unconscious reverberations of the Holocaust and its accompanying imagery in others. Such a therapist would be ever-mindful of the knowledge that the therapeutic enterprise operates under the shadow of the Holocaust that took place, the ensuing episodic mass slaughter since 1945, and the omnipresent threat of nuclear annihilation.

We suggest that the therapeutic community consider the thoughts, feelings, and ideation evoked by the Holocaust to be in need of analysis, working-through, and resolution in the same way that other core issues and developmental struggles are faced in the clinical encounter. The problem can only be adequately addressed if mental health professionals study the Holocaust and its legacy, reflect on it in their personal therapy, and consider it a significant issue influencing their patients' lives. Following Erikson's model of psychosocial development throughout the life-cycle,[4] we propose that *a dialectic of Holocaust integration vs. Holocaust disavowal* be considered alongside other major issues dealt with in in-depth psychotherapy. The therapist will have to measure the importance of this antithesis in each of his or her patients' lives. Erikson, as the reader familiar with his work on the life-cycle knows, proposes that human strengths and weaknesses are reflections of the manner in which we resolve the conflicts inherent in each phase of the life-cycle. Syntonic qualities, such as trust, autonomy, initiative, ideally outweigh corresponding dystonic tendencies, such as mistrust, doubt, and guilt. Applying this approach to conflict resolution to the Holocaust-related dialectic proposed above, we would identify humaneness as the basic strength following integration of the reality and implications of the Holocaust. Callousness would be the corresponding antipathic trend related, in part, to Holocaust disavowal or outright pathological denial.[5] It should be noted that there are those who, while not intentionally callous, wish to spare themselves and their offspring exposure to the dark side of life. It is well known, however, that adaptation can only be furthered by confronting and mastering aspects of ourselves that often contradict our prevailing self-perception. Otherwise, we unintentionally find ourselves less equipped to deal with that which is asocial, hostile, and potentially destructive in man and society.

The above polarity could encompass responses to post-Holocaust genocidal destructiveness, the nuclear threat, and attitudes toward the environment and ecology as a whole. In the broader social arena, the extent to which national leaders have resolved the antithesis of Holocaust integration vs. Holocaust disavowal may be used as one indicator of the genocidal potential of a given nation (consider the attitude toward the value of human life in Denmark as opposed to that of the rulers of Cambodia or Iran, to name but two countries on a sadly extensive list).[6]

Thus far, we have discussed the importance of incorporating the study of the Holocaust and its legacy into the training of the mental health professional concerned with the treatment and prevention of psychological disorders. We need to reflect on the broader responsibilities facing psychoanalysts following the Holocaust and in the face of our current global crises. We need to ask ourselves whether mainstream psychoanalysts and psychoanalytic associations ought not take a more active role in the effort to link scholarly psychoanalytic pursuits with greater sociopolitical involvement.

Consequently, we would welcome a collaboration between members of the psychoanalytic community and individuals involved with Holocaust research, prevention, and commemoration. Formal psychoanalytic study of the Nazi genocide could be linked to investigations focusing on current perilous global problems without stripping the Holocaust of its historical uniqueness. Finally, the psychoanalytic study of social pathology could lead the analyst to a greater involvement with various policy-creating institutions and decision-makers.

We of the generation born in the aftermath of the most grotesque episode in human history are called upon to cope with the reality of large-scale genocide and the real threat that those who govern us will lead us along the path toward collective suicide. Choosing a life-affirming response under such conditions is a difficult undertaking. For some, denial, accompanied by habituation to the imagery of atrocity and extinction, becomes the most tolerable route to follow. Others see in an impending nuclear cataclysm the joyous opportunity to partake in the ushering in of the eternal kingdom of God. For them the Holocaust was only a Last Supper prior to Armageddon and ultimate redemption. For our part, we think it infinitely wiser to learn from the surviving remnant of the Holocaust. These are people who saw their world-destruction fantasies become a living reality but who nevertheless, and despite overwhelming odds, have opted for a life of dignity. Shattered by their experiences, they could have opted to give up; instead, by and large, they have dedicated themselves to "reverence for life" and a concern for the well-being of others. How they have led their lives following years of endless brutality is a source of awe.

By combining the essential *menschlichkeit** which characterizes survivorhood at its best with the creative humanism of Freud's life and work, we will have created an amalgam imbued with the power of "eternal Eros" and offering us the possibility of residing in a wiser, freer, and more loving world.

REFERENCES

1. George Steiner, *In Bluebeard's Castle* (New Haven: Yale University Press, 1971), pp. 53–56.

2. Heinz Kohut's two major works are *The Analysis of the Self* (New York: International Universities Press, 1971) and *The Restoration of the Self* (New York: International Universities Press, 1977).

---

*Literally "humanity," but in the Yiddish tradition, deriving as it does from the word *mensch,* refers to an individual who is decent and compassionate.

3. For an excellent discussion of the psychological impact of the nuclear threat and, by extension, the ramifications of the Holocaust experience in the lives of children, see Robert J. Lifton and Richard Falk, *Indefensible Weapons: The Political and Psychological Case Against Nuclearism* (New York: Basic Books, 1982).

4. Erik Erikson, *The Life-Cycle Completed* (New York: Norton, 1982).

5. Although confronting the Holocaust in an effort to understand and possibly contribute to the prevention of genocidal destructiveness and more limited expressions of cruelty is the goal, this must be counterbalanced by at least some measure of disavowal so as to avert obsessive preoccupation with suffering or engulfment in despair.

6. For an outstanding and singular effort to apply psychodynamic concepts to an understanding and prevention of genocide, see Israel Charny, *Genocide: The Human Cancer* (Boulder, Colo.: Westview Press, 1982). In this work, Charny introduces his genocide early-warning system, which includes assessments of a given nation's attitude toward the value of human life.

Glossary

In preparing this glossary, the following sources have been consulted:

1. H. B. English and A. C. English, *A Comprehensive Dictionary of Psychological and Psychoanalytical Terms* (New York: Longmans, Green & Co., 1958).
2. B. E. Moore and B. D. Fine, *A Glossary of Psychoanalytic Terms and Concepts* (New York: American Psychoanalytic Association, 1968).
3. C. Rycroft, *A Critical Dictionary of Psychoanalysis* (Middlesex: Penguin Books, 1968).

ALEXITHYMIA. The inability to identify and express feelings and fantasies.

ANHEDONIA. The absence of pleasure or unpleasure where normally expected.

CATHEXIS. The investment of psychic energy in an external or internal object.

DEFUSION. The partial undoing of the fusion of Eros and Thanatos; a regression to a state in which the two instinctual trends are less completely harmonized. Ant. *fusion*.

EGO-IDEAL. An image of what one aspires to be, developing out of identifications with others; the protective and rewarding psychic functions which set up ideals and values, in contrast to the *superego,* which functions as a critical and punishing conscience.

EROS. The "life instincts," or those instincts whose aims are sexual gratification and the perpetuation of life.

EXTERNALIZATION. The tendency to project into the external world one's instinctual wishes, conflicts, moods, and ways of thinking. *Projection,* a related defense mechanism, is a process whereby a painful impulse or idea is attributed to the external world.

ISOLATED CEREBRAL LATERALIZATION. An interruption of the preconscious stream between the two hemispheres which causes a separation of word-presentations from thing-presentations, causing impoverishment of dreams, fantasies, and symbolization. Syn. *functional commissurotomy*.

NEUTRALIZATION. The process by which infantile sexual and aggressive impulses are modified and 'tamed,' and lose their infantile quality. Sublimation is an example of the more general process of neutralization.

OBJECT. That toward which action or desire is directed; that which the individual requires in order to achieve instinctual satisfaction. Objects are usually persons, parts, or symbols of one or the other.

OBJECT CONSTANCY. The ego's ability to maintain and retain an internal representation of the object independently of the object's presence or absence in the external world; it denotes the ability to retain the libidinal cathexis of this internal representation independent of the presence or absence of needs.

OBJECT LIBIDO. Libido which is invested in objects, as opposed to narcissistic libido, which is invested in the self. Syn. *object love*.

OBJECT LOSS. The actual loss of a loved person through separation, illness, or death; the experience of loss of love in the subject's inner world without the actual occurrence of the real loss or threat of loss of a loved person.

OBJECT RELATIONS. Relationships taken in their widest sense to include not only relations where there are direct instinctual gratifications but also relations where instinctual gratification is sublimated, as occurs in friendships and the love between parent and child.

PRE-OEDIPAL STAGE. The stages of libidinal development which precede the Oedipal, when the child's love is given almost exclusively to the mothering object (usually extending from birth to approximately 3½ years).

REGRESSION. A defensive process by which the individual avoids (or seeks to avoid) anxiety by (partial or total) return to an earlier stage of libidinal and ego development, the stage to which the regression occurs being determined by the existence of fixation points.

THANATOS. The death instinct. An instinct whose derivatives consist of impulses to injure or destroy oneself or others, and whose ultimate aim is death.

TRANSFERENCE. The projection of feelings, thoughts, and wishes onto the analyst, who has come to represent an object from the patient's past. *Countertransference* is the analyst's transference to his patient.

Contributors

Nanette C. Auerhahn, Ph.D., associate for research in psychology at the Video Archive for Holocaust Testimonies at Yale University; adjunct faculty at the Wright Institute in Berkeley.

Martin S. Bergmann, co-chairperson, Group for the Psychoanalytic Study of the Effect of the Holocaust on the Second Generation at the New York Psychoanalytic Society; co-editor of *Generations of the Holocaust;* staff, New York Freudian Society.

Sidney Furst, M.D., faculty, Department of Psychiatry, Columbia University; training and supervising analyst at the New York Psychoanalytic Institute; professional director of the Psychoanalytic Research and Development Fund; editor, *Psychic Trauma.*

Frances G. Grossman, Ph.D., faculty, Postgraduate Center for Mental Health; visiting faculty, Norwich University; winner of Holocaust Memorial Award (New York Society of Clinical Psychologists) for work on children's concentration camp art.

John Hanson, Ph.D., professor, Department of English, Virginia Commonwealth University; author, "Nazi Aesthetics" in *Psychohistory Review,* 1981.

Klaus Hoppe, M.D., Ph.D., associate professor of clinical psychiatry, University of California at Los Angeles Medical Center; director of research, Hacker Clinic.

Henry Krystal, M.D., professor of psychiatry, Michigan State University; faculty member, Michigan Psychoanalytic Institute; editor, *Massive Psychic Trauma* and *Psychic Traumatization.*

Dori Laub, M.D., chairman, Education Committee, Video Archive for Holocaust Testimonies at Yale University; associate clinical professor of psychiatry, Yale University.

Robert Jay Lifton, M.D., professor of psychiatry, Yale University; author, *Death in Life: Survivors of Hiroshima, The Broken Connection,* and other books.

Steven A. Luel, Ed.D., assistant professor of education and psychology, Touro College, New York.

Paul Marcus, Ph.D., staff psychologist, Children's Community Mental Health Center, Staten Island Mental Health Society; Adjunct Assistant Professor of Psychology, Queens College.

Rafael Moses, M.D., visiting professor of psychiatry, Hebrew University; past president, Israel Psychoanalytic Society; co-editor, *Psychological Bases of War.*

E. Mansell Pattison, M.D., professor and chairman, Department of Psychiatry, Medical College of Georgia; author, *The Experience of Dying, Clinical Psychiatry and Religion,* and other books.

Jack Terry, M.D., faculty, Department of Psychiatry, Cornell University Medical College; member, New York Psychoanalytic Society.

Martin Wangh, M.D., training and supervising analyst, New York Psychoanalytic Institute; visiting scholar, Harry S. Truman Research Institute for the Advancement of Peace, Hebrew University.